W9-AYG-410

Prayers
and Poems
for Children

Adaptations by
Sarah Toast

Illustrations by
Thomas Gianni

Interior art consultation by
David M. Howard, Jr., Ph.D.

Louis Weber, C.E.O.
Publications International, Ltd.
7373 North Cicero Avenue
Lincolnwood, Illinois 60646

Manufactured in U.S.A.

8 7 6 5 4 3 2 1

ISBN: 0-7853-1159-9

PUBLICATIONS INTERNATIONAL, LTD.
Little Rainbow is a trademark of Publications International, Ltd.

dad was alive and well and working on a gas rig off Canvey Island. The memory still made him cringe with embarrassment, and he wasn't sure now if he'd felt any relief at knowing his dad wasn't dead.

The details fell into place gradually, as he got older and learned to decipher his mum's muttered comments. "Greener pastures" meant another woman, a girlfriend. As far as Andy knew, his parents had never got a divorce. He thought his dad had sent money for a while, but it had long since stopped.

At first, his mum had had a job as a cashier at the supermarket, but after a couple of years, one day she'd just stopped going to work. He never knew what had happened. For a time they seemed to live on bread and Marmite, and then his mum had got the job at the pub, and for a while after that things had been better.

Sometimes there were "uncles," but they never seemed to stay for long, and Andy was always glad to see the back of them.

From his seat on the park steps, he watched other families, his curiosity tinged with envy. Mothers handing round ice creams, fathers playing football with sons. He couldn't imagine what that would be like. His mum had never come to the park with him, although he had another vague memory of his dad bringing him to see the dinosaurs once.

There were other boys, too, in the long August afternoons, about his age and on their own like him—sunburned savages who roamed the park in baggy shorts and expensive trainers with blinding-white laces. There were two, in particular, who came almost every day on bikes that he knew cost more than his mum made in a month. They raced and wheeled, then stood astride their bikes, watching him from the corners of their eyes. He couldn't tell if their gazes held interest or menace, but on this day, he hugged the guitar a little closer and glanced at his watch.

He had a schedule to keep now. The park, then an hour

or two in the library, then home to get his own tea. Then, as the sun sank behind the houses on the west side of Woodland Road and the air began to cool, he'd sit on the steps with the guitar on his knees and wait.

He knew to the minute when he'd hear the little Volkswagen chugging up the hill.

"A hotel, you said?" asked Gemma when she was buckled into the passenger seat of Melody's bright blue Renault Clio. Having thrown on trousers and boots and her cream-colored wool coat over a sweater, Gemma had pulled the tumble of her hair into a short haphazard plait. She saw that her partner, however, wore a dark trouser suit set off by a turquoise blouse, and had not a hair out of place in her dark, lustrous bob. Melody Talbot was the only woman Gemma knew who could wear a suit without looking dowdy, and on this miserable morning she found it a trifle annoying.

Melody downshifted through the light at Holland Park Avenue. "Some place called the Belvedere."

The streets were glistening from the fine drizzle, and Gemma was glad, at least, that they wouldn't be working outside. "Has the super been notified?" she asked. Their team's detective chief superintendent, Diane Krueger, would coordinate the investigation from South London headquarters.

"She's on her way into the station."

"The team?"

"Techies en route, as is the Home Office pathologist. And Shara will be there before us, as she lives in Brixton."

Gemma glanced at Melody, alert for any inflection in Melody's tone. As soon as Melody had passed her sergeant's exam, Gemma had requested Melody's transfer to her new South London team.

They were short staffed, the team having lost not only its

DCI, the officer Gemma had replaced, to a severe heart attack, but also a detective sergeant who had transferred to another division.

But Melody had not got off to a good start with the team's detective constable, Shara MacNicols, although that had not been Melody's doing.

Shara was a young single mum and a good copper, but possessive of what she felt was her patch. Gemma didn't like the friction on her team, but knew the situation needed both time and delicate handling. She sympathized with Shara—she'd been on her own with a small child, trying to make it in the job in a system that had seemed weighted against her—and she knew that to Shara it looked as if Melody had been brought in over her head because she was white and came from an obviously privileged background.

In truth, it was the chip on Shara's shoulder that was holding her back, but the young woman would never believe that. And then, Gemma thought with a glance at her partner and a suppressed smile, there were Melody's suits. She supposed she couldn't blame Shara for marking Melody out as a highflier.

"Do we have an ID on the victim?" she asked, putting aside the problem of her team's dynamics.

Melody had no need to consult notes. "A Mr. Vincent Arnott. At least according to the driving license in his wallet. The hotel clerk told uniform that he always signed in as Mr. Smith."

"How original," said Gemma, then frowned. "Always? He was a regular? What sort of hotel is this?"

"I don't know it." Melody glanced at the car's sat nav. "It's the other side of Crystal Palace from the park. Church Road."

"The only thing I know about Crystal Palace is the football team," said Gemma. In the light Saturday traffic, they'd reached the Battersea Bridge. Looking down as they crossed the Thames, she saw that the water was as gunmetal gray as the sky.

As they drove through Battersea, she thought of her friend

Hazel, who lived in a tiny walled bungalow just off the Battersea Road, and felt a pang of regret. She'd hoped to squeeze in a weekend visit with her, but now that looked unlikely.

"I went once," said Melody, and when Gemma looked at her blankly, added, "To Crystal Palace. The park. A school trip. Was it the beginning of year three or year four?" she mused, frowning. "Anyway, it was early in term, September, I think. We'd studied pictures in class, and I remember I walked along the empty terraces, trying to imagine what it must have been like, that great glass palace. And I couldn't comprehend how there could be so little left of something so grand and marvelous."

"It burned, didn't it?"

Melody nodded. "A few years before the war. I suppose it was unlikely to have escaped the bombing, in any case, a target like that." She gestured upwards, towards the rise of Clapham Common and the wall of fog above it. "You could see it from the City, you know."

"It was that big?"

"Huge. And plunked right on top of Sydenham Hill, the highest point between London and the south coast."

"What's it like, Crystal Palace? The area, I mean." Having grown up in North London, and until this new posting, having worked mostly in West London, Gemma was still learning her new patch.

"Going upmarket a bit, I think, but I don't know it well myself. Look." Melody pointed at the blue patches appearing in the fog, and Gemma glimpsed one of the Crystal Palace television masts before cloud shrouded it once again.

Melody concentrated on her sat nav as they looped round the elegant buildings of Dulwich College, then wound up through bare trees until the road leveled again at the top of Gipsy Hill.

Gemma glimpsed pubs and shops as they looped around a

triangle of streets at the hill's summit, following the one-way system. Then as they began a gentle descent down a tree-lined road, she saw the familiar strobe of blue lights. The journey had taken them less than forty-five minutes, door to door, so they'd made good time.

"The Belvedere, I believe," said Melody as she pulled up behind the last panda car.

The hotel was on their right, a large, sprawling building, pale-pink stucco with deep-blue awnings on the lower windows. A uniformed constable was stringing blue-and-white tape across the stairs leading up to the entry. At the top of the steps, DC Shara MacNicols seemed to be engaged in a heated discussion with a stocky woman in a blue suit.

"Hotel manager?" murmured Melody as she killed the Clio's engine and snapped open her seat belt.

"That would be my guess." Gemma got out, flashing her ID at one of the uniformed constables keeping an eye on the perimeter as she and Melody made their way towards the hotel's entrance.

As they drew closer, Gemma saw that Shara had red beads in the ends of the tiny braids in her hair, a splash of color bright as berries against the gray day. The other woman's pale skin looked blotched from shock, her straw-blond hair dry and disheveled.

"You didn't check his identification?" Shara was saying as Gemma and Melody reached the two women.

"Mr. Smith, he always paid in cash. It did not seem necessary," answered the woman, and from her faint accent Gemma guessed she was Eastern European.

Shara acknowledged them with a nod. "Guv. Sarge. This is Irene Dusek. She's the night manager who checked in our victim."

"I'm Detective Inspector James, Ms. Dusek," said Gemma. "And this is Detective Sergeant Talbot." She frowned as she continued. "Ms. Dusek, I'm sure you're aware that hotels are required to take down their guests' identification details."

"Yes, but Mr. Smith, we know him. He was never any trouble, and he never stayed long."

"Well, he's a bit of trouble now, isn't he?" said Shara, and Gemma shot her a quelling look. Dusek sounded frightened, and Gemma was more concerned about information than government hotel regulations.

"What time did Mr. Smith check in last night?" she asked.

Dusek seemed to relax. "It was maybe eleven, but I am not sure exactly."

"Was someone with him?"

"Oh, no. Mr. Smith, he always comes alone."

"Did he have luggage?" asked Melody.

"Oh, I did not see. I was busy—there was a phone call. Maybe he got something from the car." Dusek shifted, and Gemma guessed she was lying.

"You saw his car?" she asked.

"No, no. But I thought—he looked like a man who would have a car. A nice car, you know."

"So this *gentleman*"—Shara put heavy emphasis on the word—"came regularly, on his own, with no luggage. And you said he didn't stay long. Did you mean he didn't usually stay the entire night? It sounds to me like you're running a brothel here."

Dusek shook her head emphatically. "No, no," the woman said. "We do nothing bad. The housekeeper said he check out early. We are respectable hotel." Her grasp of English seemed to be deteriorating under stress.

Gemma examined the frontage of the hotel, seeing no obvious secondary entrances. "Ms. Dusek, are there other accesses to the hotel?"

"We have the fire doors, of course. They are required." Dusek seemed glad of firmer ground. "On the sides and in the back of hotel."

"Okay," said Gemma. "We'll have a look at those. But first we'd better see your Mr. Smith."

Dusek gave a little sob and pressed her knuckles to her mouth. "He was nice man, always very nice. I do not understand how this thing could happen."

"That's our job to find out, Ms. Dusek. We'll need to speak to you again. Is there someone who can sit with you?"

"There is Raymond, the day clerk. And the housekeeper. She is very upset." Coatless, Dusek had begun to shiver.

"Let's get you inside, then." Gemma guided the woman into the lobby and Melody and Shara followed.

The lobby, adorned with a violently patterned carpet in pink and blue, had a slightly scuffed reception desk to one side and a sitting area with a television on the other. Grouped around one of the tables in the sitting area were a woman in a maid's smock who was sniffing into a handkerchief, a young spotty-faced man in white shirt and black trousers, and a large uniformed constable. They looked as if they might be unlikely participants in a card game, or, considering the pot and cups arrayed on the table, a tea party.

The constable rose immediately and came towards them. When Gemma had identified herself, he said, "DC Turner, ma'am. Gipsy Hill Station." He was fair and slightly bovine, but his blue eyes were sharp.

"Ms. Dusek is going to stay with you for the moment. I'll want to speak to the others later as well. Can you send the SOCOs to us when they arrive? And the doctor? Oh, and, Turner, I don't want any of the guests leaving until we've interviewed them."

"In hand, ma'am. There's only a dozen in this whole place, apparently. Not exactly a booming business. Those that have come down, I've put in the dining room."

Gemma nodded. "Good. And can you see that no one leaves through the fire doors?"

"Done, ma'am," Turner said, with obvious self-satisfaction that was redeemed by his grin.

"Cheeky sod," Shara muttered.

Although Gemma would have preferred the scene-of-crime team on hand before she viewed the body, she felt there was little point in interviewing further staff until she knew exactly what they were dealing with. "All right, Turner. We'll be—"

"Through reception, down the stairs and to your right. You'll see the constable on the door." Turner's smile had disappeared. "And you'll be glad if you missed your breakfast."

Gemma followed his directions. Any moderately favorable impression she'd had of the hotel vanished as they left the public areas. The stairwell was dim, the walls scuffed and chipped. It smelled of damp, thinly disguised by industrial disinfectant. The basement corridor was no better. Two of the fluorescent light fixtures were out, and the others hummed unpleasantly. The uniformed officer standing at parade rest towards the end of the hall was a welcome sight.

He was younger than Turner, and she suspected he had drawn the short straw.

"Ma'am." He nodded when she showed her ID, but didn't meet her eyes.

The door in front of which he stood guard was closed, but the key was in the lock.

"Has anyone touched this other than the housekeeper?" she asked.

"DC Turner was the first on scene, ma'am, but he used his gloves. I—didn't go in."

"Right, then. Good lad." Gemma pulled a pair of nitrile gloves from her coat pocket and slipped them on. "Let's have a look, shall we?"

Turning the key, she pushed the door open and stood on the threshold.

The smell hit her in a wave. Urine, feces, and the unmistakable stench of death. The hotel might be short on guests but was not stinting on its central heating. The room was like an oven, and Gemma felt the sweat prickle beneath the collar of her coat.

Gray daylight poured in through windows set high up in the room's outside wall. She blinked as her eyes adjusted, then focused on the room's double bed, illuminated by a sudden shaft of sunlight like a tableau in a medieval painting.

"Bloody hell," she said.

CHAPTER THREE

The Crystal Palace was a huge glass and iron structure originally built in 1851 for the Great Exhibition held in London's Hyde Park. Prince Albert, head of the Society of Arts, had the idea of an exhibition to impress the world with Britain's industrial achievements. Countries including France, the United States, Russia, Turkey and Egypt all attended with exhibits falling into four main categories— Raw Materials, Machinery, Manufacturers and Fine Arts.

—www.bbc.co.uk

Gemma pressed her lips together. Melody and Shara stood just behind her, their breathing loud in her ears. They all seemed suspended in that instant.

Then Shara said, "Trussed up like a bloody chicken, isn't he? But a bit scrawny, if you ask me," and that broke the tension.

Letting the air out through her nose, Gemma moved a step forward into the room, careful not to touch anything. Her first thought on hearing the description of the scene had been that a bit of autoerotica had gone wrong. Now she said, "Not likely he did this to himself, is it?"

The man lay faceup on the bed. The thin top sheet was

rumpled beneath his feet, which were bound tightly with a black leather belt. Although otherwise naked, he still wore socks, and the right one was pushed halfway down his foot, as if he'd managed to dislodge it in a struggle. The dangling sock somehow made the scene more grotesque.

His knees were drawn up. Beneath them were stains on the bottom sheet where he had voided his bowels and bladder. His hands were beneath his buttocks, and the tail end of a conservatively patterned red-and-blue necktie peeped out to one side.

"He must have been tied facedown," said Melody. "Not just the hands. Look"—she pointed at his feet—"the belt buckle and knot are on the backside of his ankles."

"So, did he turn himself over, or did someone else turn him, either before or after they strangled him?" asked Gemma. The ligature bruising was clearly visible on his throat, as was the fixed lividity, but there was no sign of the implement that had been used.

"I should be able to tell you that," said a familiar voice, and Gemma turned to see Dr. Rashid Kaleem, Home Office pathologist, and her friend. His short hair was the color of the black leather jacket that covered his T-shirt, and his smile would have done justice to a toothpaste advert.

"Rashid. I'm glad it's you." Although Gemma had met Rashid on a case in which she had not been officially involved, she'd found that he was often assigned to South London investigations, and she liked working with him. He was young, smart, precise, and he didn't treat police officers as an annoyance. The only drawback was the swoon rate among female officers.

"Someone had a bit of fun here, eh?" Rashid set his bag just outside the door and drew on gloves. "Any idea who he is?"

Gemma pointed at the neatly folded clothing on the room's single chair—a Barbour-type jacket, dark trousers, a navy pullover that looked like it might be cashmere, and a pale-blue oxford shirt. Atop the shirt lay a man's leather wallet. She turned to the constable on the door. "Who checked his wallet, DC—"

"Gleason, ma'am. It was DC Turner. He said he didn't disturb the clothes any more than necessary."

"A Mr. Vincent Arnott, according to the initial report," put in Melody. "It seems he was accustomed to checking into the hotel as Mr. Smith."

Rashid raised his dark eyebrows. "Well. It will be interesting to see if Mr. Arnott-Smith was always so orderly, or if someone else was Mr. or Ms. Tidy. Was anyone seen with him?" Although Rashid's accent was perfect BBC-received English, Gemma knew that he'd grown up on a council estate in Bethnal Green, and his easy charm concealed a fierce intellect.

"According to the night manager, he checked in alone," answered Gemma.

"Sensible of him, if he had a habit of playing away." Rashid nodded towards the corridor. "Easy enough for him to let someone in through the fire door at the end of the hall, once he was settled in the room. The SOCOs are here," he added. "Just getting their gear from the van. They won't want anyone buggering up their scene."

The pathologist had an ongoing friendly rivalry with the crime scene techs. It was important that the SOCOs had first access to the scene, but Rashid always liked to get an impression before others moved around the victim, and Gemma felt the same way. "I don't know whether the maid who discovered the body or either of the hotel clerks actually came into the room, but we'll find out," she told him.

Turning to PC Gleason, she added, "Why don't you go and have the SOCOs come in the fire door? No need to have them traipsing through reception."

"Yes, ma'am." The constable looked happy to have an excuse to get outside.

As he started towards the door, Gemma added, "See if you

can prop that door open a bit, as long as there's a PC outside. It wouldn't hurt to have some air in here." Unfortunately, they couldn't turn the central heating down until the ambient temperature had been recorded, as Rashid would need it for his time-of-death calculations.

As they waited, Gemma studied the victim.

"What do you see, boss?" asked Melody.

"White. Obviously male." That got a flash of a smile from Rashid and a breath of a snigger from Shara. "The hands are usually a good indicator of age," she went on as Rashid nodded agreement, "but as we can't see them, just going by his general condition and his face and neck, I'd put him in his late fifties to early sixties. The hair"—she gestured towards the victim's full silvery shock—"can be misleading. That type of hair can go gray or white quite early. I'd say he was reasonably fit—a golfer, maybe, by the tan." She indicated the darker area of skin below the throat. "He could play tennis, but I'm not seeing the definition in his arms or legs." Turning to Melody, she added, "Anything else jump out at you?"

Melody frowned, considering a moment before answering. "From the quality of his clothes—assuming for the moment they are in fact his—the well-kept condition of his feet, and the good haircut, I'd say he's upper middle class with a job that doesn't require manual labor."

A murmur of voices heralded the arrival of the two crime scene techs, escorted by PC Gleason. They often worked with Gemma's team, and she greeted them by name. "Sharon. Mike."

"Sounds like you've got an interesting one for us," said Sharon, a slight, dark woman who always looked as if she might be swallowed whole by the blue bunny suit.

Gemma nodded. "You could say that. I'd like the name and address from the driving license in the wallet as soon as you can get to it. The first officer on the scene extracted it to ID the victim, but he wore gloves."

"Turned our scene into a football pitch, have you?" Mike said with a good-natured nod to Rashid as he opened his evidence kit.

"Haven't touched a thing, mate," Rashid answered with a grin. "But I've got another scene to go to. Do you mind if I have a look at him, as long as you're observing?"

"Help yourself. Take notes of the good doctor's exam, will you, Sharon?" Mike answered as he took out his camera and began recording the scene.

As Rashid retrieved instruments from his bag, Gemma stepped back into the corridor, where Melody and Shara had already joined PC Gleason. The air was quite noticeably fresher and she breathed it gratefully as she watched Rashid.

Under Sharon's watchful eye, he moved round the bed with his own digital camera. Although the SOCOs would have a complete photographic record, Rashid focused on things that might be of particular interest to him when he conducted the postmortem.

Finishing with the camera, he ran his gloved fingertips gently beneath the victim's buttocks, shoulders, and his one bare heel. "Lividity is well fixed. If he was moved postmortem, it wasn't long after. Rigor is also quite advanced. Stiff as the proverbial board," he added, as he tested the flexibility of the joints. "Although if the room was sweltering like this all night, the time he was last seen may be more useful."

"The night manager says she thinks it was about eleven," said Gemma.

"Then he may have been dead within an hour, but we'll try to be a bit more accurate."

As Rashid pulled a thermometer from his bag and shifted the corpse just enough to get a rectal temperature, Gemma looked away. She had no idea why she was always a bit squeamish about this—silly, really, considering the crime scenes she took in her stride.

"Cause of death, Rashid?" asked Gemma, when he'd finished with the thermometer. "Was he strangled? And if so, with what?"

Rashid peered more closely at the face and neck. "There's some evidence of petechiae in the eyes, but that's not conclusive. And there's some bruising on the throat, possibly from a ligature, but don't quote me on it. No handprints visible. I'll know more when I can take it down to the tissue. Sometimes bruising doesn't show up on the skin, as you know."

Mike, now gloved, crossed the room and began checking the contents of the wallet. "Several major credit cards under the name of Vincent Arnott," he said. "National Health Insurance card, ditto. No banknotes, so they might have been taken. We'll check the trousers for a money fold. And the driving license, also as Vincent Arnott." Holding it by the edge, he brought it to Gemma.

She inspected the tiny photo. It certainly seemed to be the man on the bed. He had been handsome, in a severe way, with regular features set off by his thick, silver hair. She wondered if he had been vain about it.

Melody stepped closer and entered the address into her phone, then Mike bagged the wallet.

Going back to the clothing on the chair, Mike said, "Let's see what it has in its pockets," with a hiss on the sibilants, and Gemma grinned. Balding, fortyish, Mike was known for a serious addiction to fantasy novels.

After checking the shirt and pullover, he handed them to Sharon to bag. Then he unfolded the trousers, first patting the rear pockets, then reaching gently into the front. From the right-hand pocket, he pulled out a money fold with a magician's "Ta da," then riffled through the folded notes. "Roughly fifty pounds, but we'll log it. So you can probably assume he wasn't robbed, and that he was right-handed. Nothing in the left-hand pocket, so let's check the jacket."

"There's not a single crumpled receipt," said Gemma as she watched. "No cinema ticket stubs, no chewing gum, no cigarette packet wrappers, no bits of paper with scribbled phone numbers. I'd say we can assume that he folded his own clothes."

"Obsessively neat," agreed Rashid. "And apparently not because he was hiding his identity, or he'd not have been carrying ID and credit cards."

"House or flat keys." Mike held up two Yale keys on a heavy silver key ring.

"No car keys?" asked Gemma.

"Not unless he put them somewhere else in the room."

Melody had pulled up the driving license address on her phone map. "He lived in Belvedere Road. That's just on the south side of the hill. He could easily have walked here."

"Maybe this will help." Mike held up an expensive mobile phone, retrieved from an inside anorak pocket. "Let us print it before you have a go."

He dusted and taped the phone's glass surface before passing it to Gemma.

Switching it on, Gemma saw that it was fully charged. Evidently Arnott hadn't used it much the previous evening. Nor had its owner gone in for apps. The wallpaper was standard provider issue. No photos. No music. There was no e-mail account, and only a handful of numbers under the phone contacts.

"What did he need that kind of phone for?" asked Shara, who had been looking over Gemma's shoulder. She sounded disgusted. "He could have used a cheap pay-as-you-go. What a waste."

Gemma nodded absently, her attention focused on the few tagged numbers. "Home. Kathy." She glanced at Melody. "His wife, do you think? And *chambers*."

"As in a surname?" Melody asked.

"It's not capped." Gemma met her partner's widening eyes. "Oh, hell. Don't tell me the man was a bloody barrister."

. . .

By midmorning, Kincaid had run out of strategies for dealing with cranky children.

He'd dressed and gone down to make coffee while Gemma was showering, hoping to have a quick word with her about her case before she left. He'd only caught her " . . . man strangled, Crystal Palace . . ." muffled by the sound of running water.

But their movements had roused the younger children, the dogs, and the cat. By the time Gemma had clattered down the stairs like a red-haired whirlwind, the dogs were barking, Sid the cat was sitting in the middle of the kitchen table loudly demanding his breakfast, and Toby and Charlotte, both still in pajamas, were wailing over the cancellation of the day's plans.

Hugging them, Gemma had promised to be back soon, but in their household, that promise was heard too often to be given much credence. Charlotte had transferred her limpet grasp to Gemma's waist. Lifting her, Gemma gave her a squeeze, then passed her back to Kincaid. "Sorry," she whispered, giving him a quick peck on the cheek.

"No worries," he'd said, waving her off.

The morning had gone downhill from there. The little ones, tear streaked and cornflake sticky, had run upstairs and woken Kit by bouncing on the middle of his bed. A shouting match ensued, punctuated by the distressed yips of Kit's little terrier, Tess, and then Geordie joining in the fray.

Reduced to seeking peace at any cost, Kincaid sent the small children and dogs out into the garden, and was rewarded a half hour later by a tracker's dream of muddy boot and paw prints throughout the house. "But it's the Marauder's Map," Toby protested when they were asked to mop up.

"Then it will reappear, won't it?" Kincaid said. "But not until you've cleaned up every bit." His jaw was beginning to ache from clenching. The bass from Kit's iPod speakers thumped through the sitting room ceiling, proof that his son was up and now thoroughly awake.

Handing the roll of kitchen towels to the younger children, he grabbed a jacket off the hall peg and left them to it.

He went out through the sitting room's French doors into the garden. On days like this he had started to wish he smoked, just as an excuse for the break. He never remembered feeling that way on the job.

The fine mist in the air felt soft and cool against his face. Taking a deep breath, he stood gazing over the low iron fence that demarcated their small garden from the communal garden beyond. The bare trees looked ephemeral; the grass, a lush, emerald green. A wet emerald green. Living on a communal garden might be the height of aspiration in Notting Hill, and on a fine Saturday it would have its share of dogs and children, happily occupied. But not today.

It was time to regroup and formulate a plan for the day. Structure was the key—he'd learned that quickly enough. He'd taken it for granted on the job.

"Dad!" Toby burst out through the French doors waving the kitchen phone and shouting as if Kincaid were at the far end of the garden. "It's Auntie Erika. She wants to talk to you."

"Then we'll hope she's not deaf," Kincaid said, rolling his eyes as he took the phone and shooed Toby into the house. "Hello, Erika."

The *auntie* was a courtesy title. Erika Rosenthal was, if anything, closer to a grandmother to the children. "What can I do for you?" he went on. "I'm afraid Gemma's not at home."

"So I've been informed," said Erika, amusement clear in her slightly accented voice. "Under the circumstances, I thought you might like me to have the boys over for lunch."

"Lunch? Really?" Kincaid cleared his throat in an attempt to banish the hopeful squeak. "Erika, that's very kind of you, but—"

"I'm perfectly capable of managing Toby for an hour or two, Duncan. I've a pot of beef and barley soup on the cooker. It's his favorite. And I have chess and checkers at hand."

"But Kit—"

"I've already spoken to him."

Kincaid had to laugh. Capitulating, he said, "Erika, you are more than welcome. What time shall I bring them?"

"I think they are perfectly capable of walking, Duncan. They won't melt," she said with a hint of reproof. Then she hesitated. "I would have Charlotte, as well, but I'm a little lacking in entertainments for three-year-olds."

"No need to apologize," Kincaid told her. "You're doing quite enough. Charlotte and I will have no trouble entertaining ourselves."

"It's my pleasure, Duncan," Erika said, and he heard the genuine affection in her voice.

When they'd completed their arrangements, and Duncan had seen the boys off for the short walk down Lansdowne Road into Arundel Crescent, he found himself wondering what he and Charlotte would do with the rest of their day.

Kitchen and Pantry beckoned, but he told himself the café would be mad on a Saturday, jammed with tourists and marketgoers.

Then he realized he'd been given an opportunity to pay a much-needed and too-long-delayed visit. He dialed a number stored in his phone. "Louise, it's Duncan. Can Charlotte and I come to see you today? There are some things we need to discuss."

By eleven o'clock, Andy was standing on the curb in front of his Hanway Place flat, his Strat in its case, watching for Tam's silver Mini Cooper.

He'd debated about the guitar. He had different guitars for different sounds, and when he knew what he'd be playing in a session, he chose the guitar accordingly. But today he had no idea, and the Fender Stratocaster was both his oldest electric and his favorite. And if he had to admit it, the Strat was his security blanket—the instrument that felt like an extension of himself.

His favorite amp, however, was still in the back of George's van. He'd meant to ask George if he could borrow the van this morning, but things had been so frosty between them after the gig last night that he'd accepted Tam's offer of a lift back to the flat, and then agreed to let Tam drive him to Crystal Palace today.

Tam had reassured him about the amp. "They'll have plenty of equipment in the studio, and you'll not want to be carrying your Marshall up those stairs. Trust me, laddie."

And Andy had had no choice.

Peering down the narrow street, he transferred the guitar case to his left hand and flexed the fingers of his right. His knuckles were a bit bruised and swollen, but he'd followed Tam's advice, icing and elevating his hand as soon as he'd got back to the flat last night. He'd practiced a bit that morning, and although it hurt, his playing didn't seem to be impaired.

But he didn't want to think about the injury, especially not now, when he was feeling more nervous by the minute.

Why the hell had he agreed to this? Why had he pissed off his mates so badly that whatever happened today, the band was fated to split up? And why had he ever thought he could go back to Crystal Palace?

There was a swish of tires on the wet tarmac and Tam's Mini came round the tight corner from Hanway Street. When Tam came to a stop, Andy walked round the car, stowed the guitar in the backseat, and climbed into the front.

"All right, lad?" asked Tam, shooting him a concerned look as he put the car into gear.

"Yeah. Fine." Andy didn't meet his eyes.

"Bloody traffic. Oxford Street on a Saturday. Can't think why you stay in this dump." Tam was on vocal autopilot. He never failed to say that he didn't understand why Andy stayed in the flat, and Andy never failed to say that he couldn't afford to move anywhere better.

But Tam was right. He could find someplace in Hackney, like George, or Bethnal Green, like Tam and his partner Michael, or anywhere, for that matter, out of the dead center of London. The truth was that he loved being in the middle of the hustle and bustle. And he loved being able to walk to the guitar shops in Denmark Street, which had drawn him like magnets since he'd been old enough to take the bus into the city.

"I've got room for my guitars and my cat," he said.

Tam grinned. "Barely room to swing the bloody cat. What you see in that beast, I don't know."

"He's my mate, is Bert," Andy said, relaxing into the familiar argument, as he knew Tam intended. Tam, who had German shepherd dogs, pretended to have no use for cats, but whenever he came round the flat Andy caught him giving the cat a surreptitious rub behind the ears.

Coming back late from a gig one night, Andy had found the tiny, shivering kitten in the middle of Oxford Street. There'd been no one else to help, and no other place to take him, so Andy had tucked the kitten inside his jacket and carried him back to the flat. That tiny bit of fluff had grown into an enormous tomcat the color of Dundee marmalade, and now Andy couldn't imagine life without him.

"You're sure that hand is okay, son?" Tam asked, when they'd crossed the river at Waterloo.

"It's fine, Tam, really."

Tam let him be after that, and Andy was glad of the silence. He was tired, and after a bit he almost dozed in the warmth of the little car. When he opened his eyes and blinked, they were climbing Gipsy Hill.

He sat up, his nerves kicking in again as they reached Westow Hill and the triangle of streets that formed the crest of Crystal Palace. This studio was relatively new, and he didn't know it, although he remembered the steep little lane that dropped from Westow Street. He looked away as they circled past Church Road and the White Stag.

From Westow Street, Tam turned right. He bumped down a narrow way that was more of a passage than a lane, then turned left at the bottom, pulling into a small car park. To the west, the hill dropped away towards Streatham, a gray palette of rooftops seen through the delicate filigree of bare trees.

On the other side rose a higgledy-piggledy jumble of buildings, flanked by a wall with the most garish graffiti Andy had ever seen. No, not graffiti, he realized, but rather a mural with weird creatures depicted in bright, primary colors. It looked as if it had been painted by a giant alien child, and he smiled for the first time that day.

"There's a guitar shop," he said, spying the sign tucked into the lower level of one of the brick-faced buildings.

Tam popped the door locks and climbed out of the car. "Best keep you out of there, then, hadn't we? It's there we're going." He pointed towards a steep flight of open metal stairs beside the building, and Andy saw what he'd meant about the amp.

"Up there?"

"First level," said Tam, consulting a note as Andy retrieved the Strat from the back of the Mini.

"Good God." Andy stared. "How'd they get the equipment up there?"

"Stronger backs than yours or mine, I expect." Tam winked at him and led the way.

Andy held the railing in one hand and the guitar in the other. When they reached the first landing and ducked into a dark doorway, Andy felt like he'd stepped into a hobbit hole.

Caleb Hart was waiting for them in a tiny, cluttered anteroom.

He shook Tam's hand, but not Andy's, which suited Andy well enough. He gave Hart credit for knowing that guitarists could be tetchy about having their hands touched.

"I've booked us three hours in studio one, but first an hour in rehearsal space, so you can get a feel for each other." Hart glanced at his watch. "Poppy's running a bit late. Saturday trains."

"From London?" asked Andy, frowning. He knew the train from Victoria like the back of his hand. It usually ran regularly and unimpeded on Saturdays.

"Twyford to Paddington."

"Twyford? Why the hell is she coming from Twyford?" Andy felt Tam shift uncomfortably at his tone, but it was too late to call it back.

"Poppy lives outside Twyford," said Hart. He glanced at Tam as if wondering whether there was some miscommunication. "Her dad's a vicar in a village near there."

Andy just stared at him for a moment before he found his tongue. "She lives with her parents?" He turned to Tam. "She's a bloody schoolgirl *and* a vicar's daughter? What were you—"

"I was thinking that she's twenty years old and that she can sing," Tam snapped. "Don't make a complete arse of yourself, laddie. What girl that age can afford to live on her own in London?"

"Are you talking about me?" came a voice from the doorway.

They all turned, and Andy saw a slight figure, backlit.

"Poppy. Good to see you," said Hart with a smile.

"Bloody trains." She stepped into the room, and Andy saw her clearly. She wore fur-lined boots, bright flower-patterned tights, and a tiny ruffled skirt beneath a puffy jacket. Her short hair, stuck up in unruly spikes, was the color of his cat's fur, and slung over her shoulder by a strap was what looked like a case for an electric bass. No one had told him she played an instrument.

"Hi, Caleb. Tam." She nodded, then gave Andy an assessing stare. "You must be the hotshot guitarist. I'm Poppy." She held out a hand encased in a purple fingerless glove, and he shook it awkwardly.

"I'm Andy, yeah. Andy Monahan. You're freezing," he added as he felt the tips of her fingers.

"Nobody told me I'd have to climb Mount Everest. This is a cool place, though."

It was a steep hike from Gipsy Hill Railway Station up to the Crystal Palace triangle, but Andy noticed that she didn't seem the least bit winded. And she'd come up the outside metal staircase as quietly as the cat she resembled.

Caleb Hart, however, went into solicitous mode. "Let's get you upstairs, and warm. I've already got the heaters going in the big rehearsal space."

"I'm fine, Caleb," she said with a shrug. "But I want to see it. We're going up?"

"Next level."

Poppy led the way out, taking the stairs as if she had springs in the heels of her boots, her instrument case bouncing against her hip.

"You didn't tell me you'd met her," Andy whispered to Tam as they brought up the rear.

"I went to hear her at the Troubadour. You didn't think I'd get you into something without being sure she was a goer? She's something special, I'm telling you. A bloomin' prodigy."

That probably meant spoiled rotten, in Andy's experience. But she had balls for a vicar's daughter, he had to admit. At twenty, he'd been tough and independent in a street-smart way, but this girl had a poise and confidence he still hadn't managed to achieve.

Her speaking voice, however, while pleasant, was straight Home Counties middle class, and he hoped to God she didn't sing in that little-girl-breathy indie style that made him want to grind his teeth. Or even worse, some sort of faux working-class thing like Kate Nash. At least with that accent and her slight stature she was not likely to be another Adele clone.

They reached the next level and stepped into a space completely different from the cramped anteroom to the studios below.

"Very cool," said Poppy, taking it in, and Andy had to agree.

The room was long and open, with light pouring in the large windows that overlooked the tree-clad hillside to the west. There were several guitar amps, a two-mic setup, small-scale recording equipment, and, by the windows, a baby grand piano that reflected the mottled gray sky in its black-lacquered top.

"Oh, lovely, Caleb. Thank you," said Poppy, giving her manager a quick hug that was not the least bit coy. He might have been a favorite uncle.

She stripped off jacket and gloves, then bent to unlatch her guitar case. When she took out the instrument, Andy gave a low whistle in spite of himself. It was a Fender Pastorius bass, fretless—an instrument only for a very accomplished musician.

"Can you really play that thing?" he asked.

Poppy shot him a look from under brows that were a dark punctuation to her marmalade hair. "Wait and see, guitar boy."

Stung, he shot back, "A nice prezzie from your daddy?"

She stood, slipping the bass strap over her head, and seemed to collect herself for a moment. Then she looked him directly in the eyes and said levelly, "I have two younger brothers and a younger sister. We manage, but my father is a Church of England vicar, and there is no way he could afford an instrument like this. I worked all the way through school giving music lessons to spotty, hormonal boys to buy this bass, and I bloody well deserve it. So just shut the fuck up, okay?"

She waited, and when he didn't reply, she nodded, as if something had been settled between them. Then she plugged the Fender into an amp and said, "Let's see what you got, guitar boy."

CHAPTER FOUR

*The Palace was designed by Sir Joseph Paxton, and after the
Great Exhibition finished in October 1851 he had the idea
of moving it to Penge Place Estate, Sydenham, as a "Winter
Park and Garden under Glass" . . . Penge Place, now called
Crystal Palace Park, was owned by Paxton's friend and
railway entrepreneur Leo Schuster.*

—www.bbc.co.uk

Once the coroner's van arrived, Gemma left the crime scene
techs to get on with things, and DC Shara MacNicols in charge
of interviewing the hotel staff. Seeing Shara's mutinous expression, she'd said, "Unless you'd rather give the death notifica-
tion? And, Shara, I think you'll do better with sympathy here.
Whether or not the hotel was breaking any rules is not our
main concern—at least not until we know how our Mr. Arnott
came to be here," she added, and got a grudging nod in return.

When Melody had double-checked the address she'd entered for Vincent Arnott, she looped round into Fox Hill and
then up the steep incline of Belvedere Road, back towards the
Crystal Palace triangle.

"He could certainly have walked to the hotel," Melody said

as she parked at the curb and pulled up the Clio's hand brake as an extra precaution.

Glancing at the vista spread below them as she got out of the car, Gemma wondered if, on a clear day, you could see all the way to the Channel. The view up the hill was pretty impressive, too. "He'd have been fit if he did that climb on a regular basis," she said. "Never mind what else he got up to."

She examined the house, half hidden behind a fortress of hedges. It was detached, a soft, brown brick with white trim on the windows and doors, and large upper and lower bay-fronted rooms on one side. Behind the shelter of the hedges, the lawn was immaculate, and the shrubs in the beds surrounding the house were trimmed to within an inch of their lives. A late-model silver BMW was parked in the curving drive.

"Eminently respectable," mused Melody, nodding at the house. "In an eminently respectable street. Not a hair out of place."

"A bit like our man's clothes and wallet."

"A barrister's tidy mind?" suggested Melody.

"We'll see." As Gemma tightened her scarf against the wind, she noticed Melody straightening her already perfectly aligned coat. These were little adjustments to their emotional armor, she knew. No one, no matter how long they'd been on the job, liked doing death notifications. A small part of her hoped that Mr. Arnott had lived alone, but a flash of movement at the sitting room window told her otherwise. "Let's get on with it, shall we?"

They walked briskly up the drive. By the time they reached the front door, it opened, and a woman peeped out. "I'm sorry," she said, "but my husband doesn't like solicitors. Or Jehovah's Witnesses." She was small, her plain face free of makeup, her short brown hair showing an inch of white at the roots, as if she'd forgotten to have it colored, and she wore what looked like a mismatched assortment of gardening clothes.

"Mrs. Arnott?" asked Gemma. She and Melody both had their warrant cards ready. "I'm afraid we're not selling anything. We're police officers. Can we come in and speak to you?"

"Police officers? But you don't look it." Mrs. Arnott merely looked puzzled.

"We're CID, Mrs. Arnott. I'm Detective Inspector James, and this is Sergeant Talbot."

The woman blinked pale eyes and frowned. "Has there been a burglary? I'm sure I don't know anything that could help you."

"Mrs. Arnott, may we come in? I'm afraid it's personal."

"Vincent won't like it," said Mrs. Arnott, hesitating. She scrutinized Gemma's ID, then Melody's. "He says you can never trust a card or a name badge, like those people who say they're from the gas company but aren't, really. But it is cold, and I'm sure he wouldn't object to women." She opened the door a little wider and stepped back.

Gemma threw Melody a puzzled glance of her own as they followed Mrs. Arnott inside. "Is your husband at home, Mrs. Arnott?" she asked as they stood in the tiled entry hall. The inside of the house looked as neatly manicured as the outside.

"Oh, no. He must have gone to the shops."

"Must have?"

"Well, I'm not quite sure." Mrs. Arnott blinked at them again, then looked round as if her husband might appear from out of thin air. There was something childlike about her, and Gemma began to wonder if she was quite all there. "I thought he was still asleep when I got up," she continued. "But he must have gone out early for his paper. Vincent sometimes likes to go out for his paper and a coffee on a Saturday."

"It's almost noon, Mrs. Arnott," Gemma said, but gently. "So you haven't actually seen your husband this morning?"

"No. No, I suppose I haven't. We have our separate rooms, you see. Vincent says he can't do with my tossing and turning."

"And last night? Was your husband out last night?"

"He walked up to the pub. He usually does on a Friday evening. I don't care for it myself."

"Do you know what time he came in?" Gemma asked.

"Well, I can't be sure. I go to bed early. Up with the larks, you know." Mrs. Arnott smiled at them, uncertainly. "What is this about? I'm sure Vincent can help you when he gets home."

Gemma met Melody's eyes again. "Mrs. Arnott, is there someplace we can sit down?"

"I suppose we could go in the kitchen." Turning, she led them through the cream hallway past a dining room papered in pale brown toile and into a very well-appointed kitchen in the same shades of cream and tan. The neutrality of the room, however, served to emphasize the view from the large windows along the rear wall. They overlooked a garden as riotous, even in its dormant winter state, as the front was severe. This, Gemma guessed, was Mrs. Arnott's province.

"I was just going out to prune the roses," said Mrs. Arnott, with a glance at her mismatched clothes. "I thought the sun might come out for a bit."

"Let's sit down." With a hand on her elbow, Melody guided the woman to one of the chairs in the breakfast nook. Taking out her phone, she showed Mrs. Arnott the photo she'd snapped of Vincent Arnott's driving license. Gemma knew that she and Melody both had scanned the house as they walked through for family photos that might make identification easier, but none had been visible. "Is this your husband?" Melody asked.

Mrs. Arnott's eyes widened. "Of course it is. But how— why do you have his driving license? Did someone steal it?"

Gemma drew a breath. Firmly and quickly, that was best. "I'm very sorry, Mrs. Arnott," she said. "But your husband is dead."

After a quick lunch, Kincaid decided to take the car to Bethnal Green. Unlike the boys, Charlotte considered a ride in the Astra a major treat. The old green estate car had been a welcome—at least to Kincaid—gift from his parents the previous autumn. But in a neighborhood where most families considered a new Land Rover a downgrade, Kit was embarrassed by it. Toby, after his initial excitement, had begun to copy Kit's griping.

"Are we going to see the doggies?" Charlotte asked for the tenth time.

Kincaid glanced at her, strapped securely into her booster seat in the back. "No promises, love. They might not be at home."

"We want to see Jazzer and Henny," said Charlotte, her brow creasing. Jazzer and Henny were her names for Jagger and Ginger, the two German shepherd dogs that belonged to Louise Phillips's neighbors, Michael and Tam.

"And Miss Louise," Kincaid prompted.

"Yes," said Charlotte. When he glanced back, he saw that she'd tucked her face into the top of Bob's floppy head.

Louise Phillips had not only been Charlotte's father's law partner, but was now the executor of Charlotte's parents' estate.

By the time they reached Louise's flat near Columbia Road Flower Market, the morning's drizzle had let up, and Kincaid thought he might take Charlotte to her favorite cupcake shop in Columbia Road once they'd finished their visit.

"Look," said Charlotte happily as Kincaid unbuckled her from her seat. "Jazzer and Henny!"

Indeed, the dogs were looking down at them from the first-floor balcony Louise shared with her neighbors. They began to bark in ecstatic greeting.

"Some guard dogs you are," Kincaid said, laughing, as he and Charlotte climbed the outside staircase to the balcony. The dogs were now hurling themselves against the gate in tail-wagging delight.

Michael came out of the left-hand flat on the balcony. "Duncan. Louise said you were coming." A landscape designer, Michael wore his graying hair in a ponytail, and no matter the weather, seemed to be perfectly comfortable in Hawaiian shirts and shorts. "Hello, little miss," he said to Charlotte. "Someone is glad to see you." Coming to the gate at the top of the stairs, he gave a stern command to the dogs. "You two. Sit."

The dogs sat, whining in anticipation, while he opened the gate. "Sit," he repeated, as Charlotte ran to them, then added, "Kisses."

The dogs held their sits but licked Charlotte's face enthusiastically as she hugged them in turn.

"Good to see you." Kincaid shook Michael's hand. "Tam not in?" he asked.

"Recording session. I was just about to take the dogs for a walk. Would you like Charlotte to go with us?"

"That would be brilliant." Kincaid had hoped the dogs would keep Charlotte occupied while he talked to Louise, but Michael's offer was even better.

"I'll just get their leads," said Michael, then he seemed to hesitate. "We won't be long. Louise is—she tires easily."

Kincaid thought he might have said more, but the door on the right of the balcony opened and Louise stepped out. "Hello, Duncan. Hello, Charlotte." She smiled at them, but Kincaid was shocked at how thin and haggard she looked. Not that she'd ever been robust. "I've made some coffee, Duncan, if you want to come in."

He realized then that she and Michael had prearranged the dog-walking invitation for Charlotte. "Thanks, Louise. Sounds wonderful." Michael and Tam, his partner, were more than neighbors to Louise. They were, Kincaid had learned over the past few months, in essence her family, and Louise's prickliness seemed only to make them more protective of her.

Kneeling, Kincaid buttoned Charlotte's coat, then tapped the tip of her nose. "You mind Michael, now. Be a good girl."

Charlotte nodded, too excited to speak. Kincaid waited until Michael had leashed the dogs and they had all trooped down the stairs before he followed Louise inside. He glanced at Louise's sitting room as they passed through—it was, as always, cluttered with books and a veritable snowstorm of papers. The kitchen, however, she kept quite tidy. Michael and Tam liked to tease her, saying it was because she never cooked. It was, Kincaid suspected, true.

She had made coffee in a cafetière and set out two cups and saucers along with a matching sugar bowl and creamer on the small table. The pieces were delicate bone china in a bird-and-flower pattern, which surprised him. Louise was the least frilly woman he knew.

"Charlotte's looking well," she said as she gestured to him to sit, then pushed down the cafetière's plunger and filled their cups. "How is she doing?"

"Fine, as long as she's at home, or with close friends. But our attempt at school the first week of term was a disaster." He sighed and added a bit of cream to the coffee, which was delicious but strong enough to stand the spoon in. "That's one of the things I wanted to talk to you about. I can't stay off work indefinitely, and Gemma can't take any more leave, especially with the new job. This is a critical period for her."

Louise frowned, and Kincaid noticed that there were rough, dry patches on her dark skin. "You know," she said slowly, "Charlotte might have had a difficult time with school under any circumstances. She was always with Sandra or Naz or the nanny, and she had very little interaction with other children. Quite a protected environment."

Was there, Kincaid wondered, a note of censure in Louise's voice? But she went on. "Still, you have to deal with things as they are. Have you considered options? A nanny?"

"We've talked about it. But it would mean starting from scratch with a stranger." Alia Hakim, who had been Charlotte's nanny before she came to them, was now enrolled full time at college, hoping to train as a lawyer. "I've wondered if we could find someone to come part-time, then perhaps try a few hours a week in a different school. A friend"—he set down his cup and aligned the handle neatly—"a friend has suggested a school where Charlotte would have extra attention in a less stressful environment. Charlotte's made friends with her little boy, who would be in the same class, so that might help. But it's considerably more expensive, even if the school would agree to take her." He had discovered that shark feeding frenzies were tame compared with the competition involved in trying to get one's children into elite schools in Notting Hill. "Not to mention the cost of even a part-time nanny."

"But your friend might be able to pull strings with the school?"

"Possibly." He was beginning to feel acutely uncomfortable, and would have been glad for one of Louise's regular cigarette breaks, but she sat quietly, her barely touched coffee cooling in its cup. "The thing is," he went on, "I could sell the Hampstead flat, which would certainly give us the funds to pay for a few years of school fees. But it would take time."

With a lawyer's directness, Louise got straight to the point. "You want to know if the estate can fund a more expensive school?"

"Yes. No. I don't know." Kincaid shook his head and pushed away from the table. "Christ, Louise, I haven't felt like this since I was a teenager asking my dad for pocket money. I don't want to come begging for cash. But I'm at my wit's end. If we can't keep Charlotte in some sort of day care, and we can't convince social services that she's in the best possible situation . . . And if I can't go back to work . . ."

Louise held up a hand. "Duncan, stop. It's all right. I was going to ring you, but I was waiting for the contract to be finalized. The Fournier Street house has sold."

"What?" He felt a rush of relief, followed instantly by a profound sense of regret. Louise had organized the disposition of the contents and put the beautifully restored Georgian house on the market in the autumn. But it was not just a house—it was the home Charlotte's parents had made for her, where she had spent most of the first three years of her life. Gone now.

Would she remember it, when she was grown, except in dreams?

"You know I intended to set up a trust for Charlotte's education," Louise continued. "Naz and Sandra bought the house when the market was at rock bottom in the East End, and they did most of the restoration themselves. There should certainly be enough capital from the sale to provide what she needs now. So while we're waiting for completion of the sale, talk to the school. Find a nanny. Give me a written proposal with the costs set out for both school and home care. We'll go from there. And, Duncan," she went on before he could speak, "when she's settled, I think we should start the formal adoption proceedings."

"But—" He stared at her. "You said it was best to wait."

"I've been looking into things. It seems that family courts have recently become more inclined to agree to the adoption of mixed-race children by white families. We should take advantage of the trend—it may not last. Nor"—Louise shook her head and seemed to sag in her chair—"may I."

Suddenly Michael's caution, Louise's obvious exhaustion, and the fact that he'd never seen her go so long without a cigarette clicked together in his mind. His alarm bells went off full force. "Louise, what are you talking about? What's wrong?"

She sighed. "If I don't tell you, Michael or Tam will. I've a spot on my lung."

Gemma could never decide which was worse in the suddenly bereaved—paroxysms of grief or the stunned silence of shock.

At least with hysteria you felt there was something you could do, some comfort you could offer, some calming gesture you could make. But the paralyzed ones . . . She shook her head, gazing at the blank face of Vincent Arnott's wife.

"Mrs. Arnott, is there someone you can call to be with you?"

The woman just stared, apparently unable to comprehend Gemma's question.

"Mrs. Arnott?"

A slight shudder went through Mrs. Arnott's body and she gave the same odd blink Gemma had noticed before. "I don't understand. Vincent will be home soon."

"Okay," said Gemma, catching Melody's eye and giving a little shake of her head before turning back to Mrs. Arnott. "Let's make some tea, shall we? And then we'll have a little chat."

Melody rose with her and they stepped into the work area of the kitchen. "I'll try to find out if there's a relative, and if so, get a number," Gemma said quietly. "You ring headquarters, tell them we've got a positive ID. And get an FLO here as soon as possible." She thought for a moment. Both male and female family liaison officers worked regularly with her team, but in this case she thought a woman was definitely the best option. "See if we can get Marie Daeley."

While Melody excused herself, phone already to her ear, Gemma filled the kettle and quickly found tea bags and mugs, milk and sugar. There was a shopping list fixed to the shiny stainless steel door of the fridge with a magnet. The handwriting looked masculine, but a few things had been added in the margins in an almost illegible scrawl. Peering, she decided one said "birds," another "boots." Odd items for a grocery list.

The tea bags were plain-Jane Tetley's. When Gemma poured the boiling water into the mugs, the liquid turned instantly orange and smelled comfortingly malty. When the tea had steeped, she carried the three mugs to the table with the milk and sugar, and sat down across from Mrs. Arnott.

Although she hated sweetened tea herself, she added milk and a generous helping of sugar to Mrs. Arnott's. "This'll perk you up a bit," she said as she slid the mug across. When Mrs. Arnott made no move to take it, Gemma leaned over and lifted her limp hand from the tabletop. It was icy cold, and Gemma chafed it between her own for a moment, then wrapped it round the warm cup. "Have a sip now," she encouraged gently, and slowly Mrs. Arnott gripped the mug with both hands and raised it to her lips.

"That's better," said Gemma. "Do you have children, Mrs. Arnott?"

The woman seemed to make an effort to focus on Gemma's face. "No." Her voice was a whisper. "No," she said again, more strongly. "We wanted them, but . . ."

"Do you have sisters or brothers?"

"My sister. Sara. She lives in Florida." More animation now, as if this was an often repeated source of pride.

Gemma, however, controlled a grimace. The sister would be no help any time soon. "Do you have her phone number?" she asked.

"Vincent keeps a book for me. It's in the drawer." Mrs. Arnott glanced towards the work area in the kitchen; then her face creased in distress. "But I don't—Vincent rings for me. The codes—I can't remember—"

"Not to worry," said Gemma quickly. "I'll ring her for you, in just a bit. You drink some more of that tea." She waited until Mrs. Arnott had complied and her color seemed a bit better. Then she added, "I'll bet you remember which pub Vincent goes to on his Friday evenings."

"Of course." Mrs. Arnott looked at her as if she were daft. "The White Stag, at the top of the hill. Where else would he go?"

"Does he always go the same time, on Fridays?"

"When *Emmerdale* comes on."

"That's your favorite program, is it?" Gemma was trying to

visualize the telly schedule, difficult when they rarely watched at home except for the news or something special for the kids. Her mum liked *Emmerdale,* though, and she thought it came on at seven.

Now that she had a rough idea of a time and place to begin following Vincent Arnott's movements, she breathed a sigh of relief when Melody appeared in the hall doorway and motioned to her.

"You have some more tea, Mrs. Arnott. I'll be back in a tick," she said, patting the woman's arm as she slid from her chair and went to join Melody in the hall.

"Marie Daeley's on her way," Melody said quietly, "and I've got Incident pulling up whatever they can find on Mr. Arnott. I spoke to the next-door neighbor—a Mrs. Bates. According to her, Mrs. A is suffering from early-stage Alzheimer's, and the husband took care of organizing everything around the house. Mrs. Bates has the contact number for the sister. She's ringing her now, then she'll be over to help out."

"That's a relief." Gemma glanced in the kitchen, where Mrs. Arnott still sat, her back to them. "Poor woman. Anything else from the neighbor?"

"You were right. He was a barrister, but she didn't remember the name of his chambers. She had contact numbers for him, though. One looked like his mobile, the other is probably the chambers. I've put Incident on that, too."

Gemma nodded. "Any personal comments?"

"Only that they didn't socialize much, because of her condition. Mrs. Arnott—her name's Kathy, by the way—was still okay on her own during the day as long as nothing disturbed her routine, but Mrs. Bates said she knew he was worried about how much longer they could go on as they were. He'd asked several of the neighbors if they could recommend someone who could come in at least for a few hours on weekdays."

"It certainly doesn't sound likely he planned to be out more than a few hours last night. That would explain why the hotel expected his room to be empty this morning, if he made a practice of taking women there on his evening out."

"Bastard," said Melody. "He certainly didn't have to worry about his wife finding out."

"No," Gemma answered, but thoughtfully. "You remember she said they slept separately?" She looked back into the kitchen and gave a little internal shiver. "He can't have—with his wife . . . it would have been like violating a child."

"But the bondage?" Melody shook her head.

"God knows a psychologist would have a field day with that," Gemma agreed. "But I think that in the meantime we should start with the pub."

"Let's walk," said Gemma as she and Melody left the Arnotts' house. "I don't remember there being much in the way of parking spots at the top of the hill."

They'd left Mrs. Arnott with her neighbor, Mrs. Bates, who seemed both kind and sensible. "Are you sure it's Vincent?" she'd whispered, taking them aside. "I just can't believe it."

"As sure as we can be without a formal identification," Gemma told her.

Mrs. Bates blanched. "Oh, you can't expect—Kathy can't possibly—"

"No," Gemma had agreed. "But perhaps someone from his work. Or another family member. Is there anyone, do you know?"

"I don't think so. I remember his mother passed away a few years back, and I never heard him speak of any siblings." She frowned at them. "You're detectives. I thought at first a traffic accident or a heart attack, but—"

"I'm afraid we can't tell you anything more at the moment," Gemma had said, and thanked her.

"You just want to test my legs," Melody said now as they trudged up Belvedere Road.

"You're the runner. I'll bet your legs are better than mine."

"You have the advantage—yours are longer," Melody shot back.

Gemma stopped for a moment when they reached the top of the hill, surveying the pub they had passed earlier that morning. It was orange-red brick, Victorian Gothic, with a bank of mullioned windows on the ground floor. She imagined it would be pleasant in the summer with hanging baskets of flowers, and the tables on the pavement in front filled with patrons. Now, it looked a welcome shelter from the cold.

The wind had picked up as the rain tailed off, and when Gemma opened the front door, a gust pushed them inside. They were met by tantalizing odors of food, the buzz of conversation, and the clink of cutlery on plates.

A curved bar partially divided the large front room. Behind it, a young woman with curly blond hair tied back with a red bandanna drew pints with cheerful efficiency.

"What can I get for you?" she asked, smiling, as they reached the bar.

"Just some information," said Gemma, returning the smile and holding up her warrant card.

The girl's eyes widened. She glanced to either side, checking that the other customers at the bar were occupied. "Is there a problem?"

"Do you know a man who comes in here named Vincent Arnott? Early sixties, trim, white hair?" asked Melody, showing her the driving license photo on her phone.

The girl shook her head. "I don't think I've ever seen him, but then we serve a lot of people."

"We think he came in regularly on Friday nights," said Gemma. "We were wondering if he came in last night."

"Oh." The girl looked relieved. "You'll want Reg, then. I

only fill in lunchtimes on the weekends when I'm not at uni."

"Could we have a word with Reg?"

"His son had a school football match this morning." The girl glanced at the watch on her slender wrist. "I should think he'd be back any time now, if you want to wait. This bloke"—she nodded at the photo—"is he in some kind of trouble?"

"You could say that." Gemma's eyes strayed to the menu on a chalkboard and her stomach rumbled. She realized she'd had no breakfast, and that Kincaid's Friday-night pizza was but a distant memory. "Let's get some lunch while we wait," she suggested to Melody.

"I thought you'd never ask. My knees were weak, and not from climbing the hill."

A few minutes later they were seated at a table in the front window with coffee and sandwiches.

"Nice place," said Melody as she bit into homemade fish fingers in a roll. "Upmarket shabby chic."

Gemma knew exactly what she meant. Mismatched furniture, scuffed wooden floorboards, quirky lamps, but the windows and glassware sparkled, and the food was delicious. She bit into one of the homemade chips that had come with her chicken, cheddar, and smoked bacon club. "I can see why Vincent Arnott liked to come here, but it seems a far cry from the Belvedere."

"If a stone's throw." Melody wiped a smear of tartar sauce from her lip with her pinky.

Gemma nodded, wondering if there were CCTV cameras with a good view of the pub. When they had a better idea of the time frame for Arnott's movements, she'd get the techies on it.

While they were waiting for their food, she'd checked in with DC MacNicols. Now, she glanced at her phone again, just in case she'd missed a message from Kincaid, but there was nothing.

"What were you going to do with your Saturday?" she asked Melody.

"Help Doug paint his sitting room."

"The great DIY project?" Gemma asked, bemused. "How's that coming?"

"Very slowly." Melody drew out the words. "He now knows which colors are authentic Victorian reproductions, and which brands have the least emissions." She rolled her eyes. "'Just pick a color you like' obviously was not the proper way to approach something of such import with Detective Sergeant Cullen."

Doug Cullen had become Kincaid's partner when Gemma had been promoted to inspector, and although Kincaid's leave had left him assigned to a different murder team, Cullen and Melody had become cautious friends.

"Well, it is his first house," Gemma said, laughing. "You could cut him some slack." Sobering, she nibbled a corner of her sandwich and regarded Melody a little hesitantly. "We haven't seen much of him. How are things at the Yard, do you have any idea?"

"I know Doug despises working with Superintendent Slater, and the feeling seems to be mutual. I think Doug's taking out his frustration on the paint."

"Has he said anything about Duncan? About the job, I mean?"

"Only that he's eager for him to come back. Why?" Melody looked concerned now. Gemma began to regret saying anything, but Melody was the only person she could talk to about this.

"It's just that— Look, you won't say anything to Doug?"

"Not if you don't want me to." Melody put down her sandwich and gave Gemma her full attention.

"I'm probably worrying over nothing. But when Duncan told Denis Childs he needed a bit more time at home, Denis went all hale and hearty and 'Don't bother your little head about it.' Not like him at all."

"No," Melody said slowly, frowning. "But surely he's just being—"

"All warm and fuzzy?" Gemma shook her head. "Definitely not the chief super's style, however sympathetic he may be under that impassive exterior. But I—"

She stopped as a shadow fell over their table. Looking up, she saw a large man with a shaved head and a neat brown beard, wrapping a bartender's apron around his waist. "I'm Reg," he said. "Kasey said you wanted a word?"

Gemma pushed her chair back and showed him her ID. "It's about Vincent Arnott. One of your regulars, I think?"

"Sure, he comes in most Friday nights." The man grinned. "Don't tell me Vince has the law after him."

"He's dead, actually," said Gemma quietly.

"What?" The smile left the bartender's face. "You're having me on, right?" When their expressions assured him that they weren't, he pulled out a chair and sat, heavily. "I don't believe it. He was just in last night. Was there an accident or something? Look, I'm careful not to overserve my customers," he added, a defensive edge to his voice. "And besides, Vince never drives—"

"There's no evidence that he did," said Gemma quickly, not wanting to get off on the wrong foot. "What time did he come in?"

Reg seemed to relax. "A bit after seven, maybe. It was Friday-night pandemonium in here. I remember serving him after the band came on, maybe eight thirtyish, but it was his second glass of wine, at least. Someone else must have served him before that."

"Did you talk to him?"

"Not really. Couldn't hear over the music." Reg gestured towards the back of the room, to the right of the bar, and

Gemma saw that there was a small area used as a stage. "Vince was never happy when the bands were loud. He could get downright stroppy about it."

"Then why did he come?" asked Gemma.

"Oh, well, you know. We were his local." Reg shrugged, and Gemma thought she saw a flicker of discomfort.

"Did you know him well, then?"

"Just the usual bar chat. Sometimes he'd nip in for half an hour during the week, when it was quieter. I knew he lived nearby, and that he was a lawyer. A barrister, I think. He said once that his wife was ill." The discomfort was more evident now.

"That bothers you," said Melody, having picked up on it as well. "Why?"

"Look." Reg sighed. "I'm a happily married man. And a bartender, so I see a bit of everything. What other people do is not my business."

"So what did Vince Arnott do that you didn't like?" asked Gemma, ignoring his protestations.

Reg looked at them, then shrugged again. "Not to speak ill of the dead and all that, but more often than not he'd end up with a bird. Buy them a few drinks. Sometimes I think he left with them."

"Anyone in particular?"

"No. But he had a type. Blond. Middle-aged. Divorced. Out for a little weekend fun."

"Do you know if he took them to the Belvedere Hotel?" put in Melody.

Reg gave a bark of disbelief. "That shit hole? Sorry," he added, wincing. "But anyone round here knows that place is not exactly four star, and Vince was a cashmere kind of guy. Still . . ." He thought about it for a moment. "Unless he went home with the ladies, I suppose that would be the most convenient option . . ."

"Do you know if Arnott went in for anything kinky?"

"Kinky?" Reg stared at Melody, and Gemma couldn't be sure if he was shocked at the suggestion or the fact that it came from a woman as wholesome looking as Melody Talbot. "God, no. Surely not. He was Mr. Straight Ahead."

"What about last night? Was he with anyone?" asked Gemma.

"Not that I saw." Reg scratched his chin. "Oh, but there *was* the bit of argy-bargy with the guitar player."

"What?" Gemma and Melody said in unison, then after a glance at Melody, Gemma went on. "You mean he was in a fight?"

"Just a shouting match. It was the guitar player who punched the guy in the face."

"Okay, back up," said Gemma. "What guitar player?"

"The one in the band," Reg answered a little impatiently. "Look, I didn't actually see what happened. The band stopped for a break, so there was a crush at the bar. Then I hear somebody shout, and when I looked, there's this bloke holding his hand to his nose, and the guitar player's manager clamps the guitar player by the shoulders and drags him back. Then, Vince is telling off the guitar player for starting a row, and the guitar player tells him to fuck off. End of story."

"Did they know each other? Arnott and the guitar player?"

"Don't think so. Not one of our usual bands, and from what I heard, Vince was reading him the 'Behave yourself, young man,' riot act. Vince could be a bit of a prick that way, but I was happy enough. I don't like fighting in my bar."

Gemma frowned. "Did you see Arnott after that?"

"I served him another drink, maybe a bit before eleven," Reg said, brow furrowed as he thought about it. "Lost him in the crowd after that."

"And this guitar player?"

"His manager made him put an ice pack on his hand. I know because I got some from the bar for him. Then, the band played another set and I think he left with the manager. Crap band, but the guitarist was good."

"Any idea where we could find him?" asked Gemma, thinking that any lead was better than none.

"Matter of fact, I do." Reg looked pleased at being able to offer something helpful. "Only reason we put the band in last night was that Caleb Hart, the record producer, is a regular here and he wanted to hear the guy play. He's got him recording today at the studio down the hill. I can give you directions, if you like."

CHAPTER FIVE

August 1852 saw the rebuilding work begin and in June 1854 Crystal Palace was re-opened in its new location by Queen Victoria . . . The whole building was enormous—1,848 feet long and 408 feet wide including two huge towers and many fountains with over 11,000 jets rising into the air.

—www.bbc.co.uk

Andy had plugged in the Strat and began to adjust the tuning when Poppy hit the first notes of a bass riff. He looked up at her in surprise. It was distinctive, unmistakable, and not at all what he'd expected.

"Know this one, guitar boy?" Poppy asked, her grin wicked.

He finished tuning, then fell in with her, finding the notes, getting the feel for it, watching her small fingers slide on the neck of the bass. When they'd got the rhythm, she moved into the intro, leaning into her mic until she was almost kissing it, and began to sing the familiar lyrics. " 'She's a rich girl, she don't try to hide it. She's got diamonds on the soles of her shoes.' "

Andy felt the hair rise on the back of his neck. Little Poppy Jones was an alto, rich, deep, slightly husky, and she didn't sound like anyone he'd ever heard.

He glanced across the room at Tam, who nodded once. An *I told you so* nod.

They played, working and reworking their way through the song. Time grew liquid, lost in sound. From Paul Simon, Poppy segued into Rickie Lee Jones's "Chuck E's in Love," then into something he didn't recognize. Her own composition? It was jazzy, bluesy, unique, and a little rough. When Andy had the words down, he came in on backup, adding his own riffs on the Strat, and the song began to mutate into something more polished. She was good, but together they were better.

After a while, he realized Caleb Hart was filming them with a video cam, and that they'd gone well past the time Caleb had allotted for the rehearsal space. But he also knew no one wanted to burst the bubble. There would be time for that later.

What they were making, in this finite moment, was magic.

Gemma and Melody emerged from the warmth of the pub into a fierce wind blowing up Westow Street. The clouds were in tatters now, the temperature noticeably lower. Gemma buttoned her coat, then pulled up an area map on her phone.

"Shall we get the car, boss?" asked Melody. "Drive back to the scene?"

Frowning, Gemma thought for a moment. "I think one of us should check out this guitar player. So far he's the only person we know of that had any interaction with the victim." Westow Street, where Reg the barman had said they would find the recording studio, ran to their right. Belvedere Road, where they'd left the car, to their left, Church Road and the Belvedere Hotel, straight ahead. "Why don't you go to the recording studio," Gemma continued. "I'll walk down to the hotel, see if Shara or the techies have made any progress. Then we can meet back at the Arnotts' house. Maybe by that time the FLO will have Mrs. Arnott settled, and we can have a look through Arnott's things."

"Right, boss." Melody didn't look thrilled at the allocation.

"Maybe you can get an autograph," Gemma teased. "I could have sworn you had the makings of a groupie."

When Gemma reached the Belvedere Hotel once more, the coroner's van was gone. The crime scene van was still parked in the road, however, so she decided to check in with the SOCOs before she compared notes with Shara MacNicols and talked to the hotel staff.

The younger constable, Gleason, stood guard at the propped-open fire door. When she reached the room, she found that the fresh air and the removal of the body had alleviated a good deal of the stench, although an unpleasant odor still lingered.

Mike and Sharon, the techs, had bagged the victim's clothing and the bedding, and were in the process of lifting prints from the room's surfaces.

"Bloody nightmare," said Mike as he transferred a strip of tape to a card. "Prints everywhere. And fibers. The cleaning staff in this place don't exactly do spit and polish."

"I'd never have guessed." Gemma glanced in a tiny cubicle that she suspected was referred to as the "en suite" bathroom. While the basin and toilet looked fairly clean, there were drifts of hair along the skirting boards. "Ugh." She found it interesting that a man as fastidious in his home and about his clothing as Vincent Arnott could have frequented a place like this.

"We did find something," said Sharon. "A spot of what looked to be fresh blood on the sheet."

"Any corresponding injuries on the victim?" asked Gemma.

"Not that were readily visible. Rashid will be able to tell you, of course."

That was something, thought Gemma. Assuming they could get DNA, or at least blood type. If the blood was not Arnott's, and the hotel cleaner would testify that she had changed the linens after the previous guest, they might be able to tie a suspect to the time and place. Assuming, that is, that they found a suspect.

It was time she had another word with the staff.

"Cancer?" Kincaid said, on a rush of dread.

But Louise shook her head. "It's TB. Apparently it's on the rise in London, especially among the immigrant black and Indian communities. My clients, in other words."

"But TB's treatable." His relief was not mirrored in Louise's expression.

"Yes, but." She gave him a tired smile. "There's always a 'yes, but.' It seems there are more and more antibiotic-resistant strains. They've started me on the most consistently effective drug, but it will be a couple of months before they'll know if it's working."

"Months?" Kincaid said in dismay.

"The normal course of treatment is at least a year on antibiotics. And that's assuming the drug works from the beginning. And rest. Lots of rest. Not my cup of tea."

"Will you be able to keep working?"

"I'll do as much from home as I can for the time being. I've hired an assistant, and I'll go into the office a few hours a week. But there's the contagion issue." His alarm must have shown in his face because she shook her head. "I'm not coughing, and I've been very careful with my hygiene," she added, gesturing at his coffee. "I think my hands may fall off from all the bloody washing. So as long as we don't have 'intimate' contact"—she made a wry face—"they say there's little risk. But I thought it better not to have Charlotte in the flat."

"And Michael and Tam?"

"Not likely to be any 'intimate contact' there." Louise gave a hoarse chuckle. "At any rate, I've told them they should just leave me alone, the old biddies, but they won't hear of it. They'll need to be tested every few months, just in case."

"If there's anything we can do—" he began, but she was already waving away his offer.

"Just get Charlotte settled."

Next door, he found Michael and Charlotte had already returned from their walk. As often as he'd visited Louise, he'd never been in Michael and Tam's flat. The rooms were mirror images of Louise's, but considerably more tidy and organized. Potted plants the size of small trees filled the front windows, while one long wall held neatly shelved books and CDs. Several guitars on stands were tucked into a corner, and two large rectangular dog beds were positioned opposite the sofa and armchairs.

Charlotte sat in the middle of one of the dog beds, arranging dog toys neatly on the other. Jagger and Ginger lay nearby on the polished wood floor, watching her with expressions of bewilderment.

"They're very patient," Kincaid said as Michael ushered him in.

"They love kids," Michael answered. "Interesting, isn't it, how they know? They knew about Louise, too," he added more softly. "That's why we insisted she see a doctor. Damn good thing."

"How did they tell you something was wrong?" Kincaid asked, curious.

"Well, generally Louise is sort of tolerantly affectionate with them, and vice versa. But the last month or so, they've been glued to her, nudging, whining, then coming to us as if they expected us to know what to do. Finally, even we began to see how bad she looked. Then we bullied her into going to a clinic."

"How bad is it, really?" murmured Kincaid, with an eye on Charlotte, who was still absorbed in her game.

Michael shrugged. "Hard to say. I've read that if it's an antibiotic-resistant strain, it can be tough, even for those who were in good shape before they became ill."

Kincaid knew what he wasn't saying—Louise had been a heavy smoker who didn't exercise, worked too much, and ate halfway decently only when Michael and Tam fed her.

"Can I get you a coffee?" Michael asked. "I know Louise made some, but I also know she mainlines her caffeine."

"Stout," Kincaid agreed with a grin. "I think that was my limit for the next week, but thanks. Maybe another time. And I think I might have promised a certain young lady a cupcake."

"Me! Me!" Charlotte jumped up, proving she'd been listening all along.

As Kincaid bundled Charlotte back into her coat, he glanced at Michael. "I know Louise won't ring us, but you will, won't you, if there's anything—"

"Of course. Tam will be sorry he missed you."

"The guitars—are they Tam's?" Kincaid asked as the instruments caught his eye again. "I didn't know he played."

"Relics of his misspent youth. He does still play occasionally, and he's quite good. But I think it was when he realized he'd never be great that he went into managing. He's still looking for his holy grail."

The directions given by Reg the barman took Melody into a steep lane that led off to the left from Westow Street. Not only steep, but cobbled. Within ten feet, she was cursing her heels. By the time she reached the bottom, she wondered if she'd misunderstood. The lane seemed to dead-end, and there was no sign of a recording studio.

Then she saw that the lane gave a twist to the left and leveled out for a few dozen yards before it jogged downhill again. There were a few cars parked on the right. Beyond them, treetops masked the hill as it fell steeply away to the west.

But on the other side, wildly colored murals decorated the lower part of brick walls. And above, brick and metal rose into a disjointed jumble of buildings that might have been thrown together with a giant's LEGO.

She stopped, surveying the place, and then she heard it. Music. It took her a moment to separate the source of the sound from the echoes, but when she did, she realized it was coming from the top of several flights of open iron stairs.

"Bugger," she muttered. With another disgusted glance at her shoes, she headed for the stairs.

The music grew clearer as she climbed. A ripple of guitar. Bass notes providing a punchy beat. And then the voices. One female, strong, assured, slightly quirky. Then a male voice coming in on harmony, and together they soared into a melody that made her think of songs she loved but was somehow completely new.

By the time Melody reached the railed wooden platform at the top of the stairs, she'd caught her heel only once. Pausing to adjust her shoe, she peered in the window beside the closed door, but saw only blurred shapes behind her own reflection.

She knocked lightly, feeling suddenly very much the intruder. There was no answer, no break in the music, so after a moment she opened the door and stepped gingerly inside.

The room was large, with dark, scuffed wooden floors. Bits of furniture and electronic equipment were pushed haphazardly against the walls. An electric heater near the door put out a welcoming blast of heat that Melody suspected didn't penetrate far into the room.

Four people were gathered near the large windows at the western end. For a moment, she watched them unobserved, as no one seemed to notice her.

The guitarist and the girl she'd heard singing faced each other, their mics close together as they sang. The girl, in spite of her powerful voice, looked like a child in her ruffled skirt and flowered tights. She had short hair the color of orange sherbet and held a slightly odd-looking bass guitar.

The guitarist, in jeans, trainers, and T-shirt, played a battered red electric guitar as he sang, his fingers flying over the strings. He was about her own age, she guessed. Slight—too thin, really—with rumpled blond hair. Nice looking, with features that might almost have been pretty if not for the intensity of his focus.

Melody thought she'd never seen anyone so completely absorbed in the moment, every line and muscle in his body an extension of the guitar in his hands. Her breath caught in her throat and she felt a sudden skip in her pulse.

It took an effort to shift her attention to the other two people in the room.

A small man wearing a faded Scottish tam stood beside a glossy-black grand piano, watching the artists as if mesmerized. Another man, taller, with neat brown hair and beard, was filming them with what looked to Melody like a professional-quality video cam.

Then the musicians held a last sustained note, the guitarist hit a final, ringing chord, and silence descended. The tension went out of the room like a whoosh of air.

The small man gave a congratulatory whoop and crossed the intervening space to give the guitarist a thump on the shoulders. The guitarist, starting to grin, looked up and saw Melody.

His face went still, his expression suddenly unreadable. His eyes, she thought, were blue, made darker by his black T-shirt. And the knuckles of his right hand, which still rested on the body of the guitar, were bruised and swollen. There was no doubt that this was the guitarist that Reg had described.

"Hello," said the girl, with friendly interest. "Are we taking up your space? I'm afraid we've gone a bit over."

The two older men turned to her, looking slightly puzzled. Melody couldn't imagine that she, in her tailored suit and coat, could look less like an artist in need of rehearsal space. She crossed the room, her heels clicking like gunshots on the hard floor, until she stood before the guitarist.

"My name's Detective Sergeant Melody Talbot," she said, pulling her ID from her bag. "The barman at the White Stag said I might find you here, if I could have a moment of your time. I'm sorry, but I don't know your name," she added in a rush, feeling idiotic.

"Look here, lass," said the small man, bristling, "you can see we're in the middle of a recording session—"

"Tam," broke in the guitarist, his voice easy. "I don't think you want to go calling a detective sergeant 'lass.' She might clap the cuffs on you. I'm Andy," he added, meeting Melody's gaze. "Andy Monahan. What can I do for you?"

"It's about an incident at the pub last night." Melody saw that the girl looked curious, the Scot, wary. "Is there some-where we could talk?" she asked Monahan, thinking he might be more forthcoming without an audience.

"No, this is fine," he answered, but there had been a flicker of a glance towards the Scot. "This is my manager—"

"Michael Moran. But everyone calls me Tam." Tam reached out and gave her hand a hearty shake.

"Caleb Hart," said the bearded man. "Reg at the White Stag is a mate. I told him we'd be doing a session here today."

"You're the producer?" asked Melody.

Hart nodded. "And this is Poppy Jones."

"Poppy," repeated Melody, taking the girl's offered hand. "Nice name for a singer." She saw that the girl was older than she'd first thought, and Poppy confirmed it by saying, "About time it came in useful. I've been cursing my parents over it for twenty years." Her accent, unlike Andy Monahan's, was as middle class as Melody's own.

"What's this about, then?" said Monahan, making it clear that they'd covered the social niceties.

Melody tucked her ID back into her bag, giving herself a moment to frame her response. "We're investigating the suspicious death of a man found in the Belvedere Hotel this morning. According to Reg at the White Stag, you had an altercation with the gentleman in the pub last night."

She saw the instant of shock in Monahan's eyes, and the convulsive tightening of the fingers of his right hand.

"Don't know what you're on about," he began, but Tam was already shaking his head.

"An altercation?" said Tam. He put an exaggerated emphasis on the next to last syllable. "Is that what you call some pompous geezer complaining that the lad here had a bit of a row with a punter? Is it him that's dead?"

"The pompous geezer's name was Vincent Arnott. And Reg said Mr. Monahan hit someone. I'd call that more than a row." She glanced at Monahan's bruised hand.

"Well, I didn't hit *him*, if that's what you're thinking," said Monahan dismissively, but Melody could have sworn it was relief that had washed across his face and left it pale.

"Did you see Mr. Arnott after that?" she asked. "Maybe he sought you out to further his grievance."

Monahan shrugged. "Maybe he picked a fight with someone else. I didn't see him again. I played the second set, then I went home. I certainly didn't go to the Belvedere, and from what I saw of that bloke, I can't imagine he did, either. Stuffed-up prick."

He was watching her carefully, and there was, thought Melody, curiosity mixed in with the relief. And something else. She felt her throat go dry and swallowed before she asked, "Is there anyone who can vouch for you?"

"Me, lassie," said Tam, ignoring Monahan's earlier admonishment. "I was with the band the whole evening. After we broke down the equipment, I ran Andy home in my Mini."

Melody didn't intend to let Tam Moran answer for Monahan. "Where's home, Mr. Monahan?"

"Hanway Place. Oxford Street and Tottenham Court Road. And I don't have a car, if that's what you're wondering. I didn't go back to Crystal Palace." He thought for a moment, absently plucking a few strings on the guitar, but didn't take his eyes from Melody. "You said 'suspicious death.' What happened to this bloke?"

"I'm afraid that's confidential for the moment," she answered, in her primmest police-speak. It wouldn't be confidential for long, once the press got hold of the details. "Had you ever seen Mr. Arnott before? Reg at the White Stag said he was a regular there."

Monahan shook his head, frowning. "Don't think so. And we'd never played that pub before." The twist of his lips told her that it was not an experience he'd care to repeat.

"But you did hit someone last night, Mr. Monahan," Melody persisted. "Was it someone who might have known the victim? Was that why Mr. Arnott was so upset?"

"No. I don't see how—" Monahan seemed to stop himself. "It was just some guy who'd had too much to drink and objected to our covers."

Melody studied him. "Do you always beat up the audience, Mr. Monahan? Not the best practice for someone who lives by their hands, I would think."

He flushed and looked away for the first time. "I don't like being shoved. And I don't like people putting their mitts on my guitar."

"Sergeant." It was Caleb Hart, who had carefully put down his video camera and now approached her, glancing at his watch. A Rolex, if she wasn't mistaken. "If there's nothing else we can help you with, our time here is fleeting. And expensive."

Melody felt a flash of irritation at being so summarily dismissed. But remembering the music they'd been making, she felt a stab of regret as well for the bubble she'd burst. She somehow doubted that they would all come together again in the same way, at least on this day.

"If you could just give me your contact information, Mr. Monahan and Mr. Moran. I think that will be all for now." She was brusque, determined to put herself back in charge, but the harder she tried for authority, the more she felt she was making a fool of herself.

Monahan patted his jeans pockets, then, looking around, said, "Tam, have you got a card?"

His manager took a slightly weathered business card from a case in his jacket and passed it to him, along with a pen. Monahan slipped off the guitar and placed it on its stand, then walked over to the piano and used the flat surface of its top to scrawl on the back of the card. He brought it to Melody with a flourish.

"Name. Address. Mobile," he said, and there was a hint of challenge in his look as he handed it to her.

She gave her own card to Tam, then Monahan, and told herself it was an accident when his fingers brushed hers. "Thanks. You'll let me know if you think of anything else," she added, making it a statement. "Thanks for your time."

Turning, she walked to the door, very aware of the clickety-clack of her heels on the floor and of four pairs of eyes on her back.

She let herself out onto the platform, took a gulp of cold air, then started carefully down the stairs. Halfway, she stopped, hoping to hear the music start again, but there was not a sound from above.

CHAPTER SIX

Locally the place name is often [used] as an alternative to Upper Norwood or the postcode area of SE19. If you ask a London taxi driver to take you to Crystal Palace he will usually assume to take you to the end of Crystal Palace Parade at the top of Anerley Hill, which used to have a roundabout and was the former location of the Vicar's Oak.

—www.crystalpalace.co.uk

"It was huge, the Crystal Palace." *Andy threw his arms wide in demonstration, and Nadine, sitting on the far side of the step, ducked away, laughing.*

"I believe you," she said. "Really. I do. Be careful with that guitar," she admonished. "You might actually be good at playing it, one of these days."

Flushing, Andy settled the Höfner more firmly across his knees. It was the first time anyone had given him the least bit of encouragement, and coming from Nadine it meant more than anything. He practiced every day, and had taken to playing on the front steps when he knew Nadine would be home soon. A lame excuse for keeping his observation post, but she didn't seem to mind him being there.

They'd developed an unspoken routine. When Nadine had parked her rattletrap of a Volkswagen, she'd put her handbag and work things in her flat before coming out again with lemonade or fizzy drinks for them both. Sometimes she changed from her dress into shorts, and pulled her hair up into a ponytail. She looked even younger then.

Andy had found an old strap for the Höfner at a charity shop on Westow Hill, and although he thought he probably looked a right prat wearing it sitting down, he did it anyway. It made him feel more like a real guitar player. While he and Nadine drank their lemonade, he played little snippets for her. New chords, a bit of a picking pattern. Never a whole song— that would have been totally naff.

She listened, and then they'd talk. That's how he'd learned that she liked history, and that she didn't know much about Crystal Palace.

"Wasn't it just taken down in Hyde Park and put up again here, on Sydenham Hill?" she asked now.

"No, look," he protested, pulling carefully folded papers from the back pocket of his jeans. He'd made copies at the library of some of the old black-and-white photos in the reference books. Smoothing them out, he handed them to Nadine and she took them, studying the pictures intently. That was one of the things he liked about her. She listened, and she looked at things, really looked, not just glancing at something and saying, "Oh, that's nice, dear," like most adults. Or his mum.

Not that he could think about her being anything like his mum. His mum was thirty-five, and he couldn't imagine Nadine being nearly that old, even though he knew she'd been married. But when he'd got up the nerve to ask her, she'd just laughed, and told him not to be cheeky.

Pointing at the top photo, he said, "It was bigger than the original Crystal Palace, the one they built in Hyde Park."

"You've been swotting," she said. "It was for the Great Exhibition, wasn't it? The original one. In—"

"In 1851. But when they rebuilt it, it had twice as much glass as the first one. And it took twenty-three months to build," he ventured, glancing at her to see if she looked bored. "It was 1,608 feet long, 315 feet wide, and 108 feet high."

A little crease appeared between Nadine's brows as she frowned. The bridge of her nose was slightly pink and there was a dusting of freckles across it. Even Andy, with his fair coloring, had gone brown as a nut in the past few weeks.

"I thought they just took it down and put it back up again," she said. "Like one of those conservatory kits people buy for their gardens, only bigger." She was teasing him a bit, he could tell by the tone of her voice, but he liked it. "Did you learn all that in school?" she asked.

"No." When she waited for him to say more, he made a G chord on the neck of the Höfner and ran his thumb over the strings ever so lightly. "The library," he admitted, a little reluctantly. Then, having confessed, he owned up to worse. "I like it there."

"Hmm. I like libraries, too." She smiled, and from her voice he could tell she meant it. "They're quiet," she added. "And nobody bothers you."

He relaxed, feeling that she understood, but he still couldn't bring himself to tell her that it was the one place he felt free from the worry about his mother. They never talked about personal things—he didn't even know where Nadine worked—and he somehow sensed that there were boundaries he shouldn't cross.

Nadine turned to the second photo, this one of the palace's interior, showing the great arched dome filled with fountains and pools, statues, even trees. She traced the pool in the photo with a fingertip, then said softly, " 'In Xanadu did Kubla Khan a stately pleasure-dome decree: where Alph, the

sacred river, ran, through caverns measureless to man, down
to the sunless sea.' "

A cloud passed over the sun and Andy felt a cooler breath
of air lift the damp hair on his forehead. "What is that? Did
you make it up?"

"No, it's Coleridge. You won't have had that in school yet,
will you?" said Nadine, shaking her head. "Not until secondary school. But that's what it made me think of, this great
crystal palace—Coleridge's poem. As if they tried to enclose
paradise, like Kubla Khan." She handed the papers back to
him. "I wish I could have seen it, the Crystal Palace. What
happened to it?"

"It burned. In 1936." Although he knew that perfectly well,
saying it aloud made him feel funny inside. Hollow. For a moment he wasn't sure he trusted himself to say more without his
voice going wobbly. Then, gripping the Höfner a little more
tightly, he added, "You could see the fire from eight counties.
And when the sun rose the next morning, the palace was gone,
all of it. There was nothing left but rubble."

After talking to the SOCOs, Gemma left the basement and
found an irritable and frustrated Shara MacNicols in the hotel
reception area.

If the place had been unappealing that morning, it was now
considerably less so. The cheap tables were littered with plates
of drying sandwich crusts, glasses, and scummy half-drunk
cups of tea. The staff were no longer huddled together, but
had migrated to different parts of the room, as though fearing
contagion.

Shara MacNicols, studying an antiquated hotel register at
the reception desk, looked up in surprise when Gemma entered
through the interior door. "Guv. Where did you come from?"

"Downstairs. I came in through the fire door. Mike and

Sharon have almost finished processing the scene. Any prog-ress up here?"

"We've taken details from the guests and let them go. There were a couple of commercial travelers, and a few unlucky tour-ists. No one else had a room in the basement. Apparently 'Mr. Smith' asked for that room particularly when he stayed here. That's why the cleaner assumed it would be empty first thing this morning, because he never stayed the entire night."

"Did he ask for that room because of the fire door?" Gemma wondered aloud. "And if so, did he know the latch was defec-tive, or did he just have the women wait outside until he could open the door and let them in?"

Shara nodded towards the staff in the reception area. "You won't get this lot to admit it if they knew the fire door was wonky." Raymond, the young, spotty-faced clerk, was hunched over his mobile, texting as if his life depended on it. Mrs. Dusek, the manager, was chewing a cuticle as she watched them anxiously. The cleaner, still in her smock, stared vacantly into space. "They've all gone completely dumb," Shara added, sounding disgusted. "There is a handyman, but it seems it's his day off. Very convenient. I've put that green constable—Gleason—on tracking him down, but I suspect he'll have been warned."

"You've been watching conspiracy theories on the telly," said Gemma, and was rewarded with a faint smile. She started to say, "Good work, Shara," but stopped herself, knowing that her detective constable would take it as patronizing. Instead, she thought for a moment, then said, "Let's see if we can find any other guests who've stayed in one of the basement rooms recently—assuming that they've actually given their real names and details. Someone who doesn't have a vested interest in ly-ing about the door."

"Do you think it really makes a difference, guv?" asked Shara, eyeing the hotel register with distaste.

"I don't think we should just assume that Arnott's killer came to the hotel with him."

"What?" Shara gave her a look that said she thought Gemma was daft. "You mean you think some random nutter might have walked in the fire door, tied Arnott up, and strangled him? And Arnott just said, 'Well, have a go, then'?"

Gemma shrugged. "It's possible. Anything is possible at this point." Seeing that Mrs. Dusek was straining to hear her and that the spotty clerk had looked up from his texting, Gemma turned away from them and lowered her voice. "Say Arnott brought a woman here. Say the woman had a jealous husband who followed them. The husband—or boyfriend—could have waited until the woman left, then surprised Arnott. Maybe he threatened him with a knife or a gun. Maybe he hit him over the back of the head and the wound wasn't visible. Just don't theorize in advance of the facts."

"La-di-da," Shara muttered, turning back to the register with a scowl.

Gemma bit back a retort. She knew from experience that a reprimand would make Shara go silent and sulky, but it wouldn't change her mind. And that was the thing that was likely to keep Shara MacNicols from ever being a really good detective, no matter how hard she worked and how badly she wanted to get ahead in the job. Shara wanted things to be black and white and she got stroppy when you tried to get her to see past the obvious, because she felt you were wasting her time.

"Just do it," said Gemma with a sigh. "Have the other basement rooms been searched, just in case our killer took advantage of the vacancy? He—or she"—she put in before Shara could correct her—"could have left something behind."

Having told Shara that once the SOCOs were finished and the other basement rooms searched, she could seal off the downstairs and let the hotel return to normal business, she walked back along Church Road, intending to meet Melody at the Arnotts' house.

But as she neared the White Stag, she saw Melody standing in front of the pub, phone to her ear.

Disconnecting as Gemma reached her, Melody said, "Boss, I've requested all the CCTV footage for the area. I had another word with Reg"—she nodded towards the pub—"and he says the whole of Crystal Palace was blanketed with fog last night, so I don't know how much good it will do us."

"Worth a try. Any luck with your guitarist?"

"He's not my guitarist." Melody gave Gemma an odd look. "But I did talk to him. He says he didn't know Arnott. Arnott gave him a dressing down over the punch-up with a drunk punter. Then he says he played another set and his manager took him home."

"Did you double-check with the manager?" Gemma asked.

"In the flesh. He was at the studio as well. Odd little chap. He confirms Andy's—the guitarist's—story. Neither of them recollect seeing Arnott after the incident."

"A dead end, then?" asked Gemma.

"Maybe." Melody frowned and shook her head. "The thing is, I could swear the guitarist was lying about something. I'm just not sure what it was."

Doug Cullen stood on Putney Reach, staring out at the gray expanse of the Thames below Putney Bridge. Not even the hardiest of scullers was to be seen on the river today, and he couldn't blame them. It was only his restlessness that had driven him out for a walk.

He and Melody had been planning their DIY project—painting his dining and sitting rooms—for weeks, and he was disappointed by her absence. Not that he didn't understand—

the job was the job, and a murder inquiry always took precedence.

But still, nothing these last few months had turned out quite the way he'd imagined. Not that he'd expected to like working on Superintendent Slater's team while Duncan was on family leave, but he'd never dreamed they'd stick him with doing data entry. It was a murder team, for God's sake, and he was a detective sergeant, an experienced officer. When he'd complained, Slater had told him he was "making a valuable contribution," with a smirk that let him know his new boss meant his assignment to be demeaning.

None of the team had welcomed him, and he'd begun to sense something at the Yard—an atmosphere, a feeling that people were whispering behind his back. He could put it all down to paranoia, except that he so seldom saw Chief Superintendent Childs, who was Duncan's direct superior as well as Superintendent Slater's. Not that Childs had ever been one for fraternizing, but one had always known he was there, and now somehow his large presence seemed to have diminished.

With his fingers and toes numb from the cold, Doug glanced at the sky and realized he'd only a few hours left of the pale winter light. If he was going to paint in the best conditions, he'd better buck up and get at it. He didn't need Melody's help, he told himself firmly—he was perfectly capable of doing a bit of DIY on his own.

Walking the short distance home briskly, he surveyed his preparations. He had already covered the few bits of furniture Melody had helped him pick out for the sitting room. Now he arranged a canvas cloth over the floor in the center of the room and placed his ladder atop it. Opening the cream paint, he stirred it, then placed the tin on the ladder shelf. Brush in hand, he climbed carefully up, cursing the Victorians and their ten-foot ceilings. It had seemed sensible to start at the plaster rosette surrounding the chandelier and work his way outward, but he found that he had made a slight miscalculation in the positioning of the ladder. Still, he could reach the rosette if he stretched.

Doug dipped his brush, wiped the excess on the edge of the paint tin, and began. This wasn't so bad, he told himself, as the work went quickly and half the rosette was soon finished. Maybe this was just what he needed, a little instant gratification to counter the frustration of the job. He leaned out a bit farther, certain he could reach the other side of the plasterwork without moving the ladder.

And then the ladder lurched. He swung his arm, trying to counterbalance, and the paint tin went flying. It seemed to topple in slow motion, the rich cream paint drifting out in a perfect fan. Doug watched it in an instant's frozen fascination, then time clattered back with a rush and he realized that he, too, was falling.

When Melody and Gemma reached the Arnotts' house again, a Toyota sedan that Melody recognized as belonging to DC Marie Daeley, the family liaison officer, was parked behind Melody's Clio.

"Good. Reinforcements," said Gemma, and Melody knew she hadn't been looking forward to dealing with Mrs. Arnott on her own.

When they rang the bell, it was Daeley who answered. The detective constable was in her forties, with neat, graying hair, sensible clothes, and a brisk take-charge manner that usually seemed more comforting to the bereaved than outright sympathy. She was also a sharp officer who could be depended upon to inform the murder team of anything she learned that might be pertinent to their investigation.

The house smelled of coffee and seemed indefinably more welcoming than it had that morning.

"She's next door," Daeley told them as they came into the hall. "With the neighbor. Thank God for a sensible woman." Marie Daeley, it appeared, had found a kindred spirit in Mrs. Bates. "We've rung the sister in Florida, Sara Bishop. She's trying to arrange a flight for tomorrow, but even if she can manage, she won't arrive until Monday."

"How's Mrs. Arnott holding up?" Gemma asked as they followed Daeley into the kitchen.

Daeley poured them coffee, and Melody was glad of the cup to warm her hands.

"She's very confused, and it's obviously more than just the shock," answered Daeley, leaning against the worktop and sipping from her own mug. "I don't know how the husband managed as long as he did." She waved a hand in a gesture that took in the kitchen and surrounding rooms. "There are little lists and notes for her everywhere. He was a barrister, according to Mrs. Bates?"

"So it seems. We'll be contacting his chambers as soon as possible."

"It must have been difficult for him when he was in court," mused Daeley. "He had her routines all worked out for her, and he rang her at regular times during the day. According to Mrs. Bates, he was very patient with her, but he must have known he couldn't go on much longer."

"Why such determination to keep her at home?" Melody asked, trying to meld the devoted husband with the man who picked up women on a regular basis—and who had shouted at a guitarist in a pub without any apparent provocation. "Was it concern for her, or was he ashamed of his wife's illness? I'd be curious about how much his colleagues knew."

"He might have had financial motives as well," suggested Gemma. "I imagine care in a good facility would have cost him a pretty penny."

"I've had a quick look at the computer in his office," said

Daeley, "but all the accounts, including the financials, are password encrypted. The tech team should be round shortly to take it into the lab."

Gemma took her cup to the sink and rinsed it. "Thanks for that, Marie. We needed a boost. Anything else we should take note of?"

Daeley gave a little snort. "Not unless you count color-coordinated wardrobes for them both. Oh, and there's not a single medication anywhere in the house, not even aspirin or paracetamol. I suspect he couldn't be sure what his wife might take if she was left unsupervised."

"Right, then," said Gemma. "We'd better have a look, just in case. Melody, up or down?"

"I'll take down, thanks very much." Melody didn't relish the idea of going through the couple's bedrooms. House searches always made her uncomfortable. She had learned to guard her own privacy so fiercely that the invasion of someone else's was jarring. And in this case, considering the couple's domestic arrangements, more than a little creepy.

She finished her own coffee, and as Gemma climbed the stairs, Melody left Marie in the kitchen and began working her way methodically through the rooms on the ground floor.

The formal parlor and dining rooms were scrupulously clean, and excruciatingly dull. The furniture, the drapes, the china and crystal in the dining room cabinet, all of good quality and chosen, she thought, to impress, with no spark of either imagination or real appreciation. Doug's cheap and cheerful little house in Putney beat this one by a—

"Shit," she said aloud, brought up short. She glanced at her watch. Doug. She should have rung him. Well, she'd take a minute when they were through here, and at least let him know that tomorrow didn't look promising for their painting project, either.

She went towards the back of the house, into a less formal

sitting room, with chairs that at least looked comfortable and a large-screen television. A typed and laminated list of channels lay beside the remote on an end table, and a magazine rack held a few recent women's magazines that looked unread.

There was another room, on the opposite side of the television room from the kitchen, and when she glanced in, she saw that it was obviously Arnott's study. There was the computer Marie had mentioned, a new model set dead center on a heavy mahogany desk. Glass-fronted bookcases held law books and a few old novels of the manly-thriller variety.

And there was a television as well, not as large as the one in the sitting room, but new and expensive and sitting atop its own media cabinet with a DVD and a Blu-ray player. There were no DVDs visible, however, so she tried a drawer in the cabinet. It held a small collection of action thrillers, similar in nature to the novels on the shelves. The next drawer was locked. She jiggled it, frustrated, then went to the desk and began a methodical search through the drawers.

The little key was in the back of the center compartment, behind the paper clips and elastic bands. She took it over to the media cabinet and opened the locked drawer with an easy click.

Melody stared down at the DVDs, neatly aligned, spine up. She reached out a finger to touch them, then made a face and drew it back.

Instead, she went to the door and called out, "Boss. You'd better come have a look at this."

She locked the shop door from the inside and switched off the lights. Although the streetlamps had come on half an hour ago, it was not yet officially closing, and she saw a few passersby peer curiously through the glass.

Somehow she had got through the day, serving customers

with a face that felt stiff from her manufactured smile. She'd even managed to chat with a few of the regulars, girls in the casts of nearby West End shows, taking breaks between the matinees and evening performances. But as the afternoon wore on, she felt herself stretching thinner and thinner, like an elastic band near to breaking, and now even the passing glance of a shopper through the darkened glass made her feel exposed, her knees suddenly weak as jelly.

Moving away from the window, she felt for a solid wall and leaned against it, trembling. The memories she'd held at bay all that day came at her in a rush that left her gasping, hunched over with her arms wrapped protectively across her stomach.

Why had she gone back to Crystal Palace when every instinct had told her it was a mistake? She'd thought she was prepared to face the past, but she'd never expected to see *him*. She had recognized him instantly, as if fifteen years had collapsed into an instant. Then he turned, his glance passing over her, and there had been no hint of recognition in his eyes.

He had never really looked at her, she realized, that day when he had so casually torn her life to shreds. Had he been thinking about his golf game? His next seduction? The favor he was doing for one of his cronies?

Numb with shock, her white-knuckled hand clenched round the stem of her wineglass, she'd watched him as he tried to chat up a twenty-something girl with bleached hair and a little muffin roll between her T-shirt and her jeans, seen the girl reject him with a shrug.

Scowling, he'd watched the girl walk away. Then, his attention drawn to some commotion on the band's little stage, he'd slammed his glass on the bar and pushed through the crush of punters until he reached the band. He shouted something she didn't catch, but she could see that neither the words nor the object of his tirade meant anything to him, other than a way of venting his temper over the girl's rejection.

Just as she had meant nothing to him, on that long-ago day.

The anger had rolled through her then, cold and sharp and diamond hard, and she moved instinctively and without any thought of the consequences. She'd slid up next to him when he returned to the bar, bumping him, spilling a bit of wine on his trousers and brushing at it with a flustered apology—old tricks learned in Paris, automatic as breathing.

And he'd taken the bait. Oh, he'd taken the bait. She hadn't remembered his name. When he'd said, "Call me John," she'd fought a wild desire to laugh. How perfect. How bloody perfect.

So she'd flirted, let him buy her a drink, thinking she'd get him going until he was sure he'd made a conquest, then make the old *powder her nose* excuse and walk out, leaving him high and dry. Her bit of playacting had kept her mind off the other temptation, the one she knew she mustn't give in to. Not that night, not now, not with him in the bar.

But by the time he'd whispered in her ear that he knew a little place, she'd had one glass of wine too many and she was riding a reckless adrenaline high. So she kept up the game, thinking she'd tell him the truth at the last minute—high and dry wouldn't be the half of it, then.

She'd walked through the fog with him to the seedy hotel, waited in the dark for him to let her in the basement fire door as if she were the commonest whore. And once in the room, when he'd let her know what he wanted, she'd gone along with that, too, knowing he'd suggested a humiliation more perfect than anything she might have invented. Too perfect.

She clutched herself tighter, trying to still the shaking in her hands.

How could she have done such a thing? How could she, after everything she'd been through?

The flush of shame brought nausea so intense she staggered and almost fell. Then she lurched to the back of the shop, one hand over her mouth, the other grabbing the edges of display counters as if they were railings in a rough sea, all the while the smell of that horrid room, and the smell of him, filling her nostrils.

When she reached the toilet cubicle in the back of the shop, she fell to her knees, her forehead against the porcelain, and vomited until there was nothing left but dry heaves.

And still a tiny voice whispered in her head that it had served the bastard right.

CHAPTER SEVEN

The palace and the grounds became the world's first theme park offering education, entertainment, a rollercoaster, cricket matches, and even 20 F.A. Cup Finals between 1895–1914.

—www.bbc.co.uk

Melody had watched as Gemma, her lips quirked in distaste, ran a gloved finger over the videos. Gemma pulled one out, frowned, put it back, scanned another. "Could be worse," she said. "They all seem to be pretty soft core. Nothing violent— just a little male-bondage fantasy. We'll have someone run through the lot to make sure that's all there is to them."

"Shara?" Melody suggested.

"I thought you were making an effort to be mates with Shara." Gemma flashed Melody a wicked grin.

"She was a bit difficult today, at the hotel. Serves her right. And, besides, I don't want to watch them," Melody added.

"No. Neither do I," Gemma admitted. "Shara it is."

Melody had fetched an evidence bag for the DVDs from the boot of her car, and after a last word with Marie Daeley, who was still waiting for the computer boffins, they headed back to Brixton. Night had fallen while they were in the house, but unlike the previous evening, it was clear, and as Melody drove north she could see the lights of the city spread below her.

"Anything interesting upstairs?" she asked Gemma.

"Definitely separate bedrooms. And Marie was right about the color-coordinated clothing in the wardrobes. He even had little day-of-the-week tags pinned to hers."

"Another coping tactic? Or was he just obsessively controlling?"

Gemma shrugged. "In that case, why was he the one who fancied being tied up?"

"I wonder how often he indulged?" Melody mused as they joined the long queue of red tail lamps snaking downhill. "According to Reg at the Stag, Arnott liked to hook up with the occasional divorcée looking for a good time. It seems like he'd be taking a big risk of being told to bugger off—if not getting a slap in the face—if he suggested that bit of hanky-panky to your average suburban divorcée. And he wasn't prepared with gear."

"Maybe he splurged on a professional and got more than he bargained for."

Melody tapped a finger on the steering wheel, shaking her head. "He'd have had no trouble finding a call girl to cater to his tastes in the city. But at the White Stag? A call girl of any sort seems unlikely. And why would a pro tie him up and strangle him?"

"Bad for repeat business," agreed Gemma, straight-faced. Then she added, "We'd better have the SOCOs take a look at his car tomorrow, though. He might have kept a stash of something more appropriate than belts and neckties. Maybe the opportunity to access it just didn't come up last night. He didn't drive because he'd been drinking—"

"And probably because he didn't want his car connected to the hotel," Melody broke in.

"Right. And it could have been a bit awkward to suggest

to his new lady friend that they walk down to his house and retrieve his bondage gear before going to the hotel."

"A wee bit, yes," Melody agreed, and they drove the rest of the way in silence, mulling it over.

They dropped the DVDs off in Brixton, with a note asking Shara to review them in the morning, then drove on to Notting Hill. When they reached Gemma's house, they agreed they'd meet at the station at nine the following morning, driving separate cars as the day's interviews might take them in different directions. Gemma invited Melody in, but it was perfunctory. It had been a long day and Melody was sure that Gemma wanted to spend time with Duncan and the kids. She said good night and drove the mile to her own flat.

Melody loved the old mansion block of flats near the top of Kensington Park Road, but she'd lately begun to find the flat itself confining. She could see the upper end of Portobello Road from her sitting room windows, but that was the extent of her access to the outside. Not a great loss on a cold night in January, but the previous autumn she'd begun to crave contact with things green and growing.

Tossing her coat and handbag in the sitting room chair, she stood for a moment, looking down at the haze of light rising from Portobello. Even with the windows shut tight she could hear the buzz of Saturday-night revelers. It had been a hard day and she was tired, but she still felt wired, restless. She wondered how much of her unsettled state had to do with the case, and how much with the weird frisson of connection she'd felt with the guitar player that afternoon.

"Andy," she said aloud. "Not just the guitar player. Andy Monahan." For an instant, she imagined what it would be like to wander down Portobello Road with him on a night like this, arm in arm, snuggled together for warmth.

Then she shook herself, breathed, "Stupid cow," and turned away from the window.

She had decisions to make. Important ones. Should she call her parents now and tell them she'd be missing the traditional family Sunday brunch at their Kensington town house tomorrow, or wait until morning?

Wait until morning, she decided, when she could deliver the news in a rush and avoid a scolding about working too hard. One down.

Now, wine, pajamas, ready meal, and ring Doug, in that order. Easy peasy, that one. The exciting life of a twenty-something singleton in London. That would make Doug laugh, she thought with a grin, and then they could natter about whatever dreadful thing was passing for Saturday-night telly.

She'd added her suit jacket to the pile on the chair, flicked on the television with the sound muted, and was headed for the fridge when her mobile rang.

Fishing it from her bag, she glanced at the ID, then answered cheerfully, "I was just about to call you. You must have ESP."

"One thing I'm good at," said Doug. His voice sounded strange. Slurred. Was he drinking? she wondered. She'd never seen Doug have more than a beer or two, except for the time they'd finished a bottle of champagne between the two of them, and even then he hadn't been all that tipsy.

"Sorry about today," she said, still a little absently, opening the freezer door and peering into the depths. "What are you talking about?"

"Decorating. Not my cup of . . . tea." The last word faded out, as if he'd forgotten he was on the phone.

There was definitely something wrong here. Melody closed the freezer door and gave the call her full attention. "Doug? Are you all right?"

"Effing ladder," he mumbled. Doug wasn't much of a swearer under the worst of circumstances.

"What about a ladder?" Melody said sharply.

"Fell off it, didn't I? Broke damned ankle. Bloody paint

every"—he hiccupped—"where. Wanted to know if you could drive me . . . drive me home. In the morning. Doctor says swelling has to go down before they can fit a . . . boot." He snickered. "Like a car boot."

"Doug." Melody was already reaching for her discarded jacket and bag. "Where are you?"

To Gemma's surprise, Duncan opened the front door before she could get her key in the lock.

"My very own welcoming committee?" she said, brushing her cheek against his as he ushered her in, feeling his end-of-the-day stubble.

"I was in the kitchen and saw Melody pull up. I thought I'd take advantage of having you to myself for at least thirty seconds."

"Why?" She pulled away, her stomach doing its familiar clench of anxiety when she'd been away from the children too long. "Are the kids okay?"

"Of course they're okay. I've just got the little ones settled doing a puzzle in the sitting—"

There was a scrabble of toenails on the hard floor, and Geordie, their cocker spaniel, came tearing into the hall, yipping excitedly.

"Mummy's home," came Toby's shout, followed by a squeal from Charlotte.

"So much for stealth, and my thirty seconds," Duncan said with a sigh as Toby and Charlotte pelted into the hall after the dog.

Toby bounced up and down, teasing the dog, while Charlotte grabbed Gemma's legs in a hug. "We've got a puzzle," Toby informed her. "Harry Potter and the Quidditch Golden Snitch. It's got a whole hundred pieces. Char's too little to do it."

"Am not," Charlotte protested as Gemma picked her up and gave her a proper hug.

"You're big enough to be heavy, aren't you, lovey?" Gemma teased. "Where's Kit?" she asked Kincaid.

"In his room," Kincaid answered with a shrug. They were still trying to adjust to their sociable son's new teenage need for alone time. "Hard day?" he added softly, studying her.

Gemma nodded. "I'll tell you after." Charlotte wriggled down from her hip and ran back to her puzzle.

"I've got a nice bottle of sauvignon blanc chilling in the fridge. Will that help?"

"Brilliantly." Following him into the kitchen, she sank into a chair at the kitchen table, which was already set, and with the good dishes and glassware to boot.

Kincaid took the wineglass from her place, filled it from the already uncorked bottle in the fridge, and handed it to her with a flourish. "Sainsbury's finest, madam," he said. "Crisp yet delicate, with hints of pear and citrus. Or something like that."

Laughing, she took a sip, held it in her mouth, then swallowed with an appreciative sigh. "I'd agree with all of the above. Maybe you missed your calling as a sommelier. Whoa," she added as Charlotte climbed into her lap. Gemma deftly slid her wineglass out of harm's way and settled Charlotte more firmly.

"Mummy." Charlotte patted her cheek to make sure of her full attention. "We saw the doggies today. Look, I drew a picture." She handed Gemma a piece of paper she'd held crumpled in her fist.

Smoothing out the sheet, Gemma examined two oval shapes drawn in red crayon, each with smaller circles at one end—presumably the heads, complete with triangles for ears—and four stick legs. "That's lovely, darling. Is that Tess and Geordie?"

"No, no." Charlotte shook her head, curls bouncing. "We went to see Jazzer and Henny."

Kincaid turned from the cooker, where fish cakes had just begun to sizzle in the pan. The smell was delicious and Gemma's stomach rumbled. "Jagger and Ginger," he explained. "We went to see Louise. Michael was there and he and Char took the dogs for a walk."

"Louise? Why? Is everything all right?" Gemma reached round Charlotte, who was content to snuggle against her while tracing her crayoned dogs with a fingertip, and took another sip of her wine.

"Fine. Erika had the boys over for lunch, and I just thought it was a nice opportunity for a visit." He seemed to hesitate, then added, "Louise seems a bit tired."

"Who's tired?" said Kit, coming into the kitchen with Toby on his heels, and trailed, as always, by Tess, his little terrier.

"Me," answered Gemma. "And making the most of being waited on. It sounds as if you had a nice day."

"Erika gave me a cool book. It's about Darwin's garden." Kit went to sniff the fish cakes, taking the spatula from his dad and giving them an exploratory prod.

"She does spoil you two," said Gemma, but without criticism. She knew how much pleasure it gave her friend, and the little gifts were always things that interested and stimulated the boys. Gemma only hoped that Erika would one day be able to find such a close connection with Charlotte.

Kit helped his father serve the plates—the fish cakes, a chilled yogurt and dill sauce, steamed new potatoes, and a salad. They had all got settled at the table when, from the hall where Gemma had left her handbag, came the insistent ring of a phone.

"Oh, blood—I mean blimey," muttered Gemma.

Kit hopped up. "I'll get it."

He was back in a moment, and having, of course, looked at the caller ID, said as he handed it to Gemma, "It's Melody."

Gemma pushed her plate aside and answered the call. "Has something come up?" she asked.

"As in a breakthrough?" Melody answered, with a laugh

that sounded a little strangled. "Not unless you count Doug. He's broken his ankle. He's in Charing Cross Hospital."

Melody stopped at the Tesco at Notting Hill Gate and bought some grapes and a bunch of slightly wilted yellow roses. By the time she reached the hospital, she was regretting both purchases, but she carried them in anyway.

The nurse on the ward desk told her it was past visiting hours, but when Melody showed her warrant card and said she was Doug's fellow officer, she got a nod through.

"Not too long, though," the nurse added. "We've given him something for the pain, and he needs to rest."

Finding the curtained cubicle, Melody peeked in. Doug was dozing, his splinted leg propped up on pillows. He wore a pale blue hospital gown, and without his glasses and with his blond hair rumpled, he looked ridiculously young and vulnerable.

"Hey," she said softly. He opened his eyes and blinked at her. "Nice outfit you've got there," she added.

Fumbling his glasses from the nightstand, he put them on and glanced down at the gown. "I asked for pink, but they were out." He seemed to be making an effort to enunciate.

"Good thing." She sat in the plastic bedside chair, feeling awkward, and held up the Tesco bag. "Grapes," she said, retrieving her first offering. Looking round for someplace to put them, she settled for an empty spot on the nightstand. The flowers she drew out a little more reluctantly. "They're a bit sad," she apologized. "Here, I'll put them in your water jug. I'll ask the nurse for a clean pitcher before I go."

"Thanks." He looked pleased, and she felt better.

"Does it hurt?" she asked, glancing at the ankle.

"Like blazes at first. Not so much now. They say it's a clean break, but I have to stay overnight. Have to get the swelling down before they can put on the cast . . . thingy." His eyelids drooped and he blinked owlishly at her. "Don't want me playing football."

"I wouldn't put it past you after this. The lengths you'll go to for a little attention."

"Lengths to get off work, more like it."

"Or to get out of DIY."

"There is that. Sorry to ruin your Saturday night," he added.

"I had a hot date with the telly," she told him easily. "You'll owe me. Now, what's this about tomorrow morning?"

"I could take a taxi home, but they said I'd need help getting settled. Got to keep weight off the ankle for the first day or so." He licked at dry lips and took a sip of water before going on. "Hate to ask, but otherwise, I'll have to ring my mum in St. Alban's." Rolling his eyes, he added, "Fate worse than death."

Melody laughed. "I know what you mean. Not to worry. Just tell me what time," she reassured him, all the while wondering how she was going to juggle looking after Doug with the demands of a murder case.

CHAPTER EIGHT

The site attracted 2 million visitors a year and was also home to displays, festivals, music shows and over one hundred thousand soldiers during the First World War.

—www.bbc.co.uk

Gemma was halfway to Brixton the next morning when her mobile rang. A taxi horn blared beside her just as she picked up, and then a familiar voice said in her ear, "I do hope you're on hands free. Talking while driving, tut-tut."

"Rashid, hi." She flipped on her headset. "I've just crossed the Battersea Bridge, so give me a sec." Easing into the traffic passing Battersea Park, she said, "Okay, good now. What's up? You have something for me?"

"I'm on my way to a scene in Tooting Bec, but it's not one that can't wait half an hour. I thought maybe we could meet in Brixton for a chat. I'll be going right past."

Glancing at the car clock, Gemma saw that she'd be a good half hour early for the scheduled nine o'clock briefing, and from Melody's second phone call last night detailing the arrangements for Doug, she suspected Melody might be running a bit late. "Right, I can do that."

"Station?"

She thought a moment. "You know the Caffè Nero across from the tube station? Why don't you meet me there instead. I'll buy you a cuppa."

"Deal," said Rashid, and rang off.

There were disadvantages to having Rashid come into the station, Gemma had learned—mainly that every female in the building would come up with some excuse to stop and say hello. No one had warned her when she joined CID that a pathologist with rock-star looks might present a problem.

And, she admitted to herself, she wasn't averse to a little one-on-one case discussion with Rashid. Last night had not given her much chance to do more than go over the bare bones of it with Duncan. Between conferences with Melody and the normal dinner-bedtime routine with the children, she'd fallen into bed too knackered to do more than mumble a good night.

When she reached Brixton, she parked her Escort in her designated spot in the gated police station car park, then ducked out and hurried up Brixton High Street towards the place on the second level of the old Morley's Department Store. Only when the building was in sight did she remember that it was Sunday, and that the department store wouldn't open until eleven.

Rashid, however, was standing outside the Starbucks on the tube station side of the road, grinning. He wore his usual jeans and black leather bomber jacket. A woman walking by gave him a covert glance, but he seemed, as usual, completely oblivious.

"Starbucks will have to do," he said as she reached him. "Minus the view, but at least it's warm."

"As long as there's a double-strength latte, it could be the moon."

He held the door open and ushered her in with the lightest of touches on her elbow. "Early start?" he asked. "Or late night?"

"A bit of both. And Doug Cullen fell and broke his ankle yesterday. Melody's picking him up from hospital this morning, and Duncan's trying to make arrangements for the children so that he can look in on him midday."

"How the hell did Doug do that? Sitting at the computer?" Rashid asked as Gemma got in the order queue. She didn't have to ask his coffee preference. One of the T-shirts he wore regularly bore the slogan PATHOLOGISTS DRINK JET FUEL.

"Apparently he's expanding his repertoire. He fell off a ladder while trying to paint his sitting room ceiling."

"DIY will get you every time." Rashid shook his head. "Silly git. He's lucky he didn't break his neck. I've seen enough cases like that." When Gemma had picked up their coffees and they'd found a booth, he added, "Any progress with our gentleman from yesterday?"

Gemma told him what they'd learned about Arnott's movements on Friday evening and about his home situation, adding, "And we found a stash of bondage DVDs hidden in his home office, but there was no other evidence that he made a regular practice of it. I'm having his car gone over today, just in case he kept equipment or contacts stashed there." She took a sip of her latte, which was still hot enough to burn her tongue. For a moment, she envied the other patrons, most of whom were lingering over spread-out copies of the *Sunday Times* with cooling ceramic mugs rather than paper takeaway cups. "I was hoping you'd have something more helpful," she said to Rashid.

He pulled a stack of printed sheets from the leather satchel he'd had slung over his shoulder. "Here's the report with *i*'s dotted and *t*'s crossed, but in a nutshell, I can tell you that he was strangled, and that it wasn't self-inflicted. Considering the bruising from the ligature, the pressure was definitely exerted from behind, so I think he was killed facedown, then immediately turned over."

"Could it have been an autoerotic liaison gone too far?"

"Most autoerotics go it alone. And the position was wrong. Practitioners want to, um, take full advantage of the stimulus."

Even with his olive skin, Gemma could have sworn that the imperturbable Rashid Kaleem was blushing.

"Besides," he went on a little hurriedly, "the bruising was deep in the tissue. Most autoerotics just get carried away—and usually the deaths are hanging accidents—but whoever did this really meant to do damage. And there was no evidence of anal penetration or sexual activity of any kind."

The older man who had been so comfortably reading his paper in the next booth stood up, giving them a disgusted glare, and walked out.

"Oh, dear," said Gemma, glancing round to make sure there were no other patrons within hearing distance. "I'm afraid we've just ruined that poor man's breakfast."

"As long as he doesn't complain to the management." Rashid's grin was unrepentant.

"Any findings on the ligature?" Gemma asked, leaning a bit closer and keeping her voice down.

"Some luck there. First, he was gagged, but not tightly. There was a little chafing at the corners of his mouth, but no tearing, and no bruising of either lips or tongue."

"Would the gag have been enough to keep him from crying out?"

"He could have made some noise, but probably not anything intelligible."

"There was no one else in the basement rooms. And there's a TV behind the reception desk," Gemma mused. "I'd bet the night manager keeps it on for company."

"Which would have masked any sounds from downstairs, especially with the interior fire doors closed." Rashid moved his coffee so that he could flip through the report, although Gemma was quite sure the gesture was no more than habitual. She'd never known him to have to check a fact. "I did find some interesting fibers," he went on. "Lodged in the corners of the mouth, a very fine silk blend. Pale gray. And in the ligature bruising on the neck, a few bits of a fuzzy wool-acrylic, some fibers navy, some maroon."

Gemma frowned, digesting the information. "I'll see what the SOCOs turned up as soon as I get into the station. The fuzzy stuff could have come from something that shed in the room as well." She sipped her cooling latte, which now tasted of scalded milk. "Anything interesting from the tox screen yet?"

"Blood alcohol was fairly high. He certainly shouldn't have been driving. And although his judgment was almost certainly impaired, I expect he could have still put on a pretty good front." Rashid glanced at his watch, then downed the rest of his coffee in one long swallow. "I'll have more for you on the tox results in a couple of days, but I'd better get on to Tooting Bec. An elderly man dead in his home, but the medics found an empty bottle of sleeping pills, so the coroner will need a postmortem.

"Oh, one more thing," Rashid added as he rose. "The SOCOs checked with me on the victim's blood type. That spot of fresh blood on the sheet? It wasn't Arnott's."

Getting Doug in—and out of—Melody's little Renault Clio had been a bigger undertaking than she had expected. Even after she'd slid the passenger seat all the way back, he'd had to grab the car's roof and lever himself in, grimacing as he positioned the unwieldy surgical boot in the foot well.

"Sorry, sorry," she'd murmured as she eased the car into traffic, hating the sight of his white face and clenched teeth.

Fortunately, the Sunday-morning streets were as empty as they were ever likely to be, and it wasn't far from the hospital to Putney. He'd needed her arm to get out when they reached his house, and that had made him grumble under his breath.

"You'll get better at it," she said, walking beside him as he hobbled up to the front door. "Are you sure you don't need a crutch or something?"

"No, they said I just had to stay off it as much as possible the first day or two. I don't need a bloody crutch or a cane, thanks very much." He fumbled the key in the lock, then stepped into the house with an obvious sigh of relief.

Melody had to bite her lip when she followed him into the sitting room and saw the overturned ladder and the spilled paint decorating not only the drop cloth but the surrounding carpet, like a monotone Jackson Pollock painting. "Good thing you'd decided to rip the carpeting out," she said only half jokingly. They'd discovered that beneath the worn brown flat-weave carpet, the original Victorian floorboards were in almost perfect condition. "Don't worry. I'll help you clean it up later."

She uncovered the armchair Doug had protected with a sheet and pulled up an ottoman. Both were finds from the Chelsea auction house they'd visited on several occasions, and she was glad they'd escaped unscathed. As Doug sat heavily in the chair and propped up his foot, she fetched his laptop, his phone charger, and the telly remote, putting them on a side table.

Surveying him with satisfaction, she said, "All comfy now?" then clapped a hand over her mouth. "Food. I forgot about food. Do you have anything in the house?"

"I thought we'd be going out yesterday, so I was going to do the shopping today." There was a tinge of self-pity in Doug's answer, but she couldn't really blame him.

"I can dash round the corner and get you an Egg McMuffin from the McDonald's," she offered.

Doug made a face. "No, I'm fine, really. They fed me something horrible in the hospital first thing this morning."

"Cup of tea?"

"No. You go on," he insisted. "I know you're late as it is. And thanks, Melody, really."

"Okay," Melody agreed, reluctantly. "But I'm going to pop in again after the briefing."

He flapped a hand at her in a half wave, and when she looked back from the door, his eyes were already closed.

To Melody's relief, when she arrived at the station, Gemma was just hurrying in the door to the CID suite. "Boss. Glad I'm not the only one late," Melody whispered.

"*We've* just seen Rashid," Gemma muttered back as their boss, Detective Superintendent Diane Krueger, turned to look at them with disapproval.

"Nice of you ladies to come in this morning." Superintendent Krueger had not made any casual concessions to Sunday—she wore a charcoal pin-striped suit with a knee-length skirt, and had her thick brown hair pulled into a neat French twist. "I've got a media interview in an hour, and I'd like to have something to tell them. Or at least know what not to tell them."

Krueger was a striking brunette in her midforties, slender, with a face that both still and video cameras liked. Melody knew that Gemma, who was a bit self-conscious about her North London accent when she heard it recorded, was always happy when Krueger volunteered for media duty.

Shara MacNicols, there before they were, gave them a smug look. She was seated in front of a computer monitor at one of the suite's long worktables, the pile of Arnott's DVDs beside her. Melody hoped she'd been watching them with the sound turned off.

"Sorry, guv," Gemma said to the superintendent. "We've just been meeting with the pathologist. He got the postmortem done ahead of schedule." As she and Melody slid into seats at the conference table, she went on, "Surely we want to say as little as possible. As in, 'London barrister found dead in suspicious circumstances near his Crystal Palace home. Police await coroner's ruling.'"

"Thank you, Gemma. I'll be sure to let you know next time I need help with a press release." Krueger sighed and relented a little. "Of course we'll try to keep this as low key as we can, at least until we have a better idea of what we're dealing with. But there's a very active virtual forum in the area, and a member reported police activity at the Belvedere Hotel. A newspaper stringer picked it up, talked to the staff, and Bob's your uncle. The journos are already camping in front of the station, and I can't keep them from talking to the hotel staff. By tonight we're going to be front-page and the ten o'clock news. I'd like to have something a bit more definitive to tell them."

"Yes, ma'am." Gemma knew the super was right.

Crossing the room to the whiteboard, Krueger stood with marker in hand, ready to add to the information already posted. "So, what did the delicious Rashid have for us?"

"Vincent Arnott was strangled, as we assumed," said Gemma quickly, aware that Melody was not in the loop. "Rashid said it was done from behind and that it was not self-inflicted. There was no sign of sexual assault or activity."

She went on to detail Rashid's findings of the two different fibers, the gagging, and the fact that the spot of fresh blood had not belonged to the victim. "His alcohol level was high but not enough to incapacitate him. He did, after all, walk into the hotel and pay for the room, and there were no signs of further alcohol consumption."

Krueger added key points to the board. "The lack of sexual activity doesn't mean we can rule out some sort of bondage nutter. Shara, is there anything on those videos to suggest he was into cross gender?"

"Not so far. Women wearing cheap dominatrix gear, tying up middle-aged men and telling them to be good little boys. Pretty pathetic, really."

"I assume you'd recognize *expensive* dominatrix gear if you saw it?" asked Krueger. It was their guvnor's idea of a joke, and when they all smiled obediently, she continued. "We'll see if forensics can get a DNA profile from that blood spot. Maybe some perp will conveniently pop up in the database. If not, we'll at least have something that might link a suspect to the scene, if—let's make that *when*—we do turn up a viable suspect. In the meantime, do we know anything about Arnott's work situation?"

"I've got the home number for his chambers clerk," said Gemma. "I'll see if I can set up an interview for today."

"What about the CCTV?" Krueger consulted her notes. "You had that pulled, I think, Melody."

Crossing to one of the computers, Melody logged into the case file. As she brought up the CCTV footage, she said, "Unfortunately, we've only got a camera covering the pub. There was nothing along Church Road by the hotel."

"So Big Brother is not everywhere," said Krueger. "Unfortunate indeed, in this instance."

Melody turned the monitor and they all gathered round the screen. "Damn," she said when the sequence began. "It's like bloody pea soup." The angle of the camera just caught the front of the White Stag, the intersection, and a few yards of Church Road, but the swirling fog would have made the location unrecognizable if one hadn't already been familiar with it.

Melody fast-forwarded and they watched the frames jump. Groups of people entered and left the pub's front entrance, moving in jerky quick time, like an old silent film. The digital counter clicked towards eleven o'clock, and suddenly there he was.

Arnott, recognizable in a break in the fog by his shock of silver hair. Melody slowed the tape, then backed up. There, again, Arnott exiting the pub, and now they could see that there was another person with him. But the figure was smaller, and shielded from the camera by Arnott's body. The couple moved away quickly, even in real time, and vanished from view a few yards along Church Road.

"That's definitely Arnott," said Melody. "But I can't even tell if that was a man or a woman with him."

"Back up just a couple of frames," Gemma asked, then frowned as she watched the sequence again. "A woman, I think. There's something slightly possessive about his posture, and something in the way she—if it is a she—moves . . ."

Melody started to back the tape up once more, but Gemma said, "No, go on. Let's see what else there is. All we know for certain now is that Arnott did leave the pub with another person, probably a woman."

The tape ran on, and almost immediately, another group of people came out of the pub, milling about for a moment before splitting off in different directions, some to the left towards Westow Street, some to the right towards Belvedere Road. One, presumably male, with hood up and head down, crossed the intersection, but the fog swirled in and obscured him after that.

Then, from around the corner, where Melody remembered the pub had a side entrance, came an instantly recognizable figure. Andy Monahan, in a dark peacoat, head bare, guitar case over his shoulder, pulling an amp on a trolley. And with him, a thin, dark-haired young man carrying a longer, thinner case and pulling an amp as well.

A white Ford Transit van pulled up, and when the heavyset driver got out, Melody realized she'd seen him in the group that had walked towards Belvedere Road. He conferred with Andy and the dark-haired bloke, then disappeared towards the side entrance and returned carrying a drum kit. All three loaded equipment into the van, then seemed to argue for a few moments.

Then the drummer—or so Melody assumed—got into the driver's side, the dark-haired bloke got into the passenger seat, and their doors slammed shut with what seemed unnecessary force. The van sped away, leaving Andy Monahan standing with his guitar at the curb. A moment later, a Mini Cooper pulled up. Andy leaned in the window, apparently conferring with the driver. She saw him shake his head and gesture, as if reluctant or unhappy. But then he got in and the Mini zipped round the corner into Westow Street and disappeared.

Melody sat back, feeling a rush of relief she wasn't sure she could justify. "That seems to bear out what Andy—the guitarist—and his manager told me yesterday. Still, I'll confirm the make on the manager's car. And I'd like to talk to the other members of the band. They were arguing about something, and I want to know what it was."

Kincaid rang the bell at Doug's house in Putney, stamping his feet against the cold, for the day had set in crisp and—for the moment—clear. He held a paper bag from which rose the enticing aroma of hot beef burgers from the Jolly Gardeners just up the road.

He was about to ring again when he heard Doug shout, "Coming. I'm coming," then the lock clicked and the door swung open.

Surveying his erstwhile partner's rumpled hair, heavy-lidded eyes, and booted foot, Kincaid said, "You do look a sight." He held up the bag. "I thought you might like some lunch."

"Oh, God." Doug hobbled out of the way so that Kincaid could come in. "I'm starving. There's no food in the house. Melody offered to get something this morning, but I knew she'd already gone out of her way to fetch me from hospital and I didn't want to hold her up any longer."

Kincaid followed him into the sitting room, where Doug levered himself back into his armchair and propped his booted ankle on the ottoman. An old episode of *Top Gear* was playing soundlessly on the telly, and Kincaid suspected Doug had been napping. Then he took in the tipped ladder and the spilled paint. "Bloody hell!"

Doug gave a disgruntled sigh. "I think I'm going to be apologizing for my stupidity for the rest of my life. At least, as Melody reminded me, I was going to tear the carpet out anyway. I thought you were minding the kids, with Gemma on a big case," he added as Kincaid pulled up another chair and unwrapped the burgers.

"Betty invited us all for Sunday lunch. I took advantage. Told her I was sure you needed some TLC. Although Melody seems to have done pretty well in the caretaking department, I must say."

"She feels sorry for me." Doug shrugged, but he looked pleased nonetheless.

Glancing at the front window, Kincaid saw a bright blue Renault Clio pull up to the curb. "Speak of the devil." He grinned.

"Melody? Here?" Doug looked round for someplace to set his burger and began to push himself out of the chair. "She said she was coming back but I didn't think she'd manage it."

"Stay put. I'll go," Kincaid told him.

"I see we have a party," said Melody when he greeted her at the door. She held a bag identical to the one Kincaid had brought, and when she came into the sitting room and saw their burgers, she laughed. Holding up her bag, she said to Doug, "I brought you the Gardeners' Sunday roast chicken. I thought you could save half for your dinner, but now you can have the whole thing tonight."

"Thanks," Doug called out as she went to the kitchen and popped the bag in the fridge. "But what about you? No lunch?"

Melody came back into the sitting room and perched on the edge of a chair. "Sandwich at the station. And I can't stay long. Just wanted to make sure you were coping."

"How'd you get away?" Doug asked.

"Skiving." Melody gave a dimpled smile. "No, really, I've got interviews, and Putney wasn't that far out of my way."

"Interviews? Where?" Doug, obviously more interested in keeping Melody there than in eating, managed to find a spot for his half-eaten burger. He nibbled absently on a chip.

"Well, the thing is," answered Melody, "I'm not exactly sure." She outlined the morning's developments, then added, "Gemma has Shara going round the pub in Crystal Palace again—her reward for having to watch the porn videos this morning—just in case any of the Sunday patrons were there on Friday night and might remember seeing Arnott talking to, or leaving with, a woman who might possibly fit the description of the person on the CCTV. And, of course, it's always possible that someone might admit to having had a previous liaison with him."

"Of course?" said Doug. "Is it really all that likely?"

Melody shrugged. "You never know. A lonely woman, she might see it as a chance at a little attention. Maybe even an inch in the *Evening Standard*: *My Encounter with the Victim*."

"Cynic," said Doug. He looked much more chipper than when Kincaid had come in.

"What about Gemma?" asked Kincaid, wishing she had rung him with an update.

"Still slaving away at the station. The results of the search of Arnott's car should be coming in, and she's hoping the computer techs will have something from his home computer. Oh, and I think she's tracked down the clerk from Arnott's chambers. Someplace in Battersea. The clerk, I mean, not the chambers."

Doug rolled his eyes. "Obviously. And you still haven't told us where Putney was on the way to." He frowned at his garbled sentence, and Kincaid thought he was tiring. "I mean— Well, you know what I mean."

For the first time, Melody seemed a little hesitant. "I've

already spoken to the guitarist—the one that Arnott shouted at—but I want to talk to the other guys who were playing in the band on Friday night. There was something going on with them—they seemed to be arguing after the gig. It may not have any connection with the case, but I want to know what the row was about. I rang the manager, Tam, and confirmed that it was his Mini we saw on the CCTV picking up the guitarist. And I got phone numbers and home addresses for the bass player and the drummer. The bass player, Nick, lives in Earl's Court, and Tam said if I wanted to catch him I'd better go toot suite. His term, not mine. So I should be on my—"

"Melody," Kincaid broke in. "The band's manager is named Tam? And he drives a Mini?"

"Yeah. Funny little guy, but nice. He said his name is really Michael, but he wears this ratty old Scots tam—"

"Jesus." Kincaid shook his head. "I should have realized—I would have realized, if Gemma had told me . . ." He frowned at Melody. "This guitarist—what's his name?"

"Andy. Andy Monahan." Now Melody was looking puzzled. "Why?"

"Because," said Kincaid. "I know Tam Moran. And I know your guitarist, too."

CHAPTER NINE

Recording studios started setting up in the 1960s, and it was then that Denmark Street's name was etched into the archives. Denmark Street's impact on the contemporary music scene is widely regarded as far greater than the more populist location of Abbey Road.

—www.covent-garden.co.uk

"I still can't believe it," said Tom Kershaw when he opened the door of his Battersea flat to Gemma. It was the same thing he'd said to her over the phone when she'd finally reached him an hour earlier and had informed him of Vincent Arnott's death.

She'd had no trouble finding the flat by his directions. It was a relatively new gated community with its own communal garden flanking the river.

Kershaw was a thin, balding man in his forties, with a pleasant face. Now, he hesitated for a moment, glancing back into the flat, then said, "Do you mind if we talk outside? It's just that it's Sunday, and all the kids are at home." Gemma heard the sound of a piano being laboriously practiced, then a woman hushing a childish shriek. The lingering aroma of a Sunday roast wafted out.

"Not at all." Gemma smiled, wishing she'd worn a warmer coat. "It's not exactly a suitable discussion for the family."

"Won't be a tic." Kershaw shut the door, reappearing a moment later, slipping a heavy anorak over his cable-knit pullover. "We can walk round the garden." He led the way along a path through the low buildings. When they reached the riverfront garden, the wind hit Gemma full force.

"How many children do you have, Mr. Kershaw?" she asked, suppressing a shiver.

"Three. In nursery, primary, and secondary."

"Oh, really? We have three as well. Quite a handful, aren't they?"

He smiled. "Three separate school runs, but thankfully they're all quite close together. My wife's a barrister, so it's a bit of a juggling act in the mornings."

"A little conflict of interest there?" asked Gemma.

"What?" He seemed to realize she was joking. "Oh. No. Different chambers. We did work in the same set of chambers years ago, when we were both juniors, but once we started going out, Margie took the opportunity to move to another set." They'd reached a bench that faced the river, but Kershaw kept walking.

"About Mr. Arnott," said Gemma. "Had you worked with him long?"

"More than twenty years. Since I came into the chambers on a work-experience scheme." He shook his head. "You're certain he's dead?"

"Barring the formal identification, yes. His sister-in-law is arriving from the States tomorrow. I'm afraid his wife's not up to it."

"No. She wouldn't be."

"Did you know about his wife's condition, Mr. Kershaw?"

"Well, we'd all suspected for some time. Not that he ever talked about it. Vincent wasn't one to invite sympathy or advice."

It occurred to Gemma that although Kershaw had been shocked, he'd expressed no grief at the news. "You didn't like Mr. Arnott, did you?"

"No. I didn't," answered Kershaw, with apparent regret. "He wasn't what I would call a likable man. But he was a good barrister, and part of a clerk's job is to match their chambers' barristers with the right solicitors and clients. I never put Vincent with a client who needed hand-holding. He was, in fact, much better at prosecuting."

"From what I gather, he was quite solicitous of his wife."

"She was a nice woman, Mrs. Arnott. Always little presents for the staff at Christmas, cards on birthdays. Never could imagine what she saw in him." He stopped, hands in his anorak pockets, staring out at the late-afternoon sun glinting on the river. "I suppose I shouldn't say she *was*, as if it were she who had died. But it's been a couple of years since I've seen her. The last time Vincent brought her to a chambers function, she was obviously not well."

"Mr. Kershaw, do you know if Vincent Arnott had started seeing other women after his wife became ill?"

Kershaw gave her a sharp look. "Vincent had been seeing other women for years. Not as in a mistress—at least not that I know of—but he had a knack for picking out a woman who looked lonely in a wine bar."

"Prostitutes?"

"I don't think so. He was a bit too fastidious for that. But I'd say he was quite adept at the one-night stand." Frowning, he said, "Does this have something to do with his death? You've never said what happened to him, but as you're investigating I assume it wasn't natural causes."

"He was found in a hotel in Crystal Palace on Saturday morning, and yes, there was evidence of foul play. We have reason to believe he might have left a pub with a woman the previous evening. Did you ever see any indication that Mr. Arnott was into anything . . . kinky?"

"Vincent?" Kershaw looked astonished. "Kinky? I'd say you couldn't have found anyone more sexually straight ahead than Vincent." He walked on, and Gemma was glad of the movement. She'd buttoned her coat up to the collar, and like Kershaw, had stuffed her numb hands into her pockets. "But then again," Kershaw went on thoughtfully, "I never thought he liked women."

"You mean he liked men?" asked Gemma, wondering if they'd got the whole scenario wrong.

"No. I mean he didn't *like* women. When I said I tried not to assign him cases that required hand-holding, that was part of it. I learned years ago that he would never make a real effort to defend a woman. It was as if he made an automatic assumption of guilt."

When Gemma left Tom Kershaw, both with assurances of his discretion and a promise that he would provide the team with contact information and schedules for the other members of Arnott's chambers first thing in the morning, the afternoon was beginning to slide into early winter dusk.

Getting into her car, she was glad of a little residual warmth from the heater. She checked her phone—there were no messages from either her team or Kincaid.

Gemma sat and thought for a moment. Then, on impulse, she started the car and drove east. Soon she was turning into Falcon Road, and then the little side street with the concrete block of a mosque on the corner. With a council estate at the street's far end, and the in-between bits filled with Victorian terraces in various stages of repair, it seemed unlikely that the high stone wall that occupied a section near the mosque would conceal anything other than scrap.

But if you looked closely, you saw that there was a wooden gate set into the stone wall. Gemma parked the Escort, waving at the Muslim boys who were, as usual, playing football at the street's end, and pushed the intercom buzzer set very discreetly beside the gate latch.

"It's Gemma," she said when the intercom came on, and a moment later there was a buzz and the gate swung open. Her friend Hazel Cavendish hurried towards her across the patio that separated the gate from what Gemma referred to as The Secret Bungalow.

"Gemma!" Hazel crushed her in a hug. "I thought you were tied up for the weekend."

"I was," said Gemma as Hazel led her into the house. "I am. But I had an interview not far from here, and I couldn't resist the chance to see you. And to get warm," she added, rubbing her hands together. Hazel had a gas fire going in the fireplace between the small bookcases on the far side of the room, and colorful rag rugs covered the stone floor.

"I was just making tea. You must have second sight. Go warm your hands while I bring it."

In fact, Gemma was convinced that it was Hazel who had second sight. When Gemma had lived in Hazel's garage flat in Islington, Hazel had somehow always known when Gemma had needed a cuppa, a meal, a glass of wine, or a confidante. Now, even though both their lives had changed considerably, Hazel hadn't lost the gift.

Hazel returned from the small kitchen carrying a tray with a red teapot, two mugs, and a plate of biscuits. "Cranberry walnut." She gestured at the biscuits as she put the tray on the table nearest the fire. "I made them for the café yesterday."

Hazel was a licensed therapist, but after the troubles that had wreaked havoc in her own family, she'd given up her practice. Instead, she'd taken a job in a Kensington café. Hazel's husband, Tim, from whom she was separated, had stayed in the Islington house, and they shared custody of their daughter, Holly, who was Toby's age.

"Where's Holly?" Gemma asked as Hazel poured her a

steaming cup of tea and added just the amount of milk she knew Gemma liked.

"Tim's bringing her at six. I'm doing the school run tomorrow as I've got the day off."

Gemma lifted her head and sniffed. "You're cooking. It smells delicious."

"A Moroccan veggie stew." The corners of Hazel's mouth curved in a little smile.

"Hazel," said Gemma, twigging, "is Tim by any chance staying for dinner?"

"Well, it only makes sense, really. There will be plenty, and Holly likes us to eat together."

"Protesting a bit much, are we?" Studying her friend, Gemma realized that Hazel was looking very well. She'd gained some much-needed weight, her dark curls were lustrous, her eyes sparkling. "I don't suppose it's made sense for Tim to stay the night when he comes for these dinners?"

Lifting her mug to her lips with both hands, Hazel blew on the surface of the tea. She shrugged, her eyes crinkling mischievously. "Once or twice. When we've had a glass or two of wine. But he's slept on the sofa."

Laughing, Gemma said, "Hazel, you are married, in case you'd forgotten."

Hazel quickly grew serious. "I haven't forgotten. But it's . . . delicate. Almost like dating, in a weird way, and I don't think either of us want to make any false steps. Or give Holly false hope that things will be the way they used to be."

"But there is hope?" Gemma asked carefully, not wanting to push her friend.

"Oh. I think so, yes. But things will never be exactly as they were, for either of us. And I've discovered that there are things I quite like about my new life. I've realized that I was always looking after other people and never myself, and that's something I need to learn to balance. Now," she said, with a deft change of subject, "what about you? Big case on, I take it? And Duncan and the kids are occupying themselves for the weekend? Duncan seems to be managing well."

"Too well, I'm beginning to think," said Gemma, finishing a biscuit. "I know he must be worried about getting Charlotte settled and getting back to work, but he doesn't talk about it. He's relentlessly cheerful, and I swear he's turning into bloody Nigella. The dinner menus get more complicated by the day and he turns his nose up at the suggestion of takeaway."

Hazel added a little tea to her cup and stirred it, wearing what Gemma thought of as her "therapist's face."

"Yes, I know, I know," said Gemma with a sigh. "He's a very intelligent man who's used to a stimulating, high-powered job where he's in charge of everything. Signing Charlotte up for every play group in Notting Hill and taking on gourmet cooking is his way of coping with the situation. I didn't expect him to sit home and watch daytime telly. But, still, there's something . . ." She shook her head. "I don't know." When Hazel raised an eyebrow, Gemma added, "I will talk to him. Promise. But this case is worrying enough for the moment. In fact, I'm just as glad Holly isn't here. Maybe you could give me an opinion. Unofficially."

Nodding, Hazel said, "I'll do my best."

Gemma described the murder, then told her what they'd learned about Vincent Arnott. "I can't make sense of the contradictions. The man was apparently very solicitous of his wife. Obviously fastidious in the extreme." Gemma paused, frowning, and set her empty cup on the tray. "Oh, I suppose I can understand the picking-up-women thing . . . But the bondage seems an aberration for a man who controlled everything in his life with such precision."

"Actually, that's not uncommon. That was probably the only time he felt he didn't have to be in control. His wife's illness may have precipitated a long-harbored fantasy into active behavior."

Gemma watched the gas fire for a moment, contemplating that, then turned back to Hazel. "Okay. I can see that, too. But his chambers' clerk told me that Arnott didn't like women. How do you square that with his care of his wife?"

"You described her as 'childlike.' Is it possible that she was always something of an innocent, and that the dementia has only made it more apparent? It could be that they never had much of a sexual relationship, even before her illness. Or possibly not at all."

"Tom—his clerk—did say that Arnott had been having affairs as long as he'd known him, and from what I gathered, they'd worked together nearly twenty years. So what you're suggesting," Gemma added slowly, "is that Arnott saw his wife as the virgin and other women as whores?"

"That's not uncommon, either," said Hazel. "It would be interesting to know what sort of relationship your Mr. Arnott had with his mother."

"Interesting, yes," agreed Gemma. "Helpful, maybe, if he were the murderer and not the victim. But as it is, I'm not sure it would get me any closer to figuring out who killed him. Or why."

Before picking up Charlotte and Toby, Kincaid had taken Kit on a shopping trip to Whole Foods Market and let him pick out ingredients for dinner. Now, banned from the kitchen while Kit prepared a surprise, Kincaid was helping Toby and Charlotte make a pillow fort in the sitting room when he heard the click of the front-door lock and Geordie's excited yip.

"Mummy's home!" Toby shouted, sending their carefully constructed edifice slithering to the floor. Charlotte began to cry.

Scooping her up, Kincaid kissed her and said, "Never mind. We'll build it again. You can show Mummy."

When Gemma came into the room, she looked more chipper than he'd expected after her long day. "What have we here?" she said. "Do I see the remains of a castle?"

"And the walls came tumbling down," Toby intoned. "But you can help fix it, Mummy."

She tousled his hair and gave Charlotte a hug. "Where's Kit? And what is that heavenly smell?"

"You'll have to ask Kit," said Kincaid. "It's his production and I am totally, completely in the dark."

"Okay, kitchen first," Gemma told Toby. "You and Charlotte start building again, and I'll come supervise in a bit."

Kincaid followed her into the kitchen, where they found Kit, pink cheeked from the heat of the Aga.

"I hear you're the chef du jour," Gemma told him, giving him a hug as well. "Whatever it is, you could bottle the smell and sell it."

"It's mac cheese," said Kit. He grinned at their startled looks. "Gourmet mac cheese. I made up the recipe myself."

"Wow." Gemma sank into a kitchen chair with a sigh of contentment. "Gordon Ramsay couldn't do better." Then she gave Kit a steely look. "Just promise me, if you decide to be a chef, that you won't swear like him."

"All chefs swear," said Kit, unconcerned. Turning back to the work top, he lifted a vase and set it carefully in the center of the table. "And these are for you."

"Tulips! And red. My favorite. Thank you, Kit." Then she added, laughing, "But that still doesn't mean you can swear. Or maybe only a little."

He smiled back, then glanced at the kitchen timer. "The mac cheese has got fifteen more minutes. Okay if I go check my e-mail?" When they nodded, he added, "No tasting, though." A moment later they heard him galloping up the stairs.

"I think his feet have grown a size since Christmas," Kincaid said. Then, studying Gemma, he asked, "Tea? I suspect you could use a bit of fortifying."

"I'm full up with tea. And biscuits, actually. I stopped to see Hazel on my way home."

"Wine, then?" Kincaid headed for the fridge rather than the kettle.

"I wouldn't say no."

He poured her a glass from the bottle they'd opened the night before. "Personal or professional, this visit to Hazel?"

"Bit of both." After an appreciative sip of the wine, she quietly filled him in on what they'd learned that day about Vincent Arnott, then set her glass down and rubbed at her cheekbones. "We're nearing the end of the crucial first forty-eight hours, and we still don't have any really viable leads. This could turn into a monster of a case when the media get hold of the details and we haven't made any progress."

"The Mad Strangler of Crystal Palace."

Gemma grimaced. "Or worse. *Sex, Bondage, and Murder.*"

Sid, their black cat, jumped up on the kitchen table. Kincaid scooped him off and set him on the floor, where the cat rubbed round Gemma's ankles until she reached down to stroke him.

"I saw Melody today," Kincaid told her, trying to work out how to approach this delicately. He didn't want Gemma to feel he was interfering in her case, but he couldn't withhold what he knew, either. "She came by to check on Doug while I was there."

"Really? How's he doing?"

"I suspect by tomorrow he'll be pulling his hair out from boredom. Or hacking into the MoD. But the thing is, Melody was trying to track down the members of the band who were playing in the pub on Friday night, and she said she got their details from their manager."

"Well, that seems logical." Gemma looked puzzled.

"She didn't tell you the manager's name?"

"I don't think so. But I'm sure it's in her case notes."

"You'd remember if she'd told you," he said. "It's Tam. Our Tam. Louise's Tam."

Gemma just stared at him blankly for a moment. "As in Tam and Michael?" she said at last.

"The same."

"Bloody hell." She lifted her wineglass and this time took a gulp.

"It gets better." Kincaid sat down across from her. "The guitarist who got in a row with your victim in the pub on Friday night? It was Andy Monahan."

"Andy . . ." Gemma frowned; then her eyes widened in recognition. "Andy. Blondish. Bit cheeky. Always gives me a wave and a smile when I see him coming and going at Louise's. He's usually carrying his guitar case." She shook her head in disbelief. "What on earth was he doing arguing with Vincent Arnott? And that means it was Tam who gave him an alibi for the time of Arnott's murder."

"Bit awkward, isn't it? I wondered . . ." Kincaid hesitated, thinking of all the things he hadn't said, all the things he should have mentioned to Gemma—Louise's illness, the possibilities he was exploring for Charlotte . . . and his worries about the job. The bloody, bloody job.

He shrugged. He'd find the right time.

"What, love?" Gemma reached across the table to touch his hand. "Are you all right?"

He took her hand in his. "I'm fine. But . . . I wondered if you might like me to have a word with Tam. Just in case he knows anything he'd not have thought to mention to the police."

Melody had spent the afternoon shuttling between Earl's Court, Hackney, and Bethnal Green, with no success anywhere.

She had found Nick's mother at home at the family's flat on the respectable Fulham edge of Earl's Court. Nick, said his mum, was off at a coffeehouse, studying for an accountancy exam, but she wasn't sure where. Melody had left her card. She'd also tried Nick's mobile, leaving a message on his voice mail.

As she started for Hackney, she'd tried the mobile number Tam Moran had given her for George, the drummer, which again went to voice mail.

"Why do people bother having mobile phones if they never answer them," she muttered. Maybe by the time she arrived, George would have rung her back.

But when she reached the flat in the well-kept estate east of Haggerston Park, there was no one home at all. Nor was there any sign of the white Transit van she'd seen in the video footage.

She waited a bit, in case someone showed up, but the car quickly got cold without the engine running. Frowning, she dug in her bag for the card Tam Moran had given her. His home address was near Columbia Road, not far at all. She could stop by, she thought. Tam seemed like a settled chap who might be at home on a Sunday afternoon.

Kincaid had explained that Tam lived next door to Louise Phillips, who had been Charlotte's father's law partner and was now the executor of Charlotte's estate.

"And Andy Monahan?" she'd asked. "How do you know him?"

"He was a witness to a murder near his flat, in that case we worked last spring—the one that involved Erika. It wasn't until I saw him visiting Tam when I was at Louise's last summer that I knew they had a connection. I hope he's not involved in your murder."

Melody hadn't thought it very professional to add that she hoped not, too.

When she reached Columbia Road, she found Tam's flat easily enough and climbed the stairs to the first-floor balcony. But the only answer to her knock was the ferocious barking of the two German shepherd dogs she could see through the flat's front windows, and there was no sound or movement from the adjoining flat, which she assumed must be Louise's.

Discouraged, she went back to the car and sat for a moment, irresolute. Heavy clouds were massing in the west of the already darkening sky. She'd wasted the entire afternoon, and now the day was almost gone.

As she reached in her bag for her phone, intending to check in with Gemma, she knocked Tam's card from the console and it fell facedown on the passenger seat. On the back, Andy Monahan had scribbled his address and phone number.

"Hanway Place," she read. She remembered him saying it was just off Oxford Street and Tottenham Court Road. And that was right on her way back to Notting Hill.

Bugger the band, she thought. She'd talk to Andy himself, and she wasn't going to call first.

Hanway Place was a dark little alley of a street, tucked away behind the massive Crossrail construction at the intersection of Oxford Street and Tottenham Court Road. Melody double-checked the address on the card, as the building looked more like a warehouse than housing. But when she'd parked and gone to the door, she found a row of bellpushes with adjacent name holders. Most of the building appeared to be empty, but beside a flat on the first floor the tag read "A. Monahan" in the same distinctive handwriting scrawled on the back of the business card.

She pushed the bell and when the intercom clicked on, said, "It's Melody Talbot. Can I have a word?"

"Come on up," answered a crackly voice, and the door latch clicked open.

Despite the building's unprepossessing exterior, the stairwell was clean and well lit. As she climbed, it suddenly occurred to Melody that the makeup she'd put on that morning was long gone, her hair was wind mussed, and that perhaps the long turquoise top she'd pulled on over jeans and boots that morning was not the most flattering of outfits. "Don't be stupid," she whispered to herself. Monahan was not going to be expecting her to pass a police officer's dress code, and why should she care, anyway?

When she reached the first-floor landing, one of the flat doors opened and Monahan looked out at her. "I thought it was you," he said. "Intercom's a bit wonky. But what would you expect, really," he added, with a gesture that took in the building. He was wearing the wool peacoat they'd seen in the CCTV footage.

"Just coming in or going out?" she asked as he stepped aside to let her enter the flat.

"Coming in. Another day in the studio. Here, let me take your coat, if you won't freeze before the central heating kicks in." As she shed her coat, he hung it on a row of pegs beside the door, then slipped out of his own.

It gave her a moment to look round the flat. He must have caught her glance because the look he gave her was amused. "What did you expect? A squat? I have to admit the building's a bit grim. Most of the tenants have fled due to the Crossrail upheaval, but at least the place hasn't gone under the wrecking ball yet."

"No, I—It's just that it's, um, interesting." She wondered what it was about this man that seemed to put her on the wrong foot.

"Interesting. You could say that." He grinned, then looked at her more seriously. "Is this about your case? I don't know that I can tell you any more than yesterday."

"I just wanted a chat, if you've got a few minutes."

"Right, then. Sit down, why don't you? I'll make some tea. I'm parched. Unless you'd like something else? There might be a beer in the fridge," he added a little dubiously, as if not sure what might be lurking in the refrigerator's depths.

"No, tea would be lovely."

"Tea is the police officer's lot, I should think. Back in a tic, then." There was none of the edginess he'd displayed yesterday in the studio, and if he was alarmed by having a police officer appear unannounced at his flat, he certainly wasn't showing it.

Melody watched him walk into the tiny galley kitchen and switch on the lights, but she didn't sit. Instead, she looked round the room with the curiosity she had clearly failed to disguise. There was a futon that seemed, if the folded duvet and the pillow neatly placed at one end were an indication, to double as a bed, and an armchair that looked as if it had come from the same era and perhaps the same charity shop. A coffee table held stacks of guitar magazines, a laptop, and an empty mug; a side table held a hideous ceramic lamp that again might kindly have been called "vintage."

That was the sum total of furniture. The rest of the room was stuffed with the things that obviously really mattered to Andy Monahan. She counted half a dozen amps in different shapes and sizes. There were foot pedals with switches and buttons, and masses of leads running from one thing to another like a colorful nest of snakes.

And guitars. Electric. Acoustic. Guitars on stands, guitars mounted on the wall. The far end of the room held shelves and shelves of carefully aligned CDs and vinyl albums, and in the center, a sophisticated music center that included a turntable and what Melody assumed was a mixing board.

Through an open door, she glimpsed what she guessed was meant to be the flat's bedroom, but it was filled with workbenches and boxes of tools. An enormous ginger cat jumped down from one of the worktables and strolled towards her, meowing plaintively.

"That's Bert," Andy called from the kitchen. "Don't mind

him. He's never met a stranger, and he never thinks he's had enough to eat. Milk and sugar?" he added.

"Just a bit of both, please."

When Andy came back into the sitting room carrying two mugs, Melody sat on the edge of the armchair, tentatively reaching down to scratch Bert's large head.

"Don't you like cats?" Andy asked, handing her one of the mugs, but not sitting down himself. Melody thought he looked tired, but he seemed wired, almost humming with an under-current of excitement.

"I don't dislike them. I've just never had one. My parents have always had Labradors in the country—" She stopped her-self before she could say "country house." What was wrong with her? She never willingly admitted anything about her family, especially to strangers. "Why is he called Bert?" she asked, changing tack as the cat jumped up on the futon and made himself comfortable atop the pillow and duvet. His yel-low eyes narrowed to slits, then closed.

"He's my muse." When she looked puzzled, Andy contin-ued. "He's named after Bert Jansch. He was one of the best guitarists in the world." Setting his mug on a stack of maga-zines, he took one of the acoustic guitars from its stand and sat down on the futon. He ran his fingers lightly over the strings, adjusted the tuning, then began to play a rhythmic, melodic progression that made it almost impossible for Melody not to tap her feet. His face held the same intensity she'd seen yester-day in the studio, but after a moment he stopped and looked up at her. "You don't recognize it?"

"No." Melody felt as if she'd failed a test. "It's familiar, but—"

"It's called 'Angie.' Bert Jansch's anthem, if you like. Every guitarist worth his salt learns to play it."

"How old were you, then, when you learned it?"

"It was so long ago that I don't remember." Shrugging, he

put the guitar back in its stand, but she sensed he felt less comfortable without the instrument as a shield. He lifted his mug, sniffed at the tea suspiciously, then took a sip. "Milk's all right, then. Haven't been to the shops in a while," he explained.

"Were you recording in Crystal Palace again today?" she asked.

"Yeah. We were actually in the studio today. Yesterday was just rehearsal space. It was—" Shaking his head, he set his tea down again, then rose and crossed the room, picking up the guitar case she hadn't noticed by the front door. He took out the red electric guitar he'd been playing yesterday and brought it back to the futon, placing it in his lap and resting his hands on the curve of its body.

Again, Melody sensed a barely containable energy bubbling beneath the surface of his nonchalant demeanor. She leaned forward, elbows on her knees. "Look. I know I'm not very musical, but when I heard you yesterday, with the girl—"

"Poppy."

"Right. With Poppy. The two of you—it was something . . . special."

Andy Monahan looked up at her, his glance searching. "You thought so, too? I've played with a lot of people, but there's never been anything like that. I don't want to—I don't want to make too much of it. I've had my little sand castles washed away too many times."

"But if you've been playing with Poppy—"

"That's just the thing. I'd never even met her before yesterday. It was—sort of like a blind date, in musical terms. Our managers put us together."

"You played and sang like that, and it was the first time?" Melody stared at him. "Wow."

"Yeah. That's why—" He brushed his fingers across the guitar strings in an impatient gesture. The bruise on his knuckles had darkened, and Melody noticed he didn't wear a watch. "I don't know why I'm telling you this," Andy went on, not meeting Melody's eyes as he picked out a silent pattern of chords on the frets. "It's just—my mates—I can't talk to them."

"Nick and George? You've been together a long time?"

"Ten years, on and off."

Thinking for a moment, Melody decided she wasn't going to mention the fact that she'd spent the day looking for Nick and George. Or that she'd seen the CCTV footage. "So you've been good friends."

Andy nodded. "They've been . . . like family, I guess. When there was no one else."

"But you were arguing after the gig on Friday night. Before Tam picked you up."

He stared at her. "How—"

"We've been interviewing people. Trying to find anyone who saw Vincent Arnott leave the pub. So why did you have a row with your best mates?"

He shrugged again. "It's been coming for a long time. I guess you could say that Poppy was just the catalyst. The band is finished. They knew it—we all knew it—but they're still pissed at me." He sighed. "Can't say I blame them."

"So it's your decision?"

"It's— It's just that I'm better than they are. I don't mean to sound like a total jerk. Nick and George are competent musicians. The band has been fun for them. Something to do until real life kicked in."

"Or their parents kicked them out," said Melody. At his startled look, she added, "Tam gave me their home addresses. The properties aren't registered to them. So how do you manage?" She waved round the room. "The flat. The equipment."

"I've been doing session work since I was sixteen. It's my life, playing. And if you mean the guitars"—he gave her that sudden grin—"that's what guitarists do. Our downfall. We make enough to eat and pay the rent, if we're lucky, and then we buy guitars." He waved at the workroom. "If you're good with your hands, you learn to repair the ones you find in charity shops and car boot sales, or that other players have to sell to pay their rent."

Something was nagging at Melody and she suddenly realized what it was. "Andy, if you'd never played with Poppy before Saturday, you had used the studio before, right?"

"No. Tam and Caleb set that up."

"But when I mentioned the Belvedere Hotel, you knew immediately where it was. And what sort of place it was."

"I didn't say I didn't know Crystal Palace. I grew up there," he added with a grimace. "I haven't lived there in years, but the place hasn't changed much, from what I can tell. It was Caleb who set up the gig at the pub, to see me play. A sort of audition. That's part of the reason Nick and George were so out of sorts."

"Um, I'd say you were a bit out of sorts, too, if you hit a punter," Melody reminded him, glancing pointedly at his hand.

Andy flexed his fingers, looking rueful. "Yeah. That was pretty stupid. Believe me, I don't make a habit of it. But I don't like drunks. And I was already furious with Nick and George because they were deliberately sabotaging the set. Wankers. It was a lousy venue for anyone to really hear a band. I don't know why Caleb chose it, except that the management will let him put a band in on short notice."

Was that what had given her the sense that he was withholding something yesterday at the studio? Melody wondered. He hadn't wanted to talk about the rift in the band in front of Poppy and Caleb—Caleb. Melody stopped short, feeling a prize idiot.

Caleb Hart was a regular at the pub. And she had been so focused on Andy, and so mesmerized by what she'd heard, that she hadn't shown Hart Vincent Arnott's photo. Hart hadn't shown any sign of recognition when she'd mentioned Arnott's name, but he hadn't actually denied knowing him, either. And even if he hadn't recognized the name, that didn't mean he didn't know Arnott by sight. He might even have seen him that night or on previous occasions.

"Andy," she said, "how well do you know Caleb Hart?"

"Caleb? I just met him on Saturday. He came into the Stag on Friday night but I didn't see him. Fortunately he left before the end of the first set, so he didn't see me make a complete arse of myself."

"What do you know about him?"

"He manages and produces. Has some clout. You should ask Tam. They go way back."

"I'll talk to Tam. But I think it's Caleb Hart I need to speak to first." She glanced at the windows, saw that the only light now came from the glow of the sodium streetlamps. Checking her watch, she saw that it had gone six. "Damn," she breathed. The time had flown, and she hadn't even touched her tea. "Andy, I've got to go. Sorry about the—"

"Oh, shit." He was staring at the digital clock on his music center.

"What—"

"I've got a gig at the Twelve Bar tonight. Didn't realize it was so late. I need to be there to set up in half an hour."

"The Twelve Bar?"

"Denmark Street. Guitar club. A complete dive, but every good guitarist in the business has played there at one time or another."

"I can drive you," Melody offered, feeling unaccountably guilty for having made him late.

"No, it's not far, and all I need is my guitar. I'll use the club amp." Andy studied her, and for an instant she felt as immobilized as a butterfly under glass. Then he nodded, as if he'd reached a decision. "Come with me."

"But—I should—"

"Come on. If it's Caleb Hart you want, I wouldn't bet on your chances of finding him at home on a Sunday night. Besides, where's your sense of adventure?" He cocked his head and gave her a quizzical look. "And if you don't know anything about music, you owe it to yourself to learn." When he saw her perplexed expression, he laughed. "Don't you think it's time you lived up to your name, Melody Talbot?"

Andy had put the acoustic guitar he'd played for her earlier in a case, then they'd bundled into their coats and walked round the corner of Hanway Place and into the throng of Oxford Street.

"That's my Hummingbird," he'd told her, patting the case.

"Hummingbird?"

He'd smiled. "The guitar. A Gibson Hummingbird, 1976. I have better acoustics, but there's something about the sound of this one that I like. They all have personalities, voices. Like people."

"If you say so."

"You'll see."

They'd crossed Oxford Street at the lights, following the construction hoardings until they came into tiny Denmark Street from the east, passing the dark hulk of a church.

"The street of guitars," said Andy as they reached the narrow entrance to a club with a sign over the door saying 12 BAR. Melody caught a glimpse of a printed flyer taped to the window, a monochrome version of Andy's face on pink paper with his name beneath it.

"Are you famous here?" she asked.

"It's a small world."

The bloke on the desk by the door gave Andy an enthusiastic handclasp and Melody an assessing look. "Who's this, then, mate?" he asked.

"Melody. Leave her alone, Ricky. She's new."

"Have fun, then," Ricky told her with a wink. "And watch out for guitarists. They're dangerous."

"Don't pay him any mind," Andy told her as he led her to the back. "He's just jealous."

He bought her a glass of the only white wine available. When Melody took a sip, she thought it might as well be horse piss, but she certainly was not going to complain.

"It improves with age," said Andy, seeing her grimace. "When you're a hundred years old it will taste like nectar."

She'd laughed and followed him down the stairs into a basement that was smaller than the sitting room in her flat. There were no chairs or tables, just a few bar stools against the back wall between the door that led to the sound booth, and a staircase that led to a tiny balcony overlooking the room. The odor of stale tobacco smoke seemed to ooze from the concrete walls, and she thought that eons of a smoking ban would not erase it.

"Grab a seat while you can," said Andy, and when she was settled on a stool by the sound booth door, he'd chatted with the soundman, then climbed to the stage, tested his amp and his mic, and tuned the guitar. She'd watched him, feeling oddly comfortable in this strange world in which she was the outsider.

He'd come back to her, drinking a few sips of a beer as the audience trickled in, telling her little tidbits about the history of the club and the famous guitarists who had played there, greeting people who came to speak to him. Then suddenly the room was full, the soundman mumbled something unintelligible over the PA, and Andy was on the stage.

From the first moment, she realized that what she was seeing—hearing—was different from what she'd seen when he played with Poppy in the studio. There had been a tension with Poppy, a striving to meld one musician's unique voice and style with another's to create something entirely new.

But this, this was just between Andy and the guitar, and there was a grace and confidence to his playing that took her breath away. She felt, as she listened and watched him, that she knew him in a way that she had never known anyone else. And when he came back to her, at the end of the set, she knew that something fundamental had changed between them.

She'd stood outside the club for a long time. She knew how to loiter, to make herself invisible in the ebb and flow of the street. She was just a woman with her coat collar turned up, gazing intently in windows at objects she couldn't have named.

She watched the punters trickle in—ones and twos, then the occasional group of three or four. Sunday nights were bound to be quiet, but the custom was steady, and from the looks of the patrons, they were there to listen, not to drink.

The music began, too faint to identify, loud enough to be a rhythm in the blood, a counter to her heartbeat. Finally, deciding there was camouflage enough, she walked in and paid her cover to the young man at the door. He looked at her, as men did, and when he stamped her hand he kept his fingers on her wrist an instant too long.

She gave him her most impersonal smile as she drew back her hand. "Thanks," she said. "Good show tonight?"

"Couple of guys doing acoustic sets. Top notch. Bar's on your left if you want a drink. Music's downstairs." She remembered that, the tiny basement, from a visit to the place years ago.

Nodding, she walked through the narrow ground-floor room and at the bar bought herself a drink she didn't want. It would look odd to be empty-handed. Afterwards, she couldn't remember what she'd ordered, except that it had been bitter.

The music rose up to meet her as she descended the stairs. Halfway, she stopped, her throat tight, and she held on to the rail until someone bumped her from behind. "Sorry, sorry," she murmured, and made herself take the last few steps.

The small basement was as dingy as she remembered, and packed with listeners, standing as they gazed up at the tiny, chest-high stage.

Tonight he was playing an acoustic, and she wasn't sure if that was better or worse than the sight of the red Strat when she'd seen him at the White Stag.

His hair was darker now, but the stage lighting picked out the faint blond highlights. And he still played with the same intense concentration, as if nothing existed in the world except him and the guitar. She saw that expression in her dreams, even now.

The melodies wove in and out, some familiar, some not. He built on them in variations, his fingers flying over the strings and the frets, and the audience listened in perfect silence, spell-bound.

She felt a rush of pride, then reminded herself that whatever he had made of himself was no thanks to her. But she could make an apology, and if her courage had failed her before, she was determined that tonight it would not.

The set ended. He nodded, flashing a quick smile in ac-knowledgment of the echoing applause, then placed the guitar on its stand and vaulted lightly down the steps to the floor.

She took a breath, then a step forward. And he walked right past her, slipping through the crowd until he reached a dark-haired young woman sitting on one of the few stools at the back of the room. The woman was pretty, with pale skin flushed from the heat or perhaps excitement. He didn't touch her, but leaned close and said something in her ear. The woman laughed, and intimacy crackled between them like an electric charge.

Oh, God. She turned and pushed her way towards the stairs. What a fool she had been. What had she thought she could say that he would possibly want to hear, that would change anything that had happened years ago? Friday night had been folly enough, but this, this was madness.

The man at the door called out as she went past, but his words were lost as she stumbled into the street. Blindly, she turned towards Charing Cross Road, her breath coming in sobbing gulps. The weather had changed—she felt the moisture in the air, a needle sting against her face.

And she, she was no longer invisible. Pedestrians swore as she lurched against them, turning to look at her, wondering if she was drunk. Or crazy. She made herself slow down, look in windows, be ordinary.

There, a bookshop. And there, the shop with the miniature replica guitars carefully displayed on shelves in the window, each with its little tag attributing it to a famous guitarist.

A cruel joke. Shivering, she moved on. A man coming out of a kebab shop stepped right into her path. This time, he was the one apologizing, steadying her with one hand on her shoulder. But she stood, transfixed by the picture on the television mounted above the counter in the little shop.

That face—it couldn't be.

"Lady," said the man with the kebabs, "are you all right?"

"Yes. Thanks." She managed to nod, and he moved on with a shake of his head. Then she opened the door and went into the kebab shop, her eyes never leaving the television screen. It was the London segment of the ten o'clock news. The picture flashed again, and over it, a female newscaster's voice, saying, "A well-known London barrister was found dead near his home in South London. Police are asking for help with their inquiries . . ."

The sound faded out. She stood, paralyzed, as little animated rain clouds began to move across the map of Britain on the screen.

It couldn't be. It couldn't be him.

What on earth had she done?

. . .

When the second guitarist on the bill began to set up, Andy took her half-drunk glass of wine and set it on the shelf that ran along the back wall. "You don't want to stay for this," he said in her ear. "He's not as good as I am."

As he went back for his guitar, she saw him pause for just an instant, head turned towards the stairs, an odd look on his face. Then he shook his head and retrieved the Hummingbird, and before she knew it he had hustled her up the stairs and out into the street.

The weather had changed. There was mist in the air, and the heavy scent of rain.

"We'll be wading if we don't hurry," he said, and they walked fast, this time towards Charing Cross Road. Andy held the guitar case in one hand and her elbow in the other.

Melody felt so unlike herself that she might almost have been out of her body—except that every inch of her felt so joyously, triumphantly alive. The half glass of despicable wine might have been a bottle of champagne, so giddy was she.

By the time they reached Hanway Place, it had started to sprinkle. Andy unbuttoned his coat and held it over them. She felt the warmth of his arm on her shoulders as they ran the last few yards and skidded, laughing, into the doorway of his building.

"You'd better come in and get warm," he said. "I'll make you a cuppa if you'll drink it this time."

"Oh, I'm sorry. It was fine, really."

He laughed, and she felt his breath on her face. "Maybe the milk was a bit off, after all. We could have it without."

"No, really, I've got to go. Work in the morning. I—"

She felt him draw away.

"Well, then. Thanks for coming with me. I'll see you again, shall I? When you've got more investigating to do?"

"Yes, thanks. It was lovely." She cursed herself. What could she have said that would have been more stupidly inadequate for what she'd felt that evening? "I mean—"

She stopped as he leaned towards her. His lips brushed one cheek, then he turned to kiss the other just as she responded in kind. It was the friends' casual farewell, but she'd got her timing wrong, and their lips met.

They both froze. Then his arm was around her, his mouth was against hers, and Melody found she didn't care if she ever got home.

CHAPTER TEN

Part of the gardens included a prehistoric swamp complete with models of dinosaurs. They were the first prehistoric animals ever built and came only around 30 years after dinosaurs were discovered.

The boys came to the park every day now, circling him like hyenas stalking prey. First they'd ridden bikes, but now they'd graduated to skateboards, although Andy could see that neither of them was very good.

Their interest made him wary, but he had nothing else to do, and he was not going to let them drive him away from practicing his guitar in the park.

"Can't you afford new trainers, then?" said the heavier boy, wobbling as he stepped off his board and trying to make it look as though he'd meant to do it.

Andy glanced down at his shoes, a size too small now, the broken laces reknotted, and shrugged. "Maybe I'd rather spend my money on other things."

"Where'd you get the guitar, then?"

"None of your business."

"Bet you stole it," said the heavier boy. It wasn't that he was fat, thought Andy, it was just that he had a well-fed sort of arrogance about him, and his mate was a scrawny kid who always seemed a step behind.

Now the scrawny kid dared to argue. "Come on, Shaun. Where would he steal a guitar?"

"Shut up, Joe." Shaun aimed a kick at his friend's shin. "You don't know anything." He turned his attention back to Andy. "How'd you learn to play, then?"

"I practiced. That's what you do."

Shaun didn't look impressed, and Andy guessed that in a few weeks he would give up the skateboard, and that it would be the same with anything that didn't come easily.

"Play something good."

"Not for you." Fed up, Andy put the Höfner in its case. He stood up and walked away, but he could feel their eyes on his back until he was out of their sight.

But the next day they were back.

"Where do you go to school?" asked Shaun. "We've never seen you around."

Not bloody likely, thought Andy. They both had plummy accents that marked them as public school boys. "Catholic school."

"Ooh, I'll bet those priests like you, pretty boy."

Andy didn't bother coming to the defense of the teachers, who had, for the most part, been kind to him. It would only mean more ridicule. "Bugger off, why don't you?"

That only seemed to encourage them. "Where do you live?" asked Joe.

Andy nodded in the direction of Westow Hill. He wasn't about to tell them what street.

"We live in Dulwich," said Joe, which earned him a dirty look from Shaun.

"Nice for you."

Shaun frowned, and Andy could tell he wasn't used to dealing with people who weren't impressed. Even the girls who came to the park in gaggles looked at him, simpering as they ate ice creams or sat in groups, trying out makeup and weird lipstick colors. They looked at Andy sometimes, too, but unlike Shaun, he didn't look back. Joe, on the other hand, might not have existed as far as the girls were concerned.

"What about your mum and dad?" asked Shaun. "What do they do? My dad's in dot-com startups."

Andy had no idea what he was talking about. "I live with my mum. She works in a pub."

There was sudden speculation in Shaun's glance. "In the daytime?"

"She usually goes on at lunch. Why?"

"So you're home all alone."

"I don't need a babysitter, if that's what you mean." Andy glared back at him. "I can look after myself."

"I'm sure you can, goody boy." Shaun and Joe shared a sly look, some communication passing between them that Andy didn't understand. "See you around, goody boy," said Shaun. He flipped up his skateboard, jerked his head towards Joe in a gesture of command, and they walked away, whispering.

The next afternoon they sauntered up to him, minus the boards, Shaun with a packet of cigarettes in his hand.

"Want one?" Shaun shook one from the pack with passable expertise.

"No. My mum smokes. I hate it." A flash of the fire dream made Andy feel cold even in the afternoon's heat. Only night before last, he'd found his mum asleep on the sofa with a cigarette still burning in the ashtray. "Where you'd get those, anyway?" he asked. "You can't buy them."

"Yes, we can." Shaun handed a fag to Joe, then lit them both with a bright yellow Bic. "There's a Paki guy works in one of the shops along the Parade. He'll sell us anything."

Andy wondered how much money they gave the shopkeeper on the side.

Joe looked green as he drew on the cigarette and tried hard not to cough. Andy felt a little sorry for him, but he knew better than to say anything.

It was early closing day at the library, so he was off his usual schedule and he realized he'd spent longer at the park than he'd intended. Nadine would be home soon, and he had a surprise for her. He didn't want to be late. "Look," he said, "I've got to go."

"Meeting someone?" asked Shaun. "A girlfriend?"

"Wouldn't you like to know?" Snapping the guitar into its case, Andy walked away, rather pleased with his rejoinder. Stuck-up prigs, the both of them, and the last people he'd want to tell about his friendship with Nadine.

Once home, he put the Höfner away and went out into the weedy back garden. Last week, he'd scraped together the money to buy two wilted pots of geraniums the greengrocer had set out in front of his shop. He'd placed them in a little sunny spot round the side of the back steps, hoping his mum wouldn't notice them, and had watered and tended them until they'd filled out and burst into full, crimson bloom.

Now, with one last pinch of a brown leaf, he carried them through the flat and placed them carefully on either side of Nadine's front steps. Then he sat down on his own steps to wait.

Soon, her little car came chugging up the hill. When she got out, her head was bowed, her shoulders curved. She looked sad, and he suddenly hoped quite fiercely that his surprise would please her.

When she looked up and saw him, she smiled, and the feeling that washed through him was like the sun coming out. "What?" she said. "No guitar today?" Then she saw the flowers and her face went perfectly still. "Geraniums," she whis-

pered. "And red. My favorite color." She met his eyes. "Did you do this for me?"

All he could do was nod. He was suddenly frightened, although he couldn't have said why.

"It's my birthday. Did you know that?" She clutched her bag against her chest like a shield.

Andy shook his head. "No."

"Well. Then you must have extraordinary perception. Thank you, Andy Monahan." She knelt and rubbed a deep green leaf between her fingers, releasing the spicy scent. For a moment, he thought she was going to cry, and felt as speechless as he had the day he'd met her.

Then, straightening, she gave him a too-bright grin and said, "This calls for a celebration, don't you think? When it cools off a bit, I'll bring us out some tea and biscuits, and we can gaze upon the glory of geraniums."

She went in, and Andy put his hands in his pockets, wondering if he had made her happy or sad.

A shrill whistle made him look up towards the top of the street. Shaun and Joe stood there, watching him. Shaun made a rude gesture and they fell against each other, laughing, then gave him jaunty waves before turning away.

The bastards had followed him home. And they had seen Nadine.

"I wanna see Oliver," said Charlotte for the sixth time.

Kincaid had got them settled towards the back of Kitchen and Pantry, far enough away from the damp, frigid blast of air that came in every time someone opened the front door, but still positioned where they could see anyone coming in.

When he'd told Gemma last night that he'd have a word with Tam today, he hadn't mentioned that there was someone else he wanted to talk to first. Although he'd developed a camaraderie with a number of the mothers who brought their toddlers and preschoolers in for morning coffee, he'd become closest to MacKenzie Williams. She was the only one to whom he'd confided anything about Charlotte's inability to adjust to school or his worries about getting back to work. And Oliver was Charlotte's favorite of the children they met on a regular basis.

"There he is!" Charlotte bounced up and down on her bench and waved.

MacKenzie Williams waved back from the door, keeping a firm hand on three-year-old Oliver while maneuvering a folding buggy through the narrow entrance.

Heads—male and female—turned as MacKenzie walked past. She was tall and slender, with a mass of dark, curling hair that fell almost to her waist, and olive skin that belied her Scottish name. Little Oliver had inherited his mother's dark, curly hair and coloring, and together they made perfect candidates for a well-heeled-London fashion advert.

But in spite of her looks, Kincaid had found MacKenzie to be funny, down to earth, and completely unself-conscious.

Reaching them, she boosted Oliver up next to Charlotte and said to Kincaid, "You cheated. You look fresh as the proverbial daisy. I can tell you didn't run this morning."

"Couldn't deal with a wet cocker spaniel. And we can't leave him at home or he goes into a sulk that lasts for days. Get you a coffee?"

"No, thanks. I'll go if you'll keep an eye on the boy. He'll want whatever Charlotte's having."

"Mango juice."

"Mango juice it is."

When MacKenzie came back from the counter with her order, she pulled a clean notepad and a new box of crayons from her bag and settled the children with them.

"How was your weekend?" she asked, sipping a latte as the

children began to draw. Oliver was a gentle child, and Kincaid wondered, as he often did, what Kit had been like at that age.

"It didn't exactly go according to plan. Gemma had to work, and my sergeant—my *friend*," he corrected, reminding himself once again that Doug was not actually his sergeant at the moment, "fell off a ladder and broke his ankle. Stupid git," he added, but fondly. "Doing DIY."

"Ouch. Well, I'm glad it was no worse. But poor you. I'm tempted to commit hari-kari if Bill is gone at the weekend, and I only have the one to look after."

"A friend took the boys for part of Saturday, and another friend took all the kids yesterday so that I could go and give Doug a hand."

MacKenzie studied him with the frank gaze that was one of the things he liked. "You're very lucky, you know." She stirred a tiny bit of sugar into her coffee. "In my circles, friends only do favors if they know there's a payback."

"Ouch." Kincaid grimaced. "Now I feel a complete rotter, because I came this morning specifically to ask a favor of you. And I doubt I have anything to offer in return."

"Then it's a good thing I'm not like them, isn't it?" said MacKenzie, instantly grave. "What is it? Do you need me to look after Charlotte?"

"It's a bit more complicated than that." He was reluctant now to broach the request that had seemed so simple when it had occurred to him after his visit to Louise. "It's about Oliver's school."

Kincaid had learned that parents put their children on the waiting list for exclusive Notting Hill schools when their offspring were still in utero, if not before. And that until his discussion with Louise on Saturday, he'd had no hope of paying the fees. "You know things haven't worked out for Charlotte at her current school," he continued, "and we've been a bit . . . it's been difficult."

He'd not revealed the details of Charlotte's history to MacKenzie. "The school has made it clear they're not prepared to work with what they referred to as a 'special needs' child."

MacKenzie gave Charlotte a startled glance. Turning back to Kincaid, she said quietly, although the children were now deep into an animated discussion about the proper color for chickens, "That's absurd."

"Not exactly the most flexible of environments, I admit." He tried to keep the anger from his voice. "What I was wondering was if there might be any chance of a placement in Oliver's class. I think just having a friend would be a big help."

MacKenzie chewed on her lip. "But—"

"If it's the fees," he put in quickly, "there's been a development. We may have help from Charlotte's estate." He was feeling more uncomfortable by the second. "Look, MacKenzie, I'm sorry to impose on you like this. I didn't mean to take advantage of your friendship or put you in an awkward position. And I realize I have absolutely no social clout."

She smiled suddenly. "Oh, but *I* do. And I'd certainly be happy to see if I can help you get a toe in the door. But"—she waggled a finger at him before he could respond—"I will expect something in return. And I don't mean I want you to get me out of a parking ticket."

"Okay," he said warily, hoping it was something he could deliver. "If I can—"

"I'm giving a dinner party soon. I want you to come and bring Gemma. I think it's high time I met your mysterious wife."

The atmosphere in the South London CID room was not a happy one that Monday morning.

Gemma had left home while Duncan was still getting the kids up for school, hoping an uninterrupted hour with the case file and the whiteboard would produce some much-needed inspiration, or that she would see something that they had all unaccountably missed.

Not long after Gemma arrived, Shara came in, yawning.

"You're in early," said Gemma, resisting the impulse to yawn herself.

"Baby didn't sleep. It was a relief to drop the kids at day care. Seen the papers, guv?"

"God, yes," Gemma answered with a groan. She gestured towards the stack of papers on the conference table. Not only had the story made last night's late-television news, all the papers had it this morning—complete with lurid details supplied by an "anonymous" witness, whom she strongly suspected was spotty Raymond, the hotel clerk.

The worst headline blared from Melody's father's paper: *Sicko Barrister Caught Dead in Hotel Hanky-Panky*. But at least the *Chronicle* hadn't accused the police of incompetence as had some of the other tabloids. Perhaps Ivan Talbot hadn't wanted to embarrass his daughter.

The broadsheets were a bit more circumspect, expressing dismay at the death of "an esteemed member of the law community in unfortunate circumstances."

"*Unfortunate* is bloody right," said Gemma, pushing the papers aside in disgust. She'd seen the journalists camped out in front of the station again this morning when she arrived. The super was not going to be a happy bunny.

Detective Superintendent Krueger had decided late yesterday that they might as well use the television news to make a plea for information from the public relating to Vincent Arnott, but so far nothing reliable had come in. Gemma had hoped a former girlfriend would come forward, or that someone would report having seen him leave the pub.

"What's on the slate for today, then?" asked Shara.

"The sister-in-law is arriving from Florida this morning.

I'll talk to her once she's made the formal ID this afternoon. I've got a list of the other barristers in Arnott's chambers"— the promised e-mail from Tom Kershaw had been waiting in her in-box when she'd arrived—"but as it's Monday morning, most of them have cases on the docket. It'll be catch as catch can trying to get interviews. I'll try to be in Lincoln's Inn at lunchtime, see if anyone comes in on a break. What about your statements from the patrons at the White Stag yesterday?"

"I'll type up my notes, but there was nothing earthshaking. A couple of people remember Arnott shouting at the band, thought he'd had a bit too much to drink. If we had even a rough description of the woman, it might jog someone's memory."

While Shara settled down at her computer, Gemma sat at another, watching the CCTV footage loop, going backwards and forwards, slowing it down, speeding it up. She saw the band arrive, the three musicians together. Now that Kincaid had jogged her memory, she recognized Andy Monahan, even from a brief glimpse in the grainy footage. The band unloaded their equipment; then Andy and the thin bloke went into the pub. The chubby bloke drove the van away and came back a few minutes later.

At a few minutes after the time Kathy Arnott had told them her television program began, she saw Vincent Arnott come into the frame and enter the pub. It made her feel odd, to see the victim alive, walking quickly and purposefully into the pub. Alone.

Alone. Was that the key? Would the woman he'd left with have come alone as well? It was possible that she'd come with a group and separated from them once she'd met a likely prospect, but in that case, why had no one reported it?

Slowing the tape again, Gemma watched as the punters ebbed and flowed from the pub's entrance, looking for a woman arriving on her own.

She'd begun to wonder about Melody when Melody came in, looking harried and slightly flushed. "Sorry, guv," she said, hanging up her coat and dumping her bag on a chair. "Monday morning, dreadful traffic."

Gemma pushed away from the computer, her eyes stinging from concentrating on the screen. "Must have been an accident since I came in, then, but I was early. How's Doug? Did you check in on him last night?"

"Oh, no. I didn't. Never had a chance." Melody slid into one of the workstations and was already tapping up the case file on the computer, her back to Gemma. "I'll give him a shout in a bit. So, any progress today? What's on our agenda? And where's the super?"

"No sign of Krueger this morning." She looked towards their superintendent's glassed-in cubicle. The door was still closed, the blinds drawn. "That's a bit odd, the boss skiving off on a Monday morning. Maybe we should be counting our blessings. Oh, Melody," she added as it occurred to her, "what about your guitar bloke? Have any luck there?"

Melody knocked a stack of papers from the workstation surface. She knelt, muttering and scrabbling for them, and only when she'd replaced them on the desk in a neat stack did she turn to Gemma. "Not really. It seems the band is splitting up and it was just a bad night all round. I still haven't managed to track down the drummer and the bass player. But it did occur to me that Caleb Hart, the producer who booked the band into the pub, might know Arnott at least by sight. He didn't react when I mentioned Arnott's name at the recording studio on Saturday, but then I didn't show him Arnott's photo."

"That's something to follow up," said Gemma. "Oh, and I think Duncan told you that he knows the band's manager, Tam Moran? He thought he might have a word with Tam. I'm sure he could get Caleb Hart's contact information from him."

Melody stared at her, looking unaccountably dismayed.

"But—I'd thought I could—I'm sure the recording studio will know how to get in touch with Hart. Or Reg at the pub—"

The CID room door swung open and Superintendent Krueger walked in. One look at her face froze Melody in mid-sentence, and made Gemma's heart contract in anticipation of very bad news. She had an instant to hope that it wasn't their screwup.

"I've had a call from Southwark," said Krueger. "We have another victim. Male. Found dead in his flat this morning. Naked, trussed, and strangled."

CHAPTER ELEVEN

Cleaver Square is a paradox. Sandwiched between two busy streets, it provides a sense of eerie calm rarely seen outside of a Hitchcock movie. Shielded from the outside world with perfectly aligned houses and shaded by tall trees, the square is a regular host to boules games, providing the perfect soundtrack for a peaceful afternoon: the sound of the metal balls hitting the ground; the air rushing through the leaves; the sound of hurried footsteps on the gravel. Just sit on a bench, and observe.

—www.themagnificentsomething.com

The address Gemma had been given was in Cleaver Square, near the Kennington tube station. The square was a perfect rectangle of Georgian terraced houses surrounding an unfenced tree-lined garden. There was a pleasant-looking pub in the far right-hand corner, but the obvious activity was on the left side of the square, where the road was blocked by a phalanx of panda cars with blue lights flashing.

Finding a place to park between the pub and the crime scene, Gemma was pleased to see Melody's Clio pull in behind her.

"Major circus," said Melody as she got out and they walked

towards the scene. "But it's obviously not a hotel, so maybe it has nothing to do with us."

"Maybe." Gemma thought that was wishful thinking, which was not usually one of Melody's indulgences. "I'd say we're just lucky the rain has let up."

They showed their IDs to the uniformed constable doing perimeter duty by the first panda car. "South London MIT," Gemma added.

He was young enough to look impressed. "Guvnor's expecting you." He nodded towards a slender, dark-haired woman in a Burberry standing in front of a flat with a yellow door.

Gemma stared at the detective, knowing her face was familiar but not quite able to place her. "Your guv'nor," she said to the constable, "DI—" She let it hang as a question and the constable cooperated.

"DI Maura Bell, ma'am. Southwark Station.

Gemma thanked him, then muttered, "Bugger," under her breath as she and Melody walked towards the flat.

"What's up, boss?" asked Melody.

"I know her. And I'm not sure that's a good thing."

But when they reached Detective Inspector Bell and introduced themselves, Bell showed no immediate sign of recognition.

"The techs are here, and we're expecting the pathologist any moment," said Bell, with a faint trace of the Scots accent that Gemma remembered. "But I imagine you'd like to have a look straightaway." She shook her head. "This is a weird one. Certainly not your ordinary weekend domestic." She gestured towards the flat, which was surrounded by a low, wrought-iron railing. "It's the ground floor. The door was locked, the victim's keys inside. No sign of forced entry in the front or back. None of the neighbors—at least none that we've spoken to—reported a disturbance."

"He lived alone?" asked Melody.

"Apparently. His name is Shaun Francis. His sister called it in. Said they work in the same office. She was worried when he didn't show up for work this morning and didn't answer his phone. Afraid he might be ill. Turned out to be an understatement. She came over and let herself in with her own set of keys." Bell nodded towards the panda car farthest from the flat. "She's quite shocked. I've got her sitting with one of the PCs for the moment."

"I'd rather have a look inside before we speak to her," said Gemma.

"Be my guest." Bell tapped on the yellow door and a constable opened it immediately.

The main entrance led into a central hallway, lit by the fanlight above the door. A staircase led up to the next two floors, and an interior door stood open on the left. This, Gemma surmised, was the ground-floor flat, but she paused before entering. "Both outer and inner doors were locked?"

"Yes. No one's home in either of the upstairs flats or the basement flat."

"A nasty surprise when they get home, then," said Gemma. "But we'll definitely need statements. It's possible they heard something they didn't identify as odd at the time." After another glance around the hallway, she stepped into the flat, followed by Melody and Bell.

Behind her, Melody murmured, "I hate seeing these Georgian houses converted into flats, but this one doesn't seem to have been done too badly."

"I try to keep in mind that they didn't have plumbing," said Bell. "Lessens the pain considerably. As does the fact that the servants lived in the basement."

Shooting a glance at Gemma, Melody whispered, "Bit prickly," as they moved into the room.

Gemma had more sympathy with Bell's attitude, considering that she came from a family whose ancestors would undoubtedly have labored in the basement and carried the chamber pots up and down the stairs.

A very small foyer with coat hooks and an umbrella stand led into a sitting room filled with light from the two large front windows. Gemma's first thought was that the flat was very deliberately masculine. Taupe walls with gleaming white trim, large expensive-looking sofa and chairs in coordinating taupe fabrics. Crimson accents. Expensive media gadgets and contemporary art that looked as though it might be original. A new issue of *GQ* was thrown casually across a stack of Sunday's papers on the coffee table, and a set of keys lay in a porcelain bowl on a console table in the foyer.

"Interior designer," Melody said with conviction. "And he used a good one. Didn't mind spending money."

Nothing in the sitting room seemed disturbed or unusual, so Gemma walked on, towards the open kitchen tucked into the middle of the flat. Although small, it was fitted out with the latest decor and appliances, but she saw no evidence that its owner had actually cooked.

By the time she reached the door to the bedroom just beyond the kitchen, the smell that had been tickling the back of her nostrils became unpleasantly pronounced. Decay, human waste, and something else she couldn't quite identify.

"Oh, bloody hell," she said as she looked into the room.

Two unfamiliar SOCOs in bunny suits were processing the scene, but they didn't block the view of the bed. The sheets were pulled back, as they had been at the Belvedere. But this was no cheap, rickety hotel bed. Massive and modern, it dominated the room, and made the figure lying facedown upon it seem even more grotesque.

This man was younger. Much younger. Brown hair that looked—at least from the back—as if it had been expensively barbered. A slightly stocky build with the beginnings of thickening at the waist.

Sturdy ankles—ankles bound with a brown leather belt.

Wrists bound behind his back with a tie. Liberty of London, how posh, thought the part of Gemma's mind that was picking out details from the big picture. A bit feminine compared to the atmosphere of the flat. Had it belonged to the victim?

And around his neck, a fine, gray silk scarf.

"No gag this time," said a familiar voice behind Gemma. "And he's facedown."

"Good God, Rashid," she said, turning. "You gave me a fright. Don't you ever take a day off?" she added, looking at him more closely. There were dark circles under his eyes.

"Short rota. Two pathologists down with winter flu."

"Well, I'm just as glad it's you, considering." Gemma turned back to the room but was careful not to step into it. "What do you think?" she asked quietly. "Is it the same perpetrator?"

"I'd be willing to bet all my accumulated vacation time on that being the scarf used to gag Vincent Arnott."

"If that's true, why use it as the ligature this time? And why leave it behind?"

"First things first." Rashid turned to the taller of the techs. "Laurence, mate. Mind if I have a look?"

"Got your booties on?" Laurence gave him the once-over. "Right, then. Just watch your step."

Rashid crossed to the bed.

Gemma watched as the pathologist gently probed and prodded. Just behind her, she could hear Melody's breathing. DI Bell had stayed back by the kitchen, watching the proceedings from a distance.

"The flat's cool but not cold," Rashid said as he manipulated the victim's head. "Rigor is just beginning to pass off in the neck and jaw, so I'd estimate time of death at roughly twelve hours—give or take a couple, of course. Possibly between ten and midnight last night.

"I don't want to remove the scarf until I get him on the table, so I can't say anything definitive about strangulation, although the thing was certainly tied tight enough. However, from the smell of him, there was a good deal of alcohol involved." He leaned down to look more closely at the sheet. "And—"

"Vomit," said Gemma, realizing what had been lurking beneath the stronger odors.

"Yes. He might have choked on it. But there's no trace on the bed, and I didn't see any evidence of a drinking binge as I came through the flat. So if he drank enough to be sick, how did he get home? And undressed?"

"And where is the damned smell coming from?" asked Melody. There was a slight tremor in her voice.

Straightening, Rashid scanned the room. "Ah." He went towards the bathroom, which, from the layout of the flat, Gemma guessed must be tucked beneath the hall stairs. Rashid had a dancer's grace, and Gemma watched, fascinated as always, as he moved around the crime scene without seeming to disturb a molecule.

He stopped at the door of the bathroom, however, and stood looking in. "Someone undressed him. He was sick on his clothes—probably somewhere outside the flat. And it looks like there's a trace of vomit in the sink as well."

"How can you tell it was someone else?" asked Melody.

"The clothes are in a pile. Think about it. You come home blind drunk, so drunk you've been sick. You stumble around the bathroom, pulling things off and dropping them wherever they land. You're sick again. Chances are you don't get everything off before you stagger back into the bedroom and fall—probably crossways—onto the bed. You don't drop your clothes neatly atop one another in a pile. Wait a minute—" Rashid peered more closely into the bathroom, then turned back to them, looking pleased with himself. "I'll need blood work, but there may have been more to it than alcohol. There's a bottle of Valium on the sink. But"—frowning, he gazed at the body on the bed—"mixing Valium and alcohol doesn't usually cause that severe a reaction. I'd like to get him on the table as soon as possible. All right if I get my photos, Laurence?"

"I'm logging you, but be dainty, will you?" the tech replied.

"As a bloody butterfly." Rashid grinned and took his camera from the bag he'd left by the door.

"You have to appreciate a man who enjoys his work," murmured DI Bell as they moved back into the sitting room. "Or maybe I should just say 'appreciate,' full stop."

"I take it you haven't worked with Dr. Kaleem before," said Gemma, suppressing a smile.

"I haven't had the pleasure." Bell's Scottish lilt was more apparent when she was relaxed. Now she studied Gemma, looking puzzled. "I know you, though, don't I? Have we met on a case?"

"You worked a case with my husband some time ago. A warehouse fire in Southwark. Only we weren't married then. Detective Superintendent Kincaid."

Watching Bell color, she suspected the detective remembered her now, and the gaffe she had made.

But Bell said, "Doug Cullen's guv'nor?"

"Yes." Gemma wasn't going to go into the current circumstances of Duncan's leave and Doug's reassignment.

"How is he?" asked Bell. "Doug, I mean."

Melody stepped in. "He broke his ankle over the weekend, but he's doing fine. Want me to give him a message?"

"You're—" Bell looked confused.

"His friend. I've been looking after him."

"Och. No, that's all right. But thanks. Maybe I'll give him a ring—"

"Ma'am," called the constable on the door. "There's a neighbor wants to speak to you."

"Be right there," said Bell, with an air of great relief.

. . .

Kincaid was almost back to the house with Charlotte when his phone rang. If it was Gemma wanting to know if he'd spoken to Tam, he'd have to make up an excuse. He was relieved to see that it was Doug, and answered with such a cheerful "Hullo!" that there was a moment's silence on the other end of the line.

Then, "What's wrong with you?" said Doug, sounding very aggrieved. "It's Monday morning, for God's sake. Nobody should sound like an advert for sunshine and roses."

"I've just had a very productive meeting, the details of which must remain a deep, dark secret for the moment."

"A secret?" said Charlotte, tugging on his hand. "I wanna know a secret." The rain had stopped, so that sans umbrella, he was able to hold the phone in one hand and Charlotte by the other.

"You haven't talked to that manager chap yet, have you?" asked Doug.

"No. Why?"

"I want to go with you."

"You're off work with a broken ankle, mate, in case you hadn't noticed."

"Doesn't mean I can't get in and out of a car," Doug said truculently.

"I thought you were supposed to be keeping that ankle elevated for the next couple of days."

"I can prop it up wherever I am. Come on, man, I'm going bonkers here."

As he thought about the logistics, Kincaid realized there were unforeseen advantages to driving the old Astra estate car. He could put Charlotte in the very back, and Doug could sit sideways in the middle seat.

"Okay," Kincaid agreed, thinking that trying to conduct an interview with a cripple and a three-year-old would have to go down on his list of firsts. Especially when the interviewee was a friend. "I'll pick you up in about half an hour. We'll get lunch."

"Right-ho." Doug sounded only marginally more cheerful.

"Doug, what's bothering you? You're not just bored." Kincaid walked on, waiting for a response.

He'd begun to think the line had gone dead when Doug said, "There was something . . . The way Melody talked about that guitar chap yesterday—did you notice? I didn't like it. Something's up, and I want to know what it is."

Melody was still shaky with relief as she followed Gemma and Maura Bell out of the flat. Not that she'd suspected Andy of having anything to do with Vincent Arnott's death—of course she hadn't. But the fact that she'd been consorting— *consorting*? Good God. The very word made her damp down a hysterical desire to laugh.

Whatever she chose to call it, she'd crossed the line with someone connected to their investigation, and the fact that she knew that Andy Monahan had a solid alibi for the time of this victim's death made her feel both giddy and horribly awkward. If the subject of Andy's whereabouts came up for any reason, she was going to have to come clean with her boss. She flushed at the thought.

And God forbid someone mentioned it to Doug. Not that she and Doug had *that* kind of relationship, but she'd let him down last night, and even without that, she knew that he would think less of her.

How she felt about what she'd done, she had yet to figure out. In the meantime, however, she'd better concentrate on the business at hand—although even that admonition didn't stop the little shiver of remembered desire that ran through her.

Gemma and DI Bell were talking to a woman who stood behind the low iron railing of the flat next door. She was stout, gray haired, and tweedy, and in her arms she held a Yorkshire terrier with a pink bow in its hair.

"It's Verne," she was saying, her honking voice raised to a decibel level that indicated she suffered from hearing loss. "Myra Verne. Lived here since 1972. The garden flat. Cheap in those days, the flats round here, though you wouldn't think it now."

"Mrs. Verne," said Gemma, "if you could—"

"It's Miss. Never married. Never saw the point in being saddled with a man to look after."

"Quite right, I'm sure, Miss Verne." Gemma gave her a conspiratorial smile. "But about last night—"

"Something's happened to that young man next door, hasn't it? The one in the ground-floor flat. Spells his name S-h-a-u-n instead of S-e-a-n. Bloody pretentious, if you ask—"

"Miss Verne," interrupted Maura Bell, "if you could just tell us—"

"That's exactly what I'm doing, young woman." Myra Verne's tweedy shoulders stiffened in offense, and the Yorkie gave a sympathetic growl that might have been mistaken for a mosquito whine.

Gemma gave Bell a quelling look. "Miss Verne, you were saying?" Accustomed, Melody knew, to the boisterous good nature of her own dogs, Gemma reached out to stroke the Yorkie.

"Princess doesn't like strangers," warned Miss Verne. "She didn't like him, either." She jerked her head towards the next-door flat. "He had the nerve to complain about her barking in the garden. It's her garden, isn't it? She has every right." She clutched the dog to her bosom more tightly. "Yuppies," she added with venom, and it took Melody a moment to realize she didn't mean the dog. "They've taken over the square, with all their flat conversions and German appliances."

Gemma tried again. "Miss Verne—"

"So what sort of fix did he get himself into? I know there's something, with that woman coming out of the flat this morning howling like a banshee and then the cavalry arriving in full force."

Melody could see that even Gemma was losing patience. "Miss Verne," said Gemma firmly, "we're not at liberty to say. Did you see or hear anything last night that led you to think that Mr. Francis might be in some sort of trouble?"

"He was off to the pub when I went out to put my rubbish in the bin. About seven or half past, when I'd finished my supper. Every night he was there, even on a Sunday. I think he ate all his meals at the place, too." Miss Verne sniffed in disapproval.

"You mean this pub?" Gemma gestured towards the pretty place in the corner of the square. "The Prince of Wales?"

Having seen the appealing menu on the pub's outdoor blackboard, Melody shuddered to contemplate Miss Verne's idea of a proper meal.

"It used to be a nice quiet place. But now, even in the winter, people bring their dogs and carry their beers into the square as if it was a public park. It drives Princess mad."

"Quiet, all right," muttered Maura Bell. "Supposedly in the sixties it was the hangout of the Richardsons, the rival gang to the Krays. If you ask me, the lawyers and politicians are an improvement, although maybe not any more honest," she added.

Gemma gave Bell a startled glance. "Lawyers?"

"It's all lawyers and MPs round here these days," answered Miss Verne. "As I was saying. Damned yuppies."

"Shaun Francis was a lawyer?"

"Trainee barrister, or so he said. Although I don't see how a trainee barrister could have afforded that flat."

"Barrister?" Gemma repeated faintly, looking at Melody. "Surely not—" She caught herself and turned back to the neighbor. "Miss Verne, will you excuse us? You've been most helpful and we will want to get a full statement from you in writing, if you'll just bear with us for a few minutes."

She walked away before their witness could protest, motioning Melody and Maura to follow. When they were out of Miss Verne's hearing, she hissed, "Another barrister? Strangled? Dear God. This is turning into a royal balls-up. What the hell is going on here?"

"Something Shakespeare would have loved," said Melody.

CHAPTER TWELVE

Spitalfields takes its name from the hospital and priory, St. Mary's Spittel that was founded in 1197. Lying in the heart of the East End, it is an area known for its spirit and strong sense of community. It was in a field next to the priory where the now famous market first started in the thirteenth century.

—www.spitalfields.co.uk

When Kincaid had rung Tam, asking if they could meet, Tam had suggested not his and Michael's flat near Columbia Road, but the Canteen restaurant at Spitalfields Market.

Kincaid had insisted on leaving Doug and Charlotte by the Lamb Street entrance while he parked the car, to put less stress on Doug's ankle, and now as he caught them up and they crossed the central space in the market, he could see Tam seated in the outside area of the restaurant. Because the market was covered and at least partially enclosed, the restaurants were able to maintain a semblance of pavement cafés, with a little help from outdoor heaters.

"Will this suit?" asked Tam, standing. He pumped Kincaid's hand, then Doug's, then shook Charlotte's hand and Bob the elephant's plush paw very solemnly.

He'd already had the staff bring a booster seat for Charlotte, and as he lifted her into it, he said, "I think there's a wee surprise for you, lassie."

Carefully arranged at Charlotte's place were an activity book, crayons, and a paper lion badge. "See, there's a place to put this fellow in the book." Tam showed her where to put the lion. "And the next time you come, you can get a different animal to add to your collection."

"There's a place for an elephant," said Charlotte, entranced. She looked at Kincaid. "Can we come again soon, Papa? I might get the elephant."

"I should think we could manage that." Kincaid gave Tam a curious glance. "What did we do to deserve such largess, Tam?"

"Ah, well, it's not entirely in your honor, I have to admit." Tam settled his faded hat a little more firmly on his head. "But I felt the need for a celebration, and who better to share it with than such friends? But let's order—I could eat a horse."

The restaurant specialized in traditional English food, so after some discussion on the nature of rarebit—Kincaid assuring Charlotte that it was a cheesy sauce and had nothing to do with rabbits—he chose the Welsh rarebit with a poached egg for her and the smoked haddock for himself. Tam and Doug went the whole hog—so to speak—for the roast pork of the day.

When the waiter had taken their orders, Kincaid scrutinized his friend. "So, what's all this, Tam?" A spark of hope flared. "Is it Louise? Some good news about her diagnosis?"

Tam's face fell. "No, things are just the same there, I'm afraid. Michael's cooking for her every night. We'll rub along as best we can."

"What, then? You've won the lottery?"

Tam grinned, although his Scottish dental work was a sight perhaps best not seen too often. "Close enough, maybe, for my business. Maybe as close as I'll ever come, and I've seen a good few musicians come and go over the years. But this time, Duncan, I just may have hit the pot of gold."

"Someone new?"

"No, it's my lad Andy. I got him a gig playing guitar for a girl singer, and her manager filmed them—just rehearsal time, mainly, and a bit yesterday in the studio. He did some editing, then put it up on YouTube just to see what kind of response it would get." Tam shook his head. "I'd never have believed it. The bloody thing is going viral. In a day. We're scrambling now to get the contracts in place so we can get the song up for downloads. It's— I've never seen anything like it." For a moment, Tam looked as if he were going to cry. "I havenae even told Michael yet. Afraid to jinx it. That's why I didn't want you to come to the flat."

Kincaid saw that what had seemed a simple enough errand had suddenly become much more complicated, not to mention that at Tam's mention of the guitar player, Doug had begun to glower.

He plunged in. "Tam, I didn't ring you about Louise. In fact, it was Andy Monahan I wanted to talk to you about."

Tam stared at him. "You've seen the video already?"

"No. It's about the man who was murdered in Crystal Palace. The one that Andy had the row with in the pub on Friday night."

"What?" Tam stared at him. "There wasn't any row. The daft bugger came up and shouted at Andy during the break."

"Did you actually see it?"

"No." Tam sounded less certain. "I just came in on the aftermath. I'd walked Caleb—that's Caleb Hart, the girl singer's manager—to his car. Andy had blown him away in the first set, in spite of the other two acting like prize pillocks."

"The other guys in the band, you mean?"

"Oh, they're all right, those lads, but they're not in the same league and they know it, and everyone was out of sorts over a gig that was meant to showcase Andy. Look, Duncan, what's this all about? We've already spoken to that sergeant lassie that came to the studio on Saturday—bit prim, but the lad seemed taken with her. And I thought you were off work looking after the wee one here." He glanced at Charlotte, who was still immersed in her activity book.

"Tam, it's Gemma's case. I told her I'd talk to you."

"And that 'sergeant lassie' is Detective Sergeant Melody Talbot," put in Doug, obviously offended on Melody's behalf. Kincaid was tempted to kick him under the table.

"But I don't understand." Tam's buoyant mood had evaporated like a pricked balloon. "What do you want with Andy?"

They all fell silent as the waiter brought their food. Kincaid helped Charlotte make a start on her Welsh rarebit, but no one else touched their steaming plates. "The thing is," Kincaid said, "Andy Monahan was the last person known to have had any contact with the victim—Vincent Arnott—before Arnott was found dead. Are you sure he didn't know the man?"

"Why would he? I only booked the band in that pub because Caleb Hart asked me to."

"What about Caleb Hart? Could he have known Arnott?"

Tam frowned. "Well, he didn't say so. But I suppose it's possible."

"You said Hart left the pub after the first set. Do you know where he went?"

"He said he had a meeting. But, Duncan, you can't think Caleb Hart had anything to do with this." Tam sounded horrified.

"The only verifiable thing I know is that Andy played the second set with the band, and that you picked him up outside the pub afterwards. You told Melody—Sergeant Talbot—that you drove him home. I know where Andy lives, and I think it's highly unlikely he could have got back to the Belvedere Hotel in Crystal Palace from Oxford Street in time to murder Vincent Arnott. Anyone else could be in the frame."

Tam dropped his cutlery on the plate with a clatter. "What is this, bloody Big Brother? And how do you know where Andy lives?" His raised voice was enough to make Charlotte look up anxiously at Kincaid.

"Is Tam mad at you, Papa?" she asked. "I don't like people being mad."

"No, sweetie." Kincaid shook his head at Tam, then helped Charlotte cut up some more of her rarebit and toast. "Would Bob like some Welsh rabbit, too?" He mimed feeding the plush elephant an imaginary bite, and Charlotte giggled.

"There was a CCTV camera outside the pub," Kincaid explained quietly to Tam. He picked up his own knife and fork and started on his haddock, irritated with himself for having let the conversation get out of hand. He'd needed reminding that he was here as a friend, not a policeman. "And the reason I know where Andy lives is another story that has nothing to do with any of this," he went on. "I knew Andy before I ever met you."

"He never said."

"He'd have had no reason. He was a witness in a case. He didn't do anything wrong, and now I only want to help the both of you if I can."

"I'm sorry, Duncan," said Tam more calmly. "Didn't mean to lose my temper. But you have to understand how important this is." He leaned over the table in entreaty. "Andy—well, Andy's special. I suppose he's a bit like a son to me. I saw him play in a club when he was just barely out of school, signed him then and there. He hadn't any family, so I've always tried to look after him if I could. And now, this thing with Caleb and the girl—I don't know that either of us will ever have another chance like this. If there's anything you can do to clear this up—"

"Well, why don't I talk to Caleb Hart? Unofficially. Maybe I can stave off the official interview if he can account for his whereabouts after he left the pub that night."

Tam took a bite of his pork and chewed thoughtfully. "Caleb and I go back a long way. I know he's had some problems in the past, but he's always been straight with me. And he did me a favor by asking me if I had a session guitarist to work with his girl, when he knew how good she was. So I owe him. If you could do it, maybe, delicate like?"

"Delicacy is my middle name."

Tam looked unconvinced, but he sighed and said, "His office is just round the corner, in Hanbury Street."

Melody could see that Gemma was not amused by her "Let's kill all the lawyers" reference.

"*Henry the Sixth*?" said Maura Bell. "I did Shakespeare at school, too, you know," she added to Melody, as if Melody had questioned her scholastic credentials.

"Just don't anyone breathe the words *serial killer,*" said Gemma. "There's got to be some connection between these two men, other than being barristers who frequented pubs before they were strangled. But we have got to make certain that no one says anything to the press about the manner of death.

"We couldn't keep what happened at the Belvedere quiet because of the hotel staff. But here, the sister's the only one who saw anything, right, Maura?"

"I've had a PC with her in the car, and I think she was too shocked to talk to anyone."

"Let's try to keep it that way. Melody, can you go have a word at the pub while I speak to the sister? Oh, and look out for a puddle of sick as you go."

"Thanks, boss," said Melody, but despite the sarcasm she was happy enough to have a few minutes to herself.

Melody surveyed the square. Assuming Shaun Francis had been at the Prince of Wales, and he had been drunk and ill, would he have gone round by the pavement to get home, or taken the most direct route, across the unfenced garden?

Garden, she thought, even in the dark, so she cut through it herself, walking carefully, eyes on the ground. She saw it about halfway across, rain diluted, but unmistakably a pool of vomit.

"Oi!" she shouted at the constable who'd checked their IDs, motioning him over. "Mark this, will you?" she asked. "And have someone keep an eye on it until the SOCOs can get to it."

"Whatever you say, ma'am," the constable responded, giving her a skeptical look.

"Yours is not to question why," she responded, grinning, and he tipped his cap to her in a mock salute.

"Cheeky sod," she muttered, making sure he heard her as she walked away.

As she neared the pub, cooking odors wafted out to greet her and she realized she was starving. She admonished her stomach to behave itself as she studied the pub.

The Prince of Wales was a charming place, with a narrow redbrick Georgian facade. Even in January, flowers cascaded from planters above the bright blue ground-floor awnings, and the lunchtime crowd was still braving the cold to enjoy drinks at the tables in the small forecourt.

She imagined coming here with Andy for a leisurely drink, then quickly banished the thought as she felt the color rise in her face. How did she even know he would want to see her again, much less go out with her?

She went into the pub and threaded her way to the bar.

"What can I get you?" asked the barman when she'd got his attention.

"A chat." She showed him her ID.

His eyes widened. "Is this about all the commotion on the other side of the square? I wondered what was going on." He was young, friendly, and good looking, and from the assessing look he gave Melody, not unappreciative. All the better, she thought, and smiled at him.

"It is, actually. I have some questions about last night and about one of your patrons. A regular, I think—Shaun Francis."

"Shaun? Yeah, I'd say regular—regular as clockwork. Eats—and drinks—here most nights." He glanced out the front window at the police cars on the other side of the square. "Lives across the way. Not sure which flat. Has something happened to him?"

Melody avoided the question. "Was he here last night?"

The barman wiped a glass with a towel for a moment, frowning. "Yeah. At least early on. He had something to eat—a salad, the smoked mackerel, I think. That, and a gin and tonic. He said he was doing a bit of slimming, so no beer and no chips."

"That takes the fun out of things a bit, I should think."

He met her eyes. "I'll bet you can have all the beer and chips you want." Definitely a practiced flirt.

"About Shaun Francis," said Melody. "Do you mean he didn't stay long last night?"

"No, just that I only served him the once. It was bloody sardines in here last night. Three of us on the bar. And as the rain had let up, there was a full crowd outside as well."

"When you served him the meal and the G and T, what time was it?"

"Half seven, maybe. Why all the—"

"Was he with anyone?"

The barman thought, then shook his head. "Not that I noticed."

"Was there anyone in particular he talked to regularly? Friends he met up with?"

Shrugging, the barman said, "Oh, you know, lawyers. We have a lot of lawyers and MPs round here, and the occasional actor or media type. Most of the lawyers seem to know each other. But—" He paused, then gave a flick of the towel and went on. "Shaun likes to talk about himself. He can usually find someone to impress, but I don't notice people seeking him out." He grimaced. "Ouch. That sounds a bit hard. I probably shouldn't be saying this."

"Tell me anyway. You can put it down to police coercion." Melody propped her elbows on the bar and gave him her most encouraging look.

He raised an eyebrow. "Handcuffs and all?"

That cut a little close to the bone, thought Melody, but merely said, "Go on, then."

"It's just that the bar staff has learned to avoid Shaun like the plague on quiet nights. No one wants to get stuck listening to an hour's monologue on some important case he's just tried, or hear about some new gadget he's bought for his flat." He glanced round, making sure the patrons on either side were involved in their own conversations, then added more quietly, "To be honest, Shaun's a bit of a prick."

Just as Gemma glanced towards the car where Shaun Francis's sister was sitting with the uniformed PC, the mortuary van pulled up. "Oh, bugger," she said to Maura. "I'd like to spare her seeing the removal. Tell them to hold off for a bit, even if Rashid's finished. Let me interview her, then we'll get her prints for elimination and see if we can arrange for someone to see her home."

She'd started towards the panda car when her phone rang.

"Hullo, love," said Kincaid when she answered. "I hate to interrupt, but I thought you'd want to know I've spoken to Tam. I don't think either Tam or Andy Monahan can have had anything to do with your murder on Friday night. But Tam says that Caleb Hart, the producer who arranged the band's gig, left after the first set. He said he had a meeting."

"Did Tam know if he knew Vincent Arnott?" Gemma asked, watching one of the SOCOs cross the garden to the spot where she'd seen Melody flag the vomit sample.

"Not that Tam was aware. But he's given me Caleb Hart's office address, and I'm not far from there. It's in Hanbury Street."

"Hanbury Street? What are you doing there?"

"I'm at Spitalfields Market, actually." When he paused, she heard voices in the background, one of them definitely Charlotte's. "Look, love," Kincaid went on, "it's complicated. And I know I'll be treading on your territory if I talk to Hart. But it turns out that Tam has a vested interest in Caleb Hart's feathers not being ruffled any more than necessary at the moment—I'll explain when I see you. Tam thought I might smooth the way."

"You can't take Charlotte with you to interview a witness—or a potential suspect," she protested.

"I've got Doug with me. He can look after her here at the market for a few minutes."

"Doug? What the—no, no, just tell me later." Gemma weighed just how much trouble she might get into over Duncan's interference against the expediency of getting information quickly. "Okay. But make sure it's clear you're there on Tam's behalf and that it's not official. And while you're at it, ask him where he was last night between ten and midnight."

Kincaid's comprehension was instant. "What's happened?"

"Another dead lawyer. A barrister, but young this time. Found in his flat in Cleaver Square by his sister this morning. That's where I am now."

"Same method?"

"It looks that way, but this time the killer left the scarf. Oh, and, Duncan, you remember the DI you worked with in Southwark on the arson case?"

"Maura Bell." He sounded suddenly cautious.

"It's her investigation. Or it was, until they called us in."

"Ah, well. You might want to wear your stab vest. She's a wee bit territorial."

The female constable who had been sitting in the car with Shaun Francis's sister got out as Gemma approached. "I'm glad to see you, ma'am." Nodding towards the car, she added, "She's calmed down a bit now and is wanting to make phone calls. I've asked her to wait until she's spoken to you. One of the lads went round the corner to the shops and got her a cup of tea."

"Good idea." Gemma realized her hands were freezing and rubbed them together. "I'd kill for a cuppa."

"I'll go myself," said the constable. "Won't be a tic." The constable turned back. "Her name's Amanda, by the way."

"Thanks. Oh, milk, no sugar," Gemma called after her as the PC set off in the direction of Kennington Road.

Taking a breath, she walked to the car and slid in next to the woman in the backseat. "I'm Detective Inspector James," she said. "I'm the senior officer in charge of looking into what's happened to your brother. You're Amanda, right? Amanda Francis?"

The woman nodded. She was, Gemma thought, about her own age. Her brother's tendency to put on a bit of weight around his middle had in her been translated into an over-all heaviness. She wore all black, as if she'd come prepared for mourning, and her square face was red and blotched with weeping. In one blunt hand, she clutched a polystyrene cup of tea that had gone scummy on the surface, in the other, a soggy tissue.

"Tell me what happened this morning," Gemma said gently. "Why were you worried about your brother?"

"We—we're in the same"—Amanda Francis's voice caught and she stopped to clear her throat—"chambers. Shaun was supposed to be in court this morning. A big case. For all his faults, he's not likely to be late for something that's to his benefit."

"So you rang him?"

Amanda nodded. "I left half a dozen messages. By the time the hearing had started and I still hadn't heard from him, I was frantic. I thought maybe he was ill. Or—I don't know. I never imagined—" She looked at Gemma with shocked dark eyes. "How could—why would—"

Gemma patted her hand, then dug in her coat pocket for a fresh tissue from her emergency packet. There were times when mummy preparedness paid off on the job. "Let's back up a bit, why don't we? I understand your brother was a barrister, and you worked together. Are you a barrister, too?"

Taking the offered tissue, Amanda blew her already swollen nose. "No. I'm a legal secretary. I'm two years older, but when Father died, there wasn't enough money to keep both of us in good schools and then uni. So I trained as a paralegal, and then when Shaun finished his law degree, I convinced my head of chambers to take him on." Pride and resentment warred in her voice.

"Your chambers," said Gemma, keeping her voice level, "is there another barrister called Vincent Arnott?"

Amanda looked at her blankly. "Never heard of him. What has that to do with Shaun?"

Well, that was one easy connection she could cross off her list, thought Gemma. She tried another tack. "Were you close, you and your brother?"

"I don't know." Amanda's laugh was harsh. "By what standards? Other brothers and sisters? All I can tell you is that if Shaun needed something, he would call me. *Always available Amanda*, that's me." Her face crumpled. "Now what am I going to do?"

A tap at the window signaled the return of the friendly PC.

"Ta," said Gemma as she rolled the window down and took the steaming cup.

The distraction had given Amanda Francis a chance to get herself under control again.

"Amanda, had you noticed anything different about Shaun recently?" asked Gemma as she turned back to her. "New friends? New girlfriend? Was he worried about anything?"

"Shaun's girlfriends tended not to last long. And friends—he hung out with some of the guys from chambers. And the pub here." She glanced across the square. "Not that he ever invited me."

"What about yesterday? Did you speak to him? Did he say anything about his plans?"

"He was going to play squash," Amanda said with a disapproving sniff. "He was never any good at sports, but lately he'd been on this slimming thing and had started playing squash at the weekends. He'd pulled a muscle in his back and I told him it was stupid not to lay off a bit longer. But of course he didn't listen—"

She stopped, shaking her head, her eyes brimming. "How stupid. It doesn't matter now, does it? Whatever I said, or whether or not he paid attention. Did I—did I really see what I thought I saw? Did someone really do that—those—things to him?"

Glancing towards the flat, Gemma saw Rashid come out of the building and speak to Maura Bell. They'd need that print kit, and she needed to get Amanda Francis away from the scene.

"Amanda, did you drive here or come on the tube?"

"Oh, the tube. I don't have a car. I take the train into the City from Dulwich every day."

"Dulwich?" asked Gemma, alarm bells ringing. That was almost to Crystal Palace. And hadn't there been someone else mentioned who lived in Dulwich?

"I can't afford a flat in the city, like Shaun." Even now, Amanda Francis couldn't keep the bitterness from her voice. "I still live with my mum in— Oh, God." She put a shaking hand to her mouth and her words came out in a wail. "How am I going to tell my mother that Shaun is dead?"

CHAPTER THIRTEEN

Crystal Palace was cursed by bad luck and financial crisis. In 1861 the Palace was damaged by strong winds and on Sunday 30th December 1866 a fire broke out destroying the North End of the building along with many natural history exhibits.

—www.bbc.co.uk

He gave up going to the park to practice. Now that the boys knew where he lived, they seemed to appear like shadows wherever he went.

Just bullies, he told himself. He knew enough like them at school, and he'd learned that the best way to deal with their sort was to pretend they were invisible. But it had taken the joy out of playing his guitar on the steps by the Sphinx, and he felt threatened by their presence in a way he didn't quite understand.

What did they want with him? Why, when they had money and things and the freedom to go where they pleased, did they care about a poor kid from Crystal Palace?

He'd never told them his name, but one day when he'd walked his mum to the pub for her shift and she'd given him an unexpectedly affectionate hug, he turned and found them watching from outside the shop next door.

"Your mum's a bit of a slag, eh, Andy," said Shaun, and Joe snickered. "You didn't tell us she worked in a shit hole of a bar."

Andy had had enough. He was on them in an instant, grabbing Shaun by the front of his T-shirt. "You just leave me the fuck alone. And you leave my mum the fuck alone."

"Oh, look, it can swear," mocked Joe, his voice high with excitement. "What are you going to do about it? Tell your mum? Fat lot she could do."

Andy had let go of Shaun's T-shirt when he turned to Joe, and the boys fell against each other, laughing.

"You—"

"Or you could hit us with your guitar," said Shaun. "Unless something happened to it."

"Ooh, wouldn't that be a shame." Joe giggled. "Bet you couldn't afford to buy a new one."

Andy was breathing so hard his vision blurred. "Don't you dare—"

Shaun leaned closer, leering, daring him. "Or maybe you could get your neighbor to protect you. She's totally hot."

"You bastards." Andy took an ineffectual swing at Shaun, who was inches taller and a stone heavier. "You leave her—"

The shop door opened and the Pakistani owner came out. "What's this going on in front of my shop? You trying to ruin my business, you little hoodlums?" He grabbed Shaun and Joe, who were closest, by their collars. "And you, Andy Monahan, you should be ashamed of yourself. Go on now, the lot of you, or I'll call the police." He let Joe and Shaun go with a shove and they stumbled away, then turned and gave Andy and the shop owner a two-fingered salute before running off.

Burning with shame, Andy said, "Mr. Patel, I didn't—"

"I know you didn't start it, Andy. But you should keep

away from those boys. They are bad news." Clucking in disap-
proval, he went back into his shop.

After that, Andy stopped playing his guitar on the front
steps of the flat, too. He played inside, or on the back steps
overlooking the barren garden when there was a patch of
shade. Most days, he still waited for Nadine, but found he
couldn't talk to her without watching the top of the street for
those now all-too-familiar silhouettes.

Awkwardness seemed to develop between them. Where
before they had talked so easily, now there were silences he
didn't know how to fill.

"Andy, are you all right?" Nadine asked one afternoon.
"I miss you playing. Although I hear you sometimes from my
kitchen, playing on your back steps."

He shrugged, knowing he couldn't tell her the real reason. "It's
hot. My hands sweat. It gets shady in the back in the afternoon."

"Oh, right." Nadine rubbed the finger on her left hand
where Andy thought she must have once worn a wedding ring,
something he'd noticed she did when she was thinking. Or un-
happy. He knew she didn't believe him.

"I could come out later," he said hurriedly. "When it starts
to get dark. I don't need much light to play." He'd never seen
the boys after sunset. Night was now the only time he felt safe.
"It's cooler then."

"That's a deal." She smiled and he felt he'd been given a
reprieve. "I'll make lemonade and sandwiches for later then,
shall I?"

The scent of the geraniums grew stronger at dusk. Nadine
had tended them until they'd begun to spill over the pots and
trail onto the steps. That night she wore a white dress, and in
the dimness the red blossoms looked like dark blood splashed
across her skirt.

She'd brought a candle as well as the promised lemonade and sandwiches, and after they'd eaten, Andy played in the flickering light.

He'd been working on a version of Dave Brubeck's "Take Five," but this was the first time he'd tried something so difficult in front of Nadine. After the first few bars he forgot his nervousness and lost himself in the notes.

When he'd finished he looked up and grinned. "It needs the rhythm part."

"How did you learn that?" Nadine sounded awed and Andy fingered the strings on the old Höfner, suddenly shy.

"Just listening. One of my dad's old records." He couldn't afford new CDs, although he occasionally picked things up at charity shops and jumble sales.

"Andy," Nadine said slowly, "you say 'just listening' as if anyone could do that. You know that's not the case, don't you?"

He shook his head. "I got some guitar books from the secondhand shop, so I know what the chords are called. But the songs in the books are stupid. It's more fun to listen to things I like and try to make what I play sound the same."

Nadine was silent for so long that he was afraid he'd sounded a complete tosser. "I watch music videos, too," he added, "so I can see how the real guys do it. But listening is better."

"Andy . . ." This time it was Nadine who gave a little shake of her head. She'd pulled her thick chestnut hair up to cool her neck in the heat, but a loose tendril swung with the movement. "You have a gift," she said, as serious as he'd ever heard her. "And there's no one to—" She stopped, and he somehow knew that she'd been about to tread on territory they both avoided—his mum.

Nadine noticed things—how could she not, living next door? She knew the hours his mum worked, knew Andy did the shopping and the cooking and made sure his mum got to and from work every day. And although he never said, he suspected she knew that there was never quite enough money to get through the week.

Often she'd just happen to have sandwiches or biscuits for him, or she'd say she'd made more than she could eat for dinner, no point just throwing it in the bin. And he knew she kept an eye on him when he was home alone at night, which he found weirdly comforting.

But once, when she'd hesitantly asked if it might help if she talked to his mum, he'd felt such panic that he'd shaken his head and bolted into the flat. It had been two days before he'd spoken to Nadine again, and she hadn't brought it up since.

He didn't want the two halves of his life to come together. His mother didn't approve of Nadine, although he wasn't quite sure why. And Nadine—he didn't want anyone, especially her, to know how bad things really were with his mum. It made him ashamed. And afraid.

Nadine stood, suddenly. "I'll be right back. Wait for me."

He sat obediently as the minutes ticked by, watching the last of the light fade over the distant city below, playing little bits of things he'd been learning, a Django Reinhardt song, the first few bars of Bert Jansch's "Angie." He'd begun to think he'd said something wrong and Nadine wasn't coming back when he heard the soft click of her door latch.

When he looked up, he saw that she was cradling a flat, rectangular guitar case against her chest.

Sitting down, she laid the case across her knees and stroked its surface with her fingertips. "You need a better guitar." Her voice was hoarse, as if she'd been crying, but her face was concealed in shadow. She slid her hands over to the three latches and flipped them up, but still didn't open the case. "This was my husband's," she said. "I haven't opened it since he—died. But it's doing no one any good sitting in my cupboard. I want you to have it."

"But—"

"He found it in a car-boot sale. He was so proud of it, though he only messed about with playing. He hadn't any real talent, but he recognized it when he saw it. I think he'd have wanted this"—she patted the case—"to go to someone who deserved it."

"But I—"

"Shhh." She pushed open the lid, lifted out the guitar, and handed it to him. "See? It suits you."

Andy could only stare at the thing he held in his hands. "It's—"

"A 1964 Stratocaster. Fiesta red. Marshall had it valued. Everything's original—headstock, body, the pickups. There's an amp, too. You can get it tomorrow."

Finally, he looked up at her, past feeling any shame for the tears in his eyes. "But I can't possibly—"

"Yes. You can. Just play, Andy." She touched one of the geranium blossoms. "No one has been kind to me except you. Think of it as red for red."

It was an ugly building, one of the postwar concrete blocks that had filled the bombed gaps in the East End. Two stories, with graffiti covering sections of the street-level wall, although on a closer look Kincaid realized that it was not ordinary tagging but quite well-executed street art.

He entered the double glass doors at the far end to find that appearances were once again deceiving. Caleb Hart's office had an expensively fitted-out reception area that sported an equally decorative receptionist. On the wall above her desk a stylized logo read HART PRODUCTIONS.

"Can I help you?" asked the receptionist, and her tone told him immediately that this was not a place where the uninvited walked in off the street.

"I'd like to speak to Mr. Hart." Before she could utter the refusal forming on her lips, he added, "My name's Duncan Kincaid. Tell him I'm a friend of Tam Moran's." He was glad he was no longer wearing a Scotland Yard suit—he doubted it would have cut any ice here.

"I'll just check," she said, with a minute degree of thaw, and left her desk to disappear into what Kincaid assumed was the inner sanctum, rewarding him with a view of very long legs in a very short skirt.

A moment later she reappeared. "Caleb says he'll see you."

It was hardly gracious, but Kincaid considered himself lucky to have got past the guard dog.

"Thanks." He gave her his best smile, although he suspected it was wasted.

The man who came out of the inner office to greet him was tall and slender, with a neatly trimmed brown beard and glasses. Kincaid thought he looked more like a teacher than a record producer, although unlike Tam, his clothing was trendy and obviously expensive. Black shirt, black silk jacket, designer jeans, high-topped boots. Kincaid felt shabby and altogether too GAP by comparison.

"Roxy says you're a friend of Tam's," said Caleb Hart, shaking his hand. "You've just missed him by an hour."

"Actually, I've just had lunch with him. That's why I'm here." Kincaid glanced round as Hart offered him a chair, not in front of his desk, but in a very retro-contemporary conversation grouping on the other side of the room. Gold CDs and posters of bands—some of whom Kincaid recognized—were mounted on the walls and shelves, but like Hart's clothing, the display was tastefully done.

Wondering if he had taken Tam's excitement seriously enough, Kincaid's interest rose a notch. "Tam asked me if I'd have a word with you," he continued. "He told me about the video with Andy Monahan and your singer."

188 ~ DEBORAH CROMBIE

"Her name is Poppy. Poppy Jones," said Hart, looking puzzled and a little impatient. "But I'm not sure how I can—"

"Mr. Hart, just so there's no misunderstanding. I'm Tam's friend, and I know Andy. But I'm also a police officer. I wanted to make it clear, however, that I'm here in an entirely unofficial capacity."

Blanching, Hart said, "If Monahan is in some sort of trouble and Tam hasn't told me—"

Kincaid held up his hands. "No, it's not that. As far as I'm aware, Andy Monahan hasn't done anything wrong. But Tam said the police questioned Andy about a man who was verbally abusive to him in the pub on Friday night."

"The man who was murdered? Or at least I'm assuming he was murdered—the detective who came to the studio was a bit cagey."

"Exactly. His name was Vincent Arnott. Tam took Andy back to London immediately after the band finished their second set that night, so Andy can't have been involved in Arnott's death. But as Andy was the last person known to have spoken to the victim that night, Tam's anxious to clear up anything that might potentially cause him adverse publicity."

"As am I," Hart said fervently. "But I still don't see how I can help you."

"When Tam was telling me what happened, he said that the pub in Crystal Palace—the White Stag, I think?—was your regular. So I thought perhaps you'd seen Arnott before. If he'd behaved that way on previous occasions, it would make his encounter with Andy Monahan less . . . notable."

"Ah." Hart looked thoughtful. "I didn't recognize the name, and the detective didn't show me the photo. Tam didn't describe him to me."

Kincaid couldn't very well pull up the photo Gemma had sent him on his phone, so he said, "According to Tam, sixtyish, handsome, very striking silver hair."

"Tam would notice that he was good looking," Hart said with a grin. "But the description doesn't ring a bell. I haven't been to the Stag in a while, but the manager will let me book bands in on short notice, and I wanted a look at the guitarist before I put him in the studio."

"Is that what you usually do?" Kincaid asked.

"No, although generally I do like to hear session musicians before I use them. But this all came together in a bit of a last-minute rush. I'd booked the studio for Poppy, but she'd had an open-mic gig at the Troubadour the week before. Tam was there and he told me he had a guitarist that he thought would suit her perfectly."

"But you didn't trust Tam's judgment? He said you'd been friends for a long time."

Hart looked uncomfortable. "It's not that I didn't trust his judgment. But Poppy is . . . special. She's also young, and I feel a bit in loco parentis. Poppy's father is an old friend—and a vicar. I know I can't shield her from everything, but I'd like to keep her out of the drugs and alcohol scene as much as possible. Not that I actually think Poppy needs much shielding," he added a little ruefully. "She's a strong-minded girl and as dedicated a musician as any I've ever worked with. Still, I never expected what happened in the studio last Saturday."

Kincaid waited, knowing that silence was often more encouraging than a question, and after a moment, Hart went on. "In this business, you come across something like this once or twice in a lifetime, if you're very lucky. They are both exceptionally good musicians. But together, they become something more. Bigger than the parts. Unique."

"You mean like Lennon and McCartney?"

"Oh, God." Hart laughed. "No one dares make those sort of comparisons. But there is a . . . chemistry."

"Did you intend to film them?" Kincaid asked. He was genuinely curious now.

"No. Not until halfway through the first improvised jam. And then I knew I'd better capture it while I could. They will get more polished, but there will never be the same raw joy of discovery as there was that day."

"Is Tam right?" Kincaid felt a frisson of excitement. Perhaps he should have taken Tam's enthusiasm more seriously. "Could this be something really big?"

"It's a fickle business," Hart said, drumming his fingers on his knee. His thumb and forefinger bore nicotine stains, Kincaid saw, but he had not noticed the smell of cigarettes. "All you can do is trust your instincts and jump on your opportunities," Hart went on. His phone dinged, signaling a text, and he pulled it from his jacket pocket. "And I'd better be doing just th—"

Kincaid stood, shaking Hart's hand as he rose. "I've taken enough of your time. Best of luck, for all of you."

"Oh, Mr. Hart." Kincaid turned back as he reached the door. Hart was already replying to the text. "Tam said you left before the end of the first set. Why the rush, when you'd booked the band in specifically?"

"I had a meeting," Hart answered easily. "I don't miss them for anything, even work. I'm an alcoholic, Mr. Kincaid."

When Melody came out of the pub and started back across Cleaver Square, the mortuary van was driving away and Rashid's car was gone. Gemma was standing at the curb in front of the flat, conferring with Maura Bell. While Melody had been inside, the sky had gone steely gray again, and Bell had turned her trench coat collar up against the damp chill of the wind. It made her look like a Cold War spy, which, thought Melody, quite suited her.

Melody had had the barman pack up sandwiches for her and Gemma, figuring they could eat them on the fly, but she hadn't thought of Maura. Hastily, she stopped and tucked the package in her car.

When she reached them, Gemma said, "I've sent Amanda Francis home in one of the panda cars. She says Vincent Arnott didn't work in the same chambers as her brother, and as far as she knows, her brother wasn't acquainted with him."

"Dead end there, then?"

"No obvious lead, at any rate."

Melody glanced at her watch. "We were supposed to be meeting Mrs. Arnott's sister at the morgue for the formal identification."

"So much for best-laid plans."

"Aye. I was going to have my toenails done." Maura Bell's delivery was so deadpan that Melody wasn't sure she was joking until she saw Gemma smile.

The two senior officers seemed to have established a rapport, and Melody felt a twinge of jealousy that surprised her.

"I've sent Shara," Gemma told Melody. "From there she can go on to Arnott's chambers. We'll see if anyone there knew Shaun Francis. Any luck at the pub?" she asked.

"Francis was a regular, and apparently considerably more of one than Vincent Arnott was at the White Stag. According to the barman, he came in almost every night and took most of his meals there, but he didn't seem to have any particular friends."

"That seems to have been true of Arnott as well—the friend bit," Gemma said thoughtfully. "I wonder if that made them potential targets?"

"What about last night?" asked Maura.

"Francis was there. Arrived about half-past seven, had a salad and a G and T, but the barman says the place was packed and he didn't see him after that."

Gemma turned to Maura. "Any CCTV coverage?"

"Not on the square itself, no. Not exactly your usual high-crime area. I'll pull up whatever footage I can find leading in and out of the square, though."

Gazing across at the pub and its now-deserted forecourt, Gemma said, "A salad and a gin and tonic. Sounds a bit girly, doesn't it? But his sister said he was trying to lose weight, and that he'd hurt his back playing squash. That might explain the Valium."

"And if he was only eating a salad, the gin and the drug might have hit him harder than he expected." Maura shrugged. "But hard enough to let someone strip him, tie him up, and strangle him? Did you ask the sister if he had a taste for kinky sex?"

"No. She was still very shocked. And there was something . . . not quite right there. Between them, I mean. She seemed bitterly jealous of him, but at the same time, weirdly emotionally dependent."

"One for Hazel," murmured Melody. When Maura gave a questioning look, she added, "A therapist friend."

"Bitter and jealous enough to kill him?" asked Maura. "If he was really feeling ill, he might have trusted his sister to undress him and put him to bed. Or even tie him up, for all we know. And then what would be easier than to sound the alarm this morning and have an excuse to find the body?"

"Maybe." Melody was unconvinced. "But unless she has some connection with Vincent Arnott, we have two unrelated murders in forty-eight hours, committed using the same method." Doug, she thought, would be quoting handy probability statistics. "Unless she picked up Arnott at the pub in Crystal Palace," she added as it occurred to her.

Melody had said it dismissively, but Gemma was staring at her, frowning. "She doesn't seem Arnott's type, from what we've heard about him, but—"

"No need to dance around it," said Maura. "The woman's plain as a pikestaff, and I cannae see her acting the come-hither in a bar."

"No, but the thing is, I've just sent her home to Dulwich, where she lives with her mum."

"Dulwich?" said Maura, looking at them both as if they were crackers.

"A hop and a skip," supplied Melody. "More or less. A couple of stops on the train or the number three bus to Crystal Palace, or hardly any time at all if you have a car. Worth seeing if she has an alibi for Friday night, and showing a photo round the White Stag."

"I think another talk with Amanda Francis just moved up on our action list," said Gemma. "But there's something else . . . Melody, who else have we run across who lives in Dulwich?"

It took Melody a moment to bring it back, and then she had to drag the words out. "Caleb Hart. The record producer who booked An—the band—into the pub on Friday night. Reg at the Stag said he lived in Dulwich."

CHAPTER FOURTEEN

In 1911 the building was used for marking the coronation of George V and Queen Mary but after this it fell into disrepair. Two years later the Earl of Plymouth purchased the Crystal Palace, to save it from future developers, but a public subscription re-purchased it for the nation.

—Betty Carew, www.helium.com

"God, I'm starving," said Gemma as she buckled herself into Melody's passenger seat. They'd decided to leave Gemma's car at the square, as she would need to return. "But this has turned into the day from hell and I don't think lunch is an option. I want to talk to Shaun Francis's mother before the daughter's had too much time with her."

Melody started the car, then reached into the back and held up a paper bag. "Ta da. From the pub. I got us both prawn and rocket. Seemed the safest—or at least the least messy—choice."

Taking the bag, Gemma reached in and pulled out packets of crisps and two wrapped sandwiches. "Bless you. The barman must have fancied you to do them up like this. You'd better watch yourself, influencing the witnesses like that."

Melody made a strangled sound, but when Gemma looked at her she was concentrating on reversing into the road.

"Want me to feed you bits?" Gemma continued as she opened her sandwich. "Looks delicious, but it is a bit splodgy."

"I'll nibble at the traffic lights. And really, I'm not all that hungry."

Gemma gave her a concerned glance. "Are you feeling okay? Post–crime scene queasies?"

"No, I'm fine. And that wasn't half as bad as the Belvedere in Crystal Palace. Thank God Shaun Francis kept his central heating turned down."

Biting into her prawn and rocket sandwich, Gemma nodded agreement. She chewed for a moment, then said, "I can see why he ate his meals at the pub. Although maybe it wasn't the best plan for dieting." Brushing a crumb from her lip, she added, "Maura Bell wasn't nearly as hard to deal with as I expected. Duncan worked with her on that arson case in Southwark, you remember? Made her sound a bit of a dragon."

"Maybe she gets on better with women," Melody suggested.

"Could be." Gemma had left Bell in charge of the Cleaver Square scene, and felt confident in doing so. "Didn't Doug go out with her for a while?"

"Doug?" Melody shot her a shocked glance, then looked back at the road, both hands gripping the wheel. "Are you sure? He never said anything to me."

"According to Duncan. It didn't work out. Doug never told him why."

"But—" Melody shook her head. "I can't believe it. They're chalk and cheese. I mean, Doug's brilliant, and if you give him a problem to solve he's like a terrier with it. But this is the bloke who spent months trying to decide between two shades of cream for his sitting room ceiling. The bloke who actually went to the Doctor Who exhibition at Olympia and took photos of the TARDIS. He's a supergeek. And she's—I don't know. Sort of scarily efficient. And a bit snarky."

"Melody." Gemma rewrapped the second half of her sandwich. "Are you a little bit . . . peeved?"

"No. No, it's just . . . weird. And we're mates. I don't know why he didn't tell me."

"Do you tell him about your dates?"

"I don't have dates," said Melody, with unexpected emphasis, then changed the subject. "Boss, do you want to stop at the station?"

They were coming into Brixton. Gemma considered. "No. We'll get tied up." Realizing what she'd said, she added, "No pun intended. But I checked in with Shara while you were in the pub. Mrs. Arnott's sister identified the body. She didn't have anything helpful to add about her brother-in-law. According to Shara, she's more concerned about how she's going to care for her sister. Can't say I blame her. She said she didn't realize just how ill Mrs. Arnott was."

"He must have done a good job covering up for her."

"Maybe. But I think sometimes dementia sufferers can put up a pretty good front for a short time. Enough to fool someone who didn't deal with them on a daily basis. Sad."

"And Arnott's chambers?" asked Melody.

"So far, Shara had only managed to catch two out of the eighteen barristers. They expressed shock and dismay, but couldn't imagine *how something like that could have happened to their esteemed colleague, et cetera, et cetera.* I'm quoting. Shara was not a happy bunny."

"No, I imagine not. Patience is not one of her virtues. Nor is she fond of lawyers."

"I've told her to stay until everyone has come in from court, and to follow them to their local wine bar if necessary. And to find out if any of them knew Shaun Francis."

"There has got to be a connection," Melody muttered. "Two lawyers—not just lawyers, barristers—who go to pubs on a regular basis on their own, aren't particularly liked, and chat up people they don't know."

"Shaun Francis was thirty years younger," said Gemma.

"Did the barman at the Prince of Wales say anything about him picking up women?"

"No. Just that he knew some of the other lawyers who came in regularly, and that the bar staff avoided getting stuck with him because he was a bore and—although he put it more politely—a bit of a tosser."

"His neighbor and even his sister seemed to have agreed on that part." Gemma pushed a stray strand of hair from her cheek. "But I'm still not looking forward to talking to his mum."

The address Amanda Francis had given Gemma was in Desenfans Road, just outside the center of Dulwich Village. It was redbrick, semidetached, in a quiet street, the sort of comfortable suburban house that always costs much more than one thought it should. The garden on the left-hand side looked neglected, even by winter standards, and Gemma surmised that neither Amanda nor her mother were green-fingered types.

"Once more unto the breach," murmured Melody as they got out and walked to the door.

"You're liking old Will today."

"*Henry the Fifth*, this time. I had a huge crush on Kenneth Branagh," admitted Melody. "Don't ask how many times I've seen the film."

"And you were accusing Doug of geekiness."

Thus armored, they rang the bell.

Amanda Francis answered immediately. It was obvious she'd been crying again. Her face was more swollen, and she held a sodden tissue to her nose. "No one told me how I should tell her," she said. "I remembered when the police came after my father was killed. They just said it, as if there was no point dragging it out, so that's what I did. But now I don't know what to do."

"Can we see your mother?" Gemma asked.

"She's in the conservatory." Amanda led them through a dark and cluttered hall into an even darker and more cluttered sitting room. The room felt stuffed, as if it might split at the seams, and Gemma and Melody had to thread a path through the center. "Sorry," said Amanda, as if expecting their reaction. "When we had to move here, Mum couldn't bear to let go of any of the furniture from the big house. The conservatory's the only room that's bearable."

It was just that, bearable, thought Gemma as they entered the glassed-in room at the back of the house. Some very nineties-style rattan floral-cushioned furniture, a carpet, a television, and a view of a back garden as neglected as the front. At least Kathy Arnott would, for a while, have the solace of her garden. There was none here.

Weak sun broke through the clouds, illuminating the dust in the room and the woman sitting in one of the rattan chairs. Shaun Francis's mother was stockily built and dark haired, like her children. Gemma thought she might once have been pretty. She wore now the utterly blank face of grief.

Amanda knelt beside her chair. "Mummy, these are police officers. They've come to talk to you about Shaun."

Mrs. Francis looked up at them, dark empty eyes flaring with sudden hope. "There's been a mistake. You've come to tell me there was a mistake."

"No, Mrs. Francis, I'm afraid not." Gemma sat on the edge of the floral sofa. "We're very sorry for your loss. But we need to ask you some questions about Shaun. Amanda identified the—him."

"You can't believe anything the girl says." The look the woman cast at her daughter was venomous.

"Mummy, please." Amanda flushed, turning the blotches on her face a brighter red. "Don't say things like that."

"I can't be doing without my Shaun," her mother said, immutable.

"Mummy, Shaun came for Sunday lunch once a month. I do everything for you."

"He was making something of himself," said Mrs. Francis. "He had things to do. Important things."

"He didn't come to lunch yesterday because he was playing squash. How important was that?"

Gemma cast a glance at Melody, who had perched on the sofa beside her. Amanda Francis sounded close to a meltdown, and she doubted a full-blown family feud would allow them to get anything sensible out of the mother. "Amanda," she said, "maybe you could make your mother a cup of tea."

"She wouldn't drink it," Amanda answered, sulky as a child.

"Us, then. We'd love some, wouldn't we, Sergeant?" Having seen the state of the house, Gemma wasn't sure she would drink it, either, but she wanted Amanda out of the way.

"Okay." Amanda gave a reluctant nod and left the room.

Without her daughter to combat, Mrs. Francis seemed to deflate. Her eyes brimmed and a few black tears streaked down her face. Why, wondered Gemma, had she put on mascara if she spent the day alone in the room with the telly?

"What am I going to do?" wailed Mrs. Francis, her words eerily echoing her daughter's.

"Mrs. Francis, did your son know a man named Vincent Arnott? A barrister?"

"Shaun's friends were in the City. He wouldn't want to bring them here."

"Vincent Arnott was in his early sixties, Mrs. Francis. Perhaps you or your late husband might have known him."

She shook her head. "Richard's friends weren't barristers. He was an investor. Shaun was going to get it all back. He promised me."

"Get what back, Mrs. Francis?"

"I'm sorry, but there's no milk." Amanda Francis stood in the doorway. "Inspector, could we go for a walk?"

. . .

As Gemma left the sitting room, she'd whispered to Melody, "Will you get an FLO organized?"

"Right-o. But I wouldn't want to be in their shoes," Melody had murmured back.

"You'll have to forgive my mother," Amanda Francis said as she walked quickly round the corner and into Court Lane, the street that led towards the center of Dulwich Village.

"This must be very hard for her," Gemma said now, attempting diplomacy, once she'd taken a grateful breath of cold, fresh air.

"Mummy's a bit too fond of the sherry under the best of . . . circumstances." Amanda choked back a sob on the last word. "I suppose you could call this the worst of circumstances."

"What did your mother mean when she said your brother was going to 'get it all back'?" asked Gemma.

"I'll show you." Amanda's pace was fast, and Gemma realized her heaviness disguised the fact that she was strong and quite fit. "She said my dad was an investor. Makes you think stocks and bonds and something quite sensible doesn't it?" She forged ahead, the scorn in her voice coming back to Gemma on the wind. "But it wasn't like that. My father was always on to the next good thing. He played the dot-com bubble in the mid-nineties. Made millions."

They'd reached the village and Amanda slowed, allowing Gemma to catch up with her. The little row of shops and cafés was all tasteful charm—all things that might be considered necessities by those with surplus income. The signposts at the intersections were wooden, continuing the deceit of a country village set down smack in the middle of suburbia.

Gemma followed, curious, as they left the village center behind and began to see houses again. But these were grand, detached homes, many half hidden behind high evergreen hedges—most had lush winter-green lawns.

Amanda stopped in front of a particularly impressive specimen of gleaming white stucco with dark shingles on its many
gables. "This is where we grew up," said Amanda. "Until the
bubble burst. Fortunately, Father had a life insurance policy
that kept us from being destitute, although Mother has never
for one moment accepted living in what she refers to as 'reduced circumstances.'"

"What happened to your father?" asked Gemma.

"He drove his car into a bridge abutment. There were indi-
cations that he tried to brake at the last minute, so the insurance company eventually paid out. It was assumed he'd fallen
asleep at the wheel."

"You don't think so?"

"There's no way to know, is there?" Amanda shrugged, as
if it didn't matter. "There was enough money from the insurance and the sale of the house to pay his creditors and Shaun's
school fees, and to keep Mummy in what most people would
consider reasonable comfort."

"Did Shaun really promise he'd get it all back for her?"

"No. That's just one of her fantasies. Shaun spent every
penny he earned—and more—on his flat and his clothes and
his . . . amusements."

"Amusements?"

"Oh, eating every meal out. Good wines. Membership in
the best squash and racquetball club in the City. Everything
always had to be the best for Shaun."

"Amanda . . ." Gemma paused. There was no easy way to
ask the question. "Amanda, do you know if your brother was
involved in any . . . unusual . . . sexual activities?"

"You mean like—what I saw?" Amanda turned away from
the house and started slowly back towards the village center,
her shoulders hunched. "Not that I know of. But why would
he have told me? I know he went out with women, but I don't
think he liked them much. Who can blame him, with Mummy

as an example? But if he was into . . . kinky stuff . . . I'd think it would have been Shaun doing the tying up. And hitting."

"Did he ever hit you?"

"Once or twice. When we were kids."

"Amanda." Gemma stopped in front of the children's boutique, gazing absently at a flowered corduroy dress in the window that was just Charlotte's size. Then she turned to the woman beside her. "I have to ask. Where were you last night?"

"Home. With Mummy."

"And Friday night?"

Amanda seemed puzzled, but answered readily enough. "Home. Where else would I be?"

Gemma looked at Amanda Francis, with her blotched, unmadeup face, her unstyled hair, the clothes that seemed deliberately unflattering, and wondered why she felt the need for such protection. "Amanda, you have a good job. Why do you stay with your mother?"

"What else would I do?"

Melody had endured her half hour with Mrs. Francis by sending texts requesting a family liaison officer and by having a discreet look around the room. Mrs. Francis had drawn into herself, not answering Melody's attempts at conversation or questions. Melody hoped the FLO was male—she suspected that Mrs. Francis was a woman whose universe revolved around men.

On a side table, she'd found some dusty golfing trophies—presumably the late Mr. Francis's—and some photos. The newer ones showed Shaun in cap and gown, Shaun clowning for the camera in his barrister's wig, Shaun in a group that looked as if it might have been taken at his chambers Christmas party.

There were none of Amanda, but there was an older family

grouping, obviously taken when the brother and sister were teenagers and their father was still alive. Amanda had braces on her teeth and looked desperately eager to please. Shaun glared belligerently into the camera, and Melody wondered what sort of bribe it had taken to get him to the photographer's studio.

By the time Gemma returned with Amanda and they took their leave, Melody felt she'd been released from prison. Gemma had stressed to Amanda that she should not give details of Shaun's murder to her mother or to anyone else. The FLO would be able to buffer them from reporters when the press did turn up.

"I didn't dare snoop much," she told Gemma once they were in the car. "Not that I thought Mrs. F would notice, but I wasn't sure when you'd be back. Surely Amanda Francis has made some sort of . . . habitat . . . for herself in that place."

Gemma related her conversation with Amanda, then added, "I wonder if he abused his sister."

"That might make sense of some of the nasty undercurrents."

"And give her a whopping motive."

"Would Mummy give her an alibi?" asked Melody doubtfully.

"If Mrs. Francis sits in front of the telly and drinks sherry all evening, Amanda may come and go without her noticing. But that doesn't solve the problem of Vincent Arnott. And if Rashid is right about the scarf, it's not just method—there's actual physical evidence linking the two murders."

By the time they arrived back in Cleaver Square, the crime scene van was gone and the early winter dusk was falling.

"I'm going to check with Maura before I head back to Brixton," said Gemma as she unfastened her seat belt.

"I'll be right behind—" Melody stopped as her phone dinged a text. She checked it, expecting a reply to her request for an FLO for the Francises, but it read: CAN YOU COME BY FLAT? SOMETHING REALLY COOL TO SHOW YOU. A x.

Her heart thumped. So he wanted to see her again. She didn't know if she was pleased or terrified.

To Gemma she said, "I—I've something I want to check out. Won't be long. I'll see you at the station."

Gemma gave her a curious look, but nodded and said, "See you in a bit, then," as she shut the door and waved her off.

What excuse she could invent, Melody didn't know, any more than she could pretend that Oxford Street was conveniently on her way between Kennington and Brixton. But she would think of something.

The closer she got to Hanway Place, the stupider Melody felt. She should have answered the text, not just driven straight there like a lemming going over a cliff. Would he think she had nothing better to do than to show up on his doorstep practically the minute he beckoned?

Which was, of course, exactly what she was doing, but having committed herself, she wasn't going to back out.

It was dark by the time she found a place to park her car in the narrow street. She hesitated, then got out and rang Andy's bell. As she stood in the shadowy doorway, the memories from last night came flooding back. When the door latch clicked open, her knees felt so weak she wasn't quite sure she could climb the stairs.

He was waiting for her at the open door of his flat, as he had been before, but this time he was grinning with unabashed pleasure. "I'm so glad you came," he said, kissing her on the cheek and helping her out of her coat.

"It was on my way." Melody shook her head, then said, "No, it wasn't. I wanted to come." She could still feel the imprint of his lips against her cheek and was finding it hard to breathe. "But I wanted to tell you— Look, Andy, about last night, I didn't want you to think that I usually—on a first date—" She was still standing awkwardly in the middle of the room, wishing she could shrink, like Alice.

"Oh, was that a date?" He raised an eyebrow and she felt a complete idiot. Then he touched her cheek. "I don't, either, you know," he said softly, meeting her eyes. "You thought I invited every girl I took to the Twelve Bar back to bed?"

"Well, you know, big rock star and all," she teased him back, not about to admit that she had in fact thought that.

"I may have to change my strategy, though." He grabbed her hand and led her to the futon, now folded back into its sofa configuration, the rumpled sheets neatly folded. Seeming oblivious to her discomfort, Andy pulled her down beside him. "Look at this." His laptop sat open on the coffee table. He moused over the Play arrow on the video open on the screen and clicked it.

Melody watched, mesmerized. It was Andy and Poppy in the studio rehearsal space on Saturday, doing "Diamonds on the Soles of Her Shoes." The video segued to them in the recording studio, wearing headphones, singing close into studio mics, then to Andy playing a shiver-inducing riff on the melody line. The camera work and editing were smooth, but captured all the raw joy and charm that Melody had seen. The video shifted again, back to the rehearsal space, but the light had altered and Andy and Poppy were wearing different clothes. This, she thought, must have been yesterday, and you could see that even in a day, their styles had melded into something even more unique and infectious. Poppy put a thumping bass under her soaring lead vocal while Andy sang harmony. They ended perfectly on the beat, burst into laughter, and the screen went dark.

"Oh," Melody breathed. "That was brilliant. Just brilliant. How—"

"It was Caleb. He put it up last night, just wanting to see what sort of response it got. It's gone bonkers."

Melody looked back at the screen. "That many LIKEs? In a day? Bloody hell. That's not just bonkers. That's . . . that's . . . *viral.*"

"It was just a job," he said, sounding baffled. "I never expected . . . Tam and Caleb have been working on contracts and agreements all day. And Poppy seems to be taking it all in stride."

"And you?"

He took her hand and rubbed his thumb across her knuckles. It was his left hand, the unbruised one, but she noticed a healing cut across the ball of his thumb. "I feel like I've been picked up by a tidal wave and I don't know where it's going to set me down," he said slowly. "It was always the dream, you know, but I think I'd given up on it a long time ago. I've been playing professionally for more than ten years, waiting for the big rock star break. I think I'd resigned myself to a lifetime of bad bands and session work. At least the sessions marginally paid the bills and I didn't have to go to work in a bloody dry cleaners. But this—now—I don't know if I'm prepared for this."

"Andy—"

He gave her hand a squeeze. "And I'm an ass, doing the whole confessional thing, but I couldn't tell Nick or George, and I thought you'd understand. I haven't even asked you how your day went, or if I interrupted you in the middle of anything terribly important."

"We had another murder. Like the one in Crystal Palace, but this time in Kennington. A barrister found in his flat."

"You mean with all the weird shit? The tying up and stuff?"

She'd told him last night how Vincent Arnott had been found.

"Yes. I keep thinking that while we were at the club, or . . .

here . . . somebody was doing that to him. And he was young, our age, which shouldn't make it seem worse but somehow it does. If Arnott invited some woman to that seedy hotel, well, it doesn't exactly make him culpable—"

"But he exposed himself to it by his behavior?"

Melody nodded. It was odd, talking like this. Of course she discussed cases with Gemma and with Doug, but she never talked about how she *felt* about them. "He was killed in his flat. He doesn't seem to have been picking up women. According to his mother and his sister, he didn't even like them very much. All Shaun Francis did was go to the pub."

Andy's hand on hers went still. "Shaun Francis?"

"Yeah. He—"

They'd been sitting right against each other on the futon, arms and thighs touching. Now Andy let her hand go and pulled away from her as if he'd been burned. "Is this some kind of a sick joke?" His voice was shaking.

"Andy—"

"Tell me you're having me on."

"Why would I do that?" His reaction frightened her. "Andy, what is it? Don't tell me you knew Shaun Francis?"

His laugh was harsh, humorless. "Unless there's more than one. He was the biggest bastard I ever met. And I haven't seen him since I was thirteen years old."

CHAPTER FIFTEEN

A board of trustees were set up and the leader was Sir Henry Buckland. He was said to have a great love for the Crystal Palace. Buckland and his staff were soon busy in the restoration of the building. This brought visitors back and the palace was beginning to show a small profit. Buckland not only restored the building, but also the grounds surrounding it, including its fountains and gardens.

—Betty Carew, www.helium.com

"Did you go to school with him?" asked Melody.

Andy shook his head. "Fat chance, that. I was a charity pupil at a Catholic school. He went to some poncey public school."

"Then how—"

"That summer, I was just learning to play the guitar, and I used to practice in the park. He—Shaun and his . . . mate—started hanging around."

"Crystal Palace Park?"

"Yeah, but they didn't live in Crystal Palace. I never understood why they started coming there. Or why Shaun chose me as a target for his bullying. Now, I suppose it must have been the guitar." Andy flexed his hands, as if they felt empty. "Shaun couldn't stand that I could do something he couldn't, and that it was something he couldn't buy." He looked up at her, his dark blue eyes shadowed. "But I can't believe he's dead. You're sure?"

"We've just come from seeing his mum in Dulwich. And it was his sister who found him."

"His sister? I didn't know he had a sister." Andy must have interpreted Melody's expression as doubt, because he added, "We weren't *friends*. I never really knew anything about him except that he seemed to have an unlimited supply of cash and could come and go as he pleased."

"I'd say he was a mummy's boy of the worst sort. No limits." Andy nodded. "That would make sense."

"And his sister—they seemed to have had a very . . . intense . . . relationship."

"Intense?"

"The family dynamic seems to have been more than a little dysfunctional. Do you think it's possible that he abused her?"

"You don't think this sister had something to do with his death?" Andy asked, looking shocked. "You said he was tied and strangled. You can't think it was a woman that did that."

"It's possible," said Melody. "And we think Vincent Arnott left the White Stag with a woman."

"But— You said Shaun was found in his flat, not in some rubbish hotel like the Belvedere."

"He was at the pub last night—like Arnott, it was his local— across the square from his flat. The Prince of Wales in Cleaver Square. So far we don't know if anyone saw him leave."

"Cleaver Square. He did well for himself." There was a note of bitterness in Andy's voice that Melody hadn't heard before. He stood and went to one of the guitars on its stand, the one with the hummingbird on it that he had played for her only last night, and ran his fingers over the top of the headstock. She felt the physical distance he'd put between them like a rift. "And a barrister, to boot," he added, not looking at her. "Did they know each other, Shaun and the other bloke?"

"Arnott? We don't know yet." Melody rubbed her suddenly cold hands together. "Andy, I'll have to tell my guv'nor that you knew Shaun."

"Why?" He turned back to her, his expression hostile. "I told you I hadn't seen him in years. And I thought it was between us."

Melody took a breath. She had no choice. She could not withhold information that might be pertinent to the investigation. "Because I'm a cop, Andy," she said, "and it's my job. And because, other than the fact that they were both barristers and drank in pubs, you are the only connection we have between them."

Gemma was just walking into the CID room at the station in Brixton when Kincaid rang.

"Just checking in," he said. "I'm home, and the kids have had their tea. I'll put together something for us when you get here."

"You may starve to death by then. I may, too," she added, remembering she'd left the second half of her prawn and rocket sandwich in Melody's car.

"Any developments?" Kincaid asked.

Stepping back into the corridor, she told him about their visit to Dulwich.

"You think the sister might have something to do with it?" he said when she'd finished. In the background, she could hear the kids and the telly, and then the dogs barking and a slam she recognized as the garden door. She was suddenly tired and very much wanted to be home.

"If it was just her brother, maybe, but I can't make any

sense of Arnott. Although she wasn't happy about it, I got her to give me a recent photo before I left so that we could show it round both pubs. Did you speak to Caleb Hart?"

"I did." Kincaid was obviously pleased with himself. "A very smooth operator. Butter wouldn't melt in his mouth."

"What about his movements on Friday night?"

"He says he left the White Stag after the band's first set because he had an AA meeting. And he says he didn't know Arnott and didn't ever remember seeing him in the pub."

Gemma considered this. "It's a small place, the White Stag. If they both went often enough to be on familiar terms with the manager, I'm not sure I buy that. I think we'll have to have an official chat with Mr. Hart and get the details of his AA meeting."

"I didn't mention that I was acquainted with the lead investigator." There was a hint of laughter in Kincaid's voice, and she heard the clink of crystal and guessed he was pouring a glass of wine.

"I should bloody well hope not. Miss you," she added. Glancing into the CID room, she saw that Superintendent Krueger's glassed-in office at the far end was dark, although Shara MacNicols was hunched over one of the computer workstations. "The super's gone, so maybe I won't be too long. I want to see what's come in this afternoon, check in with Maura, and Melody, wherever she's got to."

"Oh, so you're on first-name terms now with DI Bell. I told Doug you were working with her and he went silent as the proverbial tomb."

"Maura asked about him, by the way. And she's been perfectly fine to work with."

"Curiouser and curiouser."

"Did Charlotte do all right with Doug while you went to see Caleb Hart?"

"They bonded over pastries at the Patisserie Valerie in

Spitalfield's Market. She's been a bit cross after all the sugar and excitement, but I'll see if she can stay up until you get home."

"Thanks, love. I'll ring you when I'm on my way."

"How did things go in lawyer land?" Gemma asked Shara as she entered the CID room.

Shara rolled her eyes, then stretched, popping the kinks out of her fingers. "I'm putting the interviews in the case file, but it's basically bollocks. Pompous twits, the lot of them." As a detective constable, Shara had some experience testifying in court, and Gemma knew it had not made her fond of lawyers. "Although the clerk, Mr. Kershaw, seems a decent bloke," Shara added. "But the senior partner, who knew Arnott best, was on holiday—who goes on holiday in bloody January, I ask you?"

"Those that can afford to get out of miserable London," Gemma answered with a smile. "Anything useful from the others?"

Shara gave her best imitation of an Eton drawl. "They were shocked, I say, shocked at the news of poor Vincent's death, and would not entertain the idea that their esteemed partner had been involved in any impropriety."

"Bugger all, then."

"Pretty much. Except that they expressed concern that the police had released any information about the case to the press. And of course they want to be informed of any developments."

"Top of my list," said Gemma, grinning.

"Yeah, well, I told them so. Very diplomatically. You'd have been proud of me." Shara turned back to the computer. "On the bright side, I've just had an e-mail from Mike. The techs found a few of the same maroon and blue fibers in the Kennington flat that were in the room at the Belvedere."

Gemma pulled out the nearest chair and sat down. "So we

have definite physical evidence that the crimes are connected. I'm not sure that's the bright side."

"You expected it," said Shara.

"Yeah, well, I wouldn't have minded being wrong on this one. Does the super know?"

"The e-mail came in right before she went home. She said you should ring her."

Gemma was not looking forward to that. "And the scarf used on Shaun Francis? Anything on that?"

"Forensics say it's a match with the fibers Rashid found in Arnott's neck. They're trying to trace the scarf."

Looking windblown and a little pale, Melody had come in on the end of Shara's sentence. "What about the scarf?" she asked as she slid out of her coat.

"I thought you'd got lost," said Gemma.

"Traffic," Melody answered. It occurred to Gemma that Melody had used the same excuse for being late that morning— and that it was very unlike her to be late for anything.

Gemma explained about the fiber matches, then turned back to Shara. "Any print matches? Or DNA from that blood spot at the Belvedere?"

"Not yet. Rashid's got the postmortem scheduled for to-morrow afternoon, and he's hoping for the preliminary tox results by then."

"So we have what looks like the same perpetrator," Gemma said slowly, "and still the only link between the victims seems to be that they were both barristers and that they were last seen in their local pubs."

"That's not all." Melody's voice was flat. She sat, hugging her arms across her chest. "I interviewed Andy Monahan, the guitarist Arnott shouted at on Friday night at the White Stag. He knew Shaun Francis, from when he was growing up in Crystal Palace. But he hadn't seen him since they were kids."

Gemma stared at her. "And you found this out when?"

"Just now. I stopped to talk to him on my way back from Kennington."

"On the way back?" Gemma shook her head, frowning. "Melody, there's something I'm not seeing here. You're telling me that Monahan had a row with Arnott on Friday night, and he just happens to have known Shaun Francis?" She wasn't liking this at all. "That puts him square in the frame."

"It doesn't," Melody protested. "We know from the CCTV footage that his manager picked him up right after the band finished on Friday night, and we have his manager's testimony, which you yourself said was reliable, that he drove him back to Central London. He can't have been involved in Arnott's death. And if Rashid is right about the time of Francis's death, he can't have had anything to do with that, either."

"Why not? You're telling me he has an unbreakable alibi?"

Melody met her gaze. "Yes. Me."

"Shara, go home," said Gemma.

Raising her eyebrows, Shara glanced at Melody, but said, "Right, guv. Glad to. Whatever you say. I'll just finish up these reports in the morning." She collected her things, and with a last little shake of her head at Melody, left the CID room.

Gemma turned to Melody. "I think you'd better explain."

"I went to see Andy—to interview him—early yesterday evening. I'd tried to track down the other blokes in the band with no luck, and then it occurred to me that Caleb Hart hadn't looked at Arnott's photo when I went to the recording studio, so I thought I'd ask Andy what he thought about Hart."

"And you're just now telling me this?"

"I—um—got a bit sidetracked, with everything that's happened today."

Gemma tried to remember when she'd seen Melody look so uncomfortable. Although on the job Melody tried very hard to downplay her upbringing and her education—had, in fact, deliberately chosen a career where those things would be a disadvantage—her background gave her a natural confidence that Gemma sometimes envied. Now she was waffling like a nervous witness. "Back to last night," said Gemma. "So you went to see Andy. When?"

"It must have been about six. Well before Shaun Francis was seen at the Prince of Wales. Andy was getting ready for a gig at the Twelve Bar in Denmark Street—that's a guitar club—and so I—I went with him. And we didn't get back to Andy's flat until late."

"What if Rashid was off on the time of death? How late?"

Melody turned a rather becoming shade of pink and tucked a strand of her hair behind her ear. "Boss, it wouldn't matter how far off Rashid was on the time."

Gemma stared at her, remembering Melody's flustered late arrival that morning, and the penny dropped. "You're telling me you spent the night with him?"

"It's not illegal." Melody crossed her arms over her chest. "And he wasn't a suspect."

"He was a peripheral witness, and now maybe something more. Melody, if you've compromised the case—"

"The fact that Arnott spoke to Andy and that Andy knew Shaun Francis years ago is no stranger a coincidence than you and Duncan knowing Andy and his manager," Melody said hotly. Then she sighed and rubbed her cheeks. "But I've told him he'll have to speak to you, and now he feels I've betrayed his confidence."

It would have been patronizing for Gemma to have told Melody she'd done the right thing. Instead, she considered what Melody had said. "I don't really know Andy, not to speak to. It was Duncan and Doug who met him on a case. I've just seen him coming and going from Tam and Michael's flat. But you haven't told me how he knew about Shaun Francis's murder."

"I told him. He'd asked me to come by the flat. He wanted to show me a video that Caleb Hart had made of Andy's sessions with Poppy over the weekend."

"A video?"

"Caleb put it up on YouTube last night. It's gone bonkers. You wouldn't believe the hits in a day."

"Oh," Gemma murmured as the light dawned. "Tam's vested interest."

"What are you talking about?"

Now it was Gemma's turn to admit that she'd bent the rules—although not, apparently, nearly as far as Melody. "Duncan and Doug talked to Tam today. And then Duncan went to see Caleb Hart. Unofficially. On Tam's behalf. Tam was worried about the business with Arnott causing Andy problems, and now I see why, if there's something big in the works. But when I told Duncan he could talk to Hart, I didn't know that it was going to get a good deal more complicated."

"Duncan and Doug? Bloody hell." Melody took a moment to digest this. "What was Doug doing out with that ankle?" she asked, then shook her head, as if, it being Doug, the question had answered itself. "Never mind. What did Duncan find out from Hart?"

"Hart said he didn't know Arnott, and that he left the pub to go to an AA meeting. I'm not sure I believe either, which means I'm going to have to get the same information through official channels, without mentioning that Duncan spoke to him. And no," she said, seeing Melody's eager expression, "you can't interview him. I made a mistake as it is, letting Duncan talk to him.

"And," she went on before Melody could interrupt, "I don't want you talking to Andy Monahan about any of this until I've had a chance to speak to him."

Melody's shoulders slumped. "Not a problem. I don't think he wants to talk to me."

There was something in the way she said the words that frightened him, and he felt suddenly that he didn't want anything to change, ever. He wanted to go on playing his guitar in his room, making his mum breakfast, having tea on the steps with Nadine. And he didn't want her to sound like someone he didn't know.

"Nadine—" He hesitated. He never called her by her name, and he'd never asked her anything personal, but he couldn't bear not speaking. "Nadine, are you all right?"

More than anything, he wanted to touch her, to offer some gesture of comfort for whatever was troubling her, but he somehow knew that was a boundary he could not cross.

In the fading light, he saw her quick half smile as she glanced at him. "I'm fine. It's just the heat, it makes me cross. I wish it would break." She gave an irritable shrug and brushed a hovering midge from her bare legs. "Don't pay me any mind." With a sigh, she handed him her empty cup and stood. "Thanks for the tea, Andy. Good night."

Before he could respond, she went into her flat and the door closed behind her with a click. He felt dismissed.

CHAPTER SIXTEEN

The final assault came on Crystal Palace on November 30th, 1936, when fire engulfed the building and within hours it was destroyed. Buckland and his daughter who had been out for an evening walk notice[d] smoke coming from the building and when they arrived, they found two of the night watchmen, trying to put out the small blaze. The fire department was called but despite the use of 89 fire trucks and 400 firemen the Crystal Palace burned to the ground.

—Betty Carew, www.helium.com

"Melody did what?" Kincaid said, one eyebrow shooting up.

It was late, but the children were at last in bed; Gemma had eaten the antipasti Kincaid had brought her from Carluccio's, and was now curled up next to him on the sitting room sofa, drinking a cup of cocoa. Geordie was snuggled against her other side, and Sid the cat was stretched out on the hearth, absorbing as much heat as possible from the gas fire flickering in the grate. The skin on his stomach glowed pink in the spots where it showed through his black coat.

"You heard me perfectly well."

"I just didn't believe it," he said, and she heard the smile in his voice. "I always imagined Melody with a proper prep school type. An investment banker, or maybe a doctor or a lawyer."

"Then you don't know her very well. If Melody didn't have a streak of the rebel, she'd never have defied her father and gone into the job."

"Still, isn't that a bit of a cliché, shagging the lead guitarist?"

Gemma smacked his arm with her free hand. "It's not funny. God knows the super isn't going to think it's funny if she finds out."

"If? You haven't told her?"

"I'm waiting for Rashid's official estimate on time of death before I add Melody's statement to the case file. I'm hoping that he'll place it before midnight and I can just say she interviewed Monahan at a club during that time frame. And when I spoke to Superintendent Krueger, her biggest concern was keeping any details of Shaun Francis's death from the media for as long as possible. The reporters were gathering by the time I got back to Cleaver Square this afternoon. They'll have Amanda Francis's address in no time."

What Krueger had actually said was, "Get me a result before this thing leaks or we'll have a media circus, and you do not want to be the star," implying that this was Gemma's first really high-profile case on the team, and she had better not screw it up.

"No pressure, then," Kincaid said lightly, and she knew he understood. "I won't say anything to Doug, but I suspect he'll find out one way or another," he added, the humor gone.

"They're just friends," Gemma protested. "It's not as if they're going out or anything."

"Not in any conventional sense, perhaps. But just hearing the way Melody talked about Andy Monahan got Doug's knickers in a twist. That's why he was so keen to go with me to talk to Tam."

"Oh, dear. Well, Melody will have to sort that one out. If Andy Monahan is involved in this case, she's got bigger problems than Doug's wounded feelings, and so do I."

"Andy couldn't have more reliable alibis than Tam and Melody."

"No. But he's off-limits to Melody for the time being. I'm sending her to Shaun's chambers first thing in the morning to see what she can turn up there. And I'm going to talk to Andy Monahan myself."

"Are you seduction proof?" He pulled her closer and put his lips against her neck.

"I have to admit, the video is pretty amazing . . ." she teased.

Kincaid had shown it to her earlier, with Kit looking over their shoulders. "That's brilliant," Kit had said. "You mean you know them?" he'd added, obviously impressed with Andy and Poppy. "Can I download the song?"

Now Kincaid nibbled her ear. "You mean the music is amazing. Just the music."

"Stop it. That tickles." Gemma wasn't ready to be distracted. "And I'm going to follow up on Caleb Hart." That thought took her back to her overriding worry. "About today—was Charlotte really all right with Doug?" Charlotte had told her all about her Na-pol-e-on, pronouncing all the syllables carefully. And she'd been very impressed with Doug's boot cast, explaining to Gemma that Doug had had an accident and that one should be careful on ladders. "And Saturday, when she went for a walk with Michael and the dogs, she was all right then, too?"

"She seemed to be fine."

Gemma pulled away and turned so that she could see his face. "Do you think she's getting better?"

He shrugged. "I think it helps that she knows them."

"Yes, but until now, she's only been willing to stay with Betty or Alia, so surely she's improving at least a little. And if we don't work out something about school for her soon—"

"Shhh." He touched her lips with his finger. "There's no point worrying about that tonight." Taking her hand, he pulled her to her feet, dislodging the disgruntled cocker spaniel from the sofa and making Sid stretch and yawn in his place by the fire. "Come on. I think it's far past time for bed."

It was only much later that she realized he'd done a very good job of changing the subject.

The next morning, Gemma drove straight to Andy Monahan's flat rather than going into the station. She doubted if musicians were early risers, but she was determined to catch him at home, even if she had to get him out of bed.

After inching her Escort up onto the curb in the narrow confines of Hanway Place, she got out and looked up at the grim facades of the buildings. The slice of sky she could see overhead was leaden gray, and the air blowing through from Oxford Street smelled of car exhaust and rancid cooking grease from the fast-food restaurants and takeaways. Beneath those scents she thought she caught the faint metallic tang of sleet.

She found the flat and was just touching the bell when the street door opened and Andy barreled out, almost knocking her down with the rectangular guitar case in his hand.

"Oh, sor—" he said, then stopped short, staring at her. "I know you. I've seen you at Louise's. You're little Charlotte's foster mum."

"It's a bit more complicated than that. I'm also Melody Talbot's boss. Detective Inspector Gemma James."

Andy looked dumbfounded. "You're a cop? But I thought it was Duncan who was—I mean—"

"We both are."

"Melody said she had to speak to her guv'nor, but I never imagined . . ."

"It is a bit weird, isn't it? Six degrees of separation and all that. Look, could we go somewhere and talk?" Thinking of

Melody, she felt suddenly uncomfortable insisting that they go back into his flat, as if she were trespassing on her partner's privacy. "There's a Starbucks just at the corner. I'll buy you a coffee."

Looking harried, Andy pulled his phone from his jeans pocket and glanced at the time. He didn't wear a watch. "I've got a session in Notting Hill in an hour. I can't be late."

"Notting Hill? With Poppy?"

"How did you—" He shook his head. "No. That's pie in the sky, that stuff. This is paying work, at one of the studios in Lansdowne House, and it's been booked for months. I can't afford to miss it."

"Twenty minutes," Gemma insisted. "I don't want to have to do this officially."

The threat had been implicit, but after a moment Andy shrugged. "Okay." He set off, leading the way round the corner into Oxford Street and dodging through the traffic.

Although he wasn't much taller than Gemma, she had to hurry to keep up, but when she reached the coffee shop he seemed to think better of his manners and stopped to hold the door for her.

As they entered, Gemma inhaled the warmth and the peculiarly comforting aroma of the place. "Why is it that no other coffee shop smells quite like Starbucks?" she asked. "It's all coffee beans. You'd think it would be the same." When Andy looked at her blankly, she said, "Never mind. What can I get you?"

"Just regular coffee. Black." He eased his guitar case in beside a chair in the front window and glanced again at the time on his phone.

Budget coffee, thought Gemma. That was how she had drunk hers when she was on her own with Toby, struggling to pay the bills, and every penny counted. As she stood in the queue, she wondered if Andy Monahan had any idea who Melody's father was, and if it would matter to him if he did. He didn't seem the sort to be impressed by money and power—he might, in fact, be terrified by the prospect.

When she came back with their cups—hers half coffee, half steamed milk, as she knew it would be a long day and she'd drop halfway through if she overdid the caffeine this early—he'd settled uneasily on the edge of his chair.

She eased the lid off her cup, using the moment to study him. He seemed very different from the cheeky bloke she'd occasionally seen coming and going from Tam and Michael's flat when she was visiting Louise. He was older than she'd thought, and perhaps, up close, more good looking, with his shadowed dark blue eyes and tousled, blond-tipped hair. And in the video, she'd seen the grace and skill in his playing, and something else that was both indefinable and undeniable. He had star quality, whatever that was, and she wondered suddenly what he would be willing to do for the success he deserved.

"Tell me about Shaun Francis," she said.

Andy gave her a startled glance, as if he'd expected her to make small talk. She tapped her watch. "You're the one on a schedule."

"I told Melody. I met him one summer when we were kids, in Crystal Palace Park. I didn't like him. I haven't seen him since."

Taking out her phone, Gemma pulled up a photo they'd copied from one in Shaun Francis's flat and handed it across to Andy.

He looked at the picture, frowning, then shook his head and gave it back to her. "If that's Shaun, I'm not sure I'd have recognized him." He rubbed his fingers on the leg of his jeans—an odd gesture, thought Gemma, as if he were erasing even such distant contact.

"Did you know he lived in Cleaver Square?"

"No. Why would I?"

"Have you ever been to the pub there, the Prince of Wales?"

"Yeah, but not for a while. I've a photographer mate who uses the Camera Club round the corner. I've been for a drink with him when he's done some publicity shots for the band, but he's been in Australia this year."

Gemma made a mental note to check how long Shaun Francis had been living in the Cleaver Square flat. "But you didn't see Shaun when you were there?"

"No, I've told you. I don't think so."

"Would Shaun have recognized you?" she asked, thinking about it the other way round. "If he'd seen you somewhere—anywhere, not just in the Prince of Wales."

He seemed taken aback. "I don't know. Maybe. I was skinny and blond all those years ago, too. But really blond," he added with the first hint of a smile she'd seen, touching his hair. "Like barley straw, and that summer it was bleached almost white from the sun. But what if he did? I don't understand what this has to do with anything."

"I don't, either." Gemma changed tack. "What about Caleb Hart? What do you know about him?"

"He's a friend of Tam's. He seems like a good guy, and he really knows his stuff, musically." Andy moved his coffee in a circle on the table, but he hadn't taken a sip. "You can't possibly think Caleb has anything to do with these—these deaths. That would be mad."

"Murders," Gemma corrected him, holding his gaze. "And I think whoever is doing this might be quite mad, actually."

It was Andy who broke the eye contact first. "I can't help you. And I've got to go." He hadn't bothered looking at the time on his phone again. Standing, he retrieved his guitar case, and Gemma resigned herself to letting him go. For the moment. She didn't think he'd lied to her, but she was equally sure that he hadn't told her the whole truth.

"Andy," Gemma said quietly as he turned towards the door, "Melody had no choice but to speak to me."

"I know," he said. "But that doesn't make it any better." And then he was out the door and gone, swallowed up by the milling crowd in Oxford Street.

Having done the post-breakfast washing-up and got Charlotte settled in the sitting room for her allotted half hour of morning telly on BBC2, Kincaid was looking out into the garden, weighing the look of the sky against the prospect of a run in the park.

He'd just decided that the best option might be to leave Geordie at home and take Charlotte for a gentle jog in the direction of Portobello Road, where they could take cover if needed.

"Slacker," he said aloud, chiding himself. But the dark day seemed to call out for color and crowds, not an isolated pounding of the paths in the park.

The doorbell rang, making him jump and startling the dogs into a frenzy of barking. Charlotte, mesmerized by the garishly colored animated figures on the television, remained unperturbed.

Wondering if Gemma had ordered something and forgotten to tell him, he went to the door and looked out the sidelight. A black Mercedes SUV he didn't recognize idled at the curb, plumes of white fog drifting from its exhaust. Frowning, he opened the door and found MacKenzie Williams standing on his doorstep.

"Duncan," she said, "sorry to drop by unannounced, but I didn't have your mobile number, and I knew where your house was because you'd told me."

"Not to worry." He was surprised, pleased, and a little disconcerted. "Are you all right? Won't you come in?"

"I'm fine, and no, I can't stay. I've got a job to go to this morning. That's why I stopped by, because I knew I'd miss you at K and P."

228 ~ DEBORAH CROMBIE

Hushing the dogs at his ankles and stepping outside, he wondered what sort of job it was. She had her long, curly hair pulled up in an untidy bunch, wore not a stitch of makeup, and looked as though she'd thrown on her old waxed jacket and faded jeans in her sleep. "I had some news for you and it couldn't wait," she went on, grinning. "There was a parents' evening at the school last night, and I've convinced the head to at least consider Charlotte for placement. You've an appointment tomorrow morning at ten." MacKenzie couldn't have looked more pleased with herself if she'd just given him the crown jewels.

"But—"

"Oliver will be in his class. I can wait in reception with Charlotte while you talk to the head. And she may want to see Charlotte as well."

"Oh, I—" Kincaid collected himself. "MacKenzie, you're brilliant. But what should I— What does one wear to an interview with the headmaster? It feels like a state visit."

"It's headmistress," MacKenzie warned. "And she won't like it if you assume otherwise." She pursed her lips, giving him a considering glance. "I'd go for nice but casual, the stay-at-home Notting Hill dad look. No suit. You'll do fine."

"Will I need any sort of paperwork or credentials?"

She laughed. "Don't worry. I've told her all about you."

"Now I really am terrified," he said, joking, but he was feeling a bit gobsmacked by the speed of MacKenzie's results, and her apparent influence. And by the fact that he had yet to speak to Gemma about any of this.

"I'll see you at the school, then, a bit before ten tomorrow? You know where it is?"

Kincaid nodded. It was east of Notting Hill Gate, and he'd seen the children coming out in their uniforms often enough.

"Got to dash. Cheerio." MacKenzie waggled her fingers at him, ran lightly to her car, and drove away, leaving Kincaid staring after her and feeling as if he'd just been blitzed by a force of nature.

He'd just come in and shut the door when his mobile rang. He swore under his breath as he realized he still hadn't given MacKenzie his number, in case of a hitch, and then he wondered if Gemma or one of the boys had forgotten something or if Doug was going stir-crazy again.

But it was Tam on the other end of the line, his voice high and his Scots accent more pronounced than usual.

"Duncan, our Andy just rang me and said Gemma turned up at his flat this morning to question him. Something about anither murder and a lad he knew from years ago, and what I'm wondering is why Gemma would think he knew anything at all about that?"

Still trying to work out whether or not that had been a question, Kincaid said, "Whoa, Tam. You knew it was Gemma's case, the murder in Crystal Palace. There's a possibility that the two might be connected."

"But why talk to Andy?" Tam asked, a bit more coherently. "How did Gemma ken that Andy knew this lad?"

"He wasn't a lad anymore. He was a junior barrister, living in Kennington. And as for how Gemma knew, did Andy not tell you?"

"He was blathering something about that dark-haired lass, the constable that came to the studio."

"Melody. And you know perfectly well she's a detective sergeant. She told Andy about the second murder, um, in passing, and Andy recognized the name. Simple enough."

There was silence on the other end. "In passing?" Tam said at last. "Are you telling me that the lad has gone and got himself involved with a lady copper? I thought he was a wee bit smitten, but not that he'd gone right off his haid."

"You should be glad, for his sake. It looks as though she's his alibi for the time of the second murder."

"And why would he need an alibi, Duncan, tell me that? I should never have spoken to you about him."

Kincaid was still standing at the front window. The sky had grown darker, and now the first fat drops of rain splashed against the pavement. "Tam—"

"Och, I'm sorry." Tam sighed. "It's not your fault. But I don't understand what's going on here. If the lad cannae have had anything to do with either of these . . . incidents, then why is he in such a lather? He's even saying he's not sure he wants to sign the contract with Caleb. I've told him he's lost all sense but I cannae seem to get through to him."

Crystal Palace, thought Kincaid. That was the common factor. The first murder had taken place there. Andy Monahan had grown up there. Andy had met the second victim there. "Tam, what do you know about Andy's background? You said he hadn't any family when you first met him, and that he was not long out of school. Has he ever talked about his childhood? Or about what happened to his family?"

"No. Not to speak of. But"—Tam sounded reluctant—"he might have said a few things over the years that gave me the impression his mum was a bit overfond of the drink. He gets a bit shirty with the lads—and sometimes the punters—if they're over the limit."

Kincaid was certain that was not quite all. "And?"

"And . . . I might have mentioned that to Caleb . . . I didn't say that the lad was teetotal, mind you, just that he's not one to overindulge. I wanted to give a good impression, seeing as how—"

"Caleb is a recovering alcoholic."

"He told you?"

"He makes no secret of it. I believe that's common in the AA program. So, you thought Caleb and Andy might have a common bond. Fair enough. Did Andy ever tell you he grew up in Crystal Palace?"

"What? No. No, he didn't." Tam sounded surprised and a little hurt. "When I met him, he was dossing on sofas in Central London and the East End. It was only when I started getting him session work that he was able to get his own place. I just assumed . . ."

Kincaid was beginning to think that it wasn't wise to make assumptions about Andy Monahan. "That's how he knew the second victim. From Crystal Palace."

"But he never said, when Caleb chose that pub . . ." Tam was silent for so long that Kincaid walked into the sitting room to check on Charlotte. She was sitting cross-legged on the floor, both dogs sprawled on her lap, perfectly happy with the extended telly time.

"Duncan," Tam said at last, "I don't know what to think, except that he's a good lad, and I'd not want to see him come to any harm, regardless of all this business with Caleb and the video. I've seen these sand castles wash away before, and I will again. It's a nice little dream, but my life will go on as it is, one way or anither, and I'm lucky with it. But Andy . . . I fear the lad is in some sort of real trouble, and I don't think he'll confide in me. Do you think he might talk to you?"

It was early evening before Andy realized they'd run out of milk. If there was anything that would make his mum more cross than usual, it was not having milk for her morning tea. She said milk made the tea easier on her stomach, which he could well believe considering the amount of cheap gin she'd been pouring down in the evenings.

She'd been worse the past few weeks, the heat, she said, getting on her nerves. And it seemed there was no relief in sight from that. The sky stayed bleached as bone, and the oc-

casional menacing rumble of thunder in the distance came to nothing.

Surely the weather would break soon, Andy thought, trudging back from the shop with the pint of milk—bought with pennies scrounged from the last of the week's grocery money—sweating in his hand. It was almost term time—but that thought made him clench the bottle more tightly. As much as his mum was drinking, he couldn't believe she'd get herself up and to the pub for work if he wasn't there to make sure of it. And if she lost her job . . .

Although the blistering sun was sinking in the west, the heat still radiating off the pavement made him feel woozy and he stumbled slightly. He'd not been sleeping well, or eating much, for that matter.

And even though he'd stopped going to the library and reading the books on Crystal Palace, the fire dream had come back. Sometimes he woke in the dark, sure he'd heard the crackle of flames. And just last night, restless in his stuffy room, he'd come down and found his mum asleep on the sofa with a cigarette burning in her hand. Again.

Since the first time that had happened, he'd been hiding them from her when he could, but it made her furious. One night she'd actually struck him. The next morning, grumbling under her breath as she absently searched drawers for the packet, then the ashtrays for fag ends, she obviously had no recollection of what she'd done. Andy wasn't sure if he'd been glad or sorry.

As he started down the incline of Woodland Road, he saw that Nadine was sitting on her steps. He waved, but she didn't seem to see him. As he got closer, he saw that she was wearing a white dress again, this time with poppy-red splashes. She was wearing makeup as well, the slash of red lipstick making her look alien, unfamiliar. And she was drinking.

She held a glass of red wine in her hand, a half-empty bottle on the step beside her. Her pots of geraniums, he realized, were withering, the leaves yellowed.

"It has legs, you know," she said when he reached her, holding up the glass and tilting it so that the liquid made thick trails on the inside of the glass. Her own legs were brown and bare, and in spite of the dress and the makeup, she wore no shoes.

Frowning, he stared down at her. "What are you doing?"

"Celebrating. Wedding. Annivers-ary." She struggled a bit with the syllables. "White, and red." Tilting her glass even further, she let a few drops of the wine fall onto the step, then rubbed at it with her finger. "Red as blood. We were arguing about where to go for our anni— You know." She smiled, but when she looked up at him her eyes were frighteningly blank, and her voice was thick and slurring a bit.

Feeling sick, Andy said, "Nadine, you shouldn't be sitting out here."

"And where should I be, Andy love?" She took another sip of the wine. "No party to go to. No dancing. That's what Marshall wanted to do, did you know that? Take me out for champagne and dancing. I said it was too expensive. He said I was a stupid cow who didn't know how to have a good time. So who's sorry now, eh?" she added in a singsong, swaying with it.

Andy fought the urge to put his hands over his ears. He didn't want to hear this. Didn't want to know this. Didn't want to think about Nadine fighting with her husband. Being with her husband. Dressing up for him, even though he was dead.

And he didn't want her sounding like someone he didn't know. Or someone he knew all too well.

"Stop it," he said. "Stop it. You're just like my mum."

"You know, maybe I am," Nadine said slowly. She frowned up at him, then looked away and sloshed more wine from the bottle into her glass, spilling drops on her dress. "I'm sure she has her reasons. And I never said I was perfect. I never promised you anything, did I, Andy?"

Sudden shame made his eyes burn with tears, blinding him. He'd thought he was special. He'd thought she cared about him.

Then fury washed over him, leaving him dizzy and shaking. "No!" he shouted at her. "No. You bloody well didn't."

He turned away from her and slammed into the flat.

The light grew dim as Andy sat hunched against the wall in the sitting room. He wasn't sure how he'd got there, or how much time had passed. The pint of milk, warm now, was on the floor beside him.

His chest ached from the heaving sobs that had finally subsided into hiccups. His eyes felt raw, scoured, his face flushed and chapped. But not even the bout of tears had eased the knot of anger inside him. He wanted to do something, anything, to make the hurt go away.

When the bell rang, he jerked to his feet, breathing hard. Was it Nadine, come to say she was sorry?

He didn't want her to see he'd been sitting in the dark. Switching a lamp on low, he walked slowly to the door, his heart thumping, and pulled it open.

But it wasn't Nadine who stood waiting. Andy stared at Shaun and Joe. "What are you doing here?"

"It's Friday night," said Shaun. "You never go out. We thought you might be lonely. And we brought you a present."

Something clinked in the paper bag Joe held against his chest.

"Go away." Andy started to shut the door, but Shaun put a hand on it.

"Hey, man, come on. We're sorry about what happened in town. We've come to make amends. Let us in."

"Besides," put in Joe, "we know you don't have anything better to do."

No, thought Andy. He didn't.

The steps next door were empty. Nothing was what he'd thought. No one was what they seemed. And he didn't have anything to do at all.

He opened the door.

CHAPTER SEVENTEEN

What really struck me as I was looking for accounts and images of the fire is the extent to which it was and continues to be seen as a spectacle, comparable with all the palace's previous performances.

Shaun Francis's chambers was a venerable establishment in the Middle Temple—meaning the offices were old, cramped, and filled to the gills with too much stuff and a very harried staff.

The head clerk answered Melody's questions politely, as did the barristers to whom he introduced her, but the first thing they all wanted to know after expressing polite dismay over Shaun Francis's death was when Amanda was coming back.

Her impression was that Amanda Francis was the glue that held the chambers together, and that her brother had been at best an afterthought, at worst a nuisance.

When she was shown into the office of the head of chambers, he was quick enough to confirm her suspicions.

"It's Spencer, Edmund, like the poet," he said, rising to shake her hand. "Except with an undistinguished *c.*"

He was past middle age, bald, short, with a stomach that strained the buttons of his chalk-striped waistcoat, and he had a voice that Melody thought would either sear righteous fire into jurors' souls or reduce them to puddles of treacly sentiment, depending on his intent. She hoped that if she ever met him in court, he would be representing the prosecution.

"We are most shocked at this news about Shaun," he went on as he gestured her into a chair. "A tragic loss. So young, such promise." When Melody merely raised a quizzical brow, he sighed. "Well, perhaps that is a bit of an exaggeration. You'll find out, I think, that Shaun Francis was not particularly well liked in the chambers. But we are certainly distressed and saddened by his death."

"Had Shaun been with you long?" Melody asked, feeling that they'd got on a more useful footing.

"Less than a year. To be honest, we took him on at Amanda's request. She began here as a trainee legal secretary ten years ago, and we are all utterly dependent on her."

"And Shaun? Were you satisfied with his performance?"

Spencer tapped a silver fountain pen on his cluttered desk for a moment before he answered. "His record in trials had not been stellar, I admit. We were, in fact, in a bit of a pickle." He looked up at her with very sharp blue eyes that crinkled at the corners. "But not one that anyone here would have bumped him off to resolve."

"Did he make things difficult for Amanda in chambers?"

"It was hard for her, yes, when he didn't prepare properly for a case. I think she felt it reflected on her."

"And if it had come to the point where you had to tell Shaun that other accommodations might better suit him, would Amanda have gone, too?"

"That I can't say."

"But you're very relieved not to have to find out."

"That, Detective Sergeant," said Spencer, "is not against the law." Although delivered with a smile, it was a dismissal, but one Melody was not quite ready to accept.

"Mr. Spencer, do you know if Shaun knew a barrister called Vincent Arnott?" She mentioned Arnott's chambers, which were in the nearby Inner Temple.

"He might have done. It's a fairly small world, you know." His gesture seemed to encompass the Inns of Court. "Vincent and I had been opposing counsels a number of times over the years, and of course you see one another in the pubs and wine bars."

"So you knew Arnott was dead?"

"One could hardly have missed the speculation in the news-papers. And no, I'm not going to ask you if it's true," he added, obviously having seen Melody begin to form a denial. "I know you're not at liberty to say, and I'm not at all sure I want to know."

"Did you consider Arnott a friend?"

Spencer deliberated, and Melody doubted he ever answered anything of importance without first weighing the pros and cons. "I wouldn't say that Vincent had friends," he answered after a moment. "He could be a tough adversary in court— admirable, of course—but he was inclined to take things be-yond the courtroom."

"How do you mean?" asked Melody.

"Oh, surely you see that in your work as well, Sergeant. He carried his cases with him on a personal level, whether he was defending or prosecuting. And more than that, if he was bested in the courtroom, he didn't forgive it."

From what Melody had learned about Vincent Arnott's pri-vate life, she didn't find this surprising. "But you don't know that he had any direct connection with Shaun Francis?"

"No. You can, of course, ask the clerk to look through our files, but if Shaun had opposed Arnott in court, I'm sure Amanda would have known it." Spencer's sharp blue eyes ap-praised her. "But you can't be thinking that Arnott had anything to do with Shaun's death, as Arnott was already dead. And if Shaun had something to do with Arnott's, then who would have killed him?"

If it had been the other way round, thought Melody as she left the chambers and wound her way through the narrow alleys leading into Fleet Street, they could have made a tidy case of it. If Shaun had been killed first, Amanda Francis could have picked up Arnott in the White Stag and killed him as revenge for her brother's murder. But then why would Arnott have killed Shaun, in this hypothetical scenario? So far, they'd found no connection between Vincent Arnott and Shaun Francis. And Melody knew she was just confusing herself with idle speculation, trying to distract herself from the constant nagging worry about Andy.

She'd spent the past twenty-four hours wondering if she had done the best or the worst thing in her life. And last night, alone in her flat, she'd sat huddled on the sofa with her finger hovering over the keypad on her phone, debating whether to call or text Andy or Doug.

In the end she had done neither. She didn't know what she could say to Andy that would make things any better between them, and contacting him would have meant disobeying a direct order from Gemma.

As for Doug, she didn't think that either Gemma or Duncan (she had no doubt that Gemma would tell Duncan) would say anything to Doug about her spending the night with Andy, but she also had no doubt that sooner or later Doug would find out. She needed to talk to him before that happened, but not over the phone.

She had, however, finally managed to contact Nick, the bass player in Andy's band, and he'd agreed to meet her at lunchtime at a pub near the Royal Courts of Justice.

The Seven Stars in Carey Street was tiny and eccentric, and Melody had suggested it as neutral ground when Nick told her he'd be studying that morning at King's College Library. It had rained while she was in Shaun's chambers, and as she walked, the pavement glistened under a still-threatening sky.

The pub was jammed when she reached it, but shoving her way inside, she saw Nick, thin and dark, at a corner table. He'd put a stack of books on the chair beside him and was looking round worriedly. She recognized him from the CCTV footage of the band loading up outside the White Stag in Crystal Palace, but realized he had no idea what she looked like.

When she'd elbowed her way through the crush, he looked up and, putting a defensive hand on the books, said, "This one's taken."

"Nick? I'm Melody Talbot."

She'd dressed for the interview at the Inns of Court, in a suit and her best red wool coat, and from Nick's surprised expression she thought he'd expected a trench coat and a badge. Maybe she should take a page from Maura Bell's book.

"Oh, sorry." Hastily, he moved the books and squeezed them precariously onto the tiny table beside an almost empty half-pint of lager. "You're not—I didn't—"

"Can I get you another?" she asked.

"Oh—" He glanced at his watch. "No, I'd better not. I've got a class. Accounting's dull enough as it is. I'd never stay awake."

"I'll try not to take up too much of your time, then," she said, sitting down. "Thanks for seeing me." The pub was loud and she had to lean close to be heard.

"You said this was about Andy. I've been ringing him but he doesn't return my calls. Is he okay?" His worry seemed genuine.

So Nick hadn't heard about the video. "Yes, he's fine. I just had a few questions about what happened at the White Stag last Friday night."

Nick was frowning at her, the remainder of his beer untouched. "You're a plainclothes detective. Why should you care about a little punch-up? That guy didn't press charges, did he?"

She remembered her first interview with Andy and Tam in the studio, and Andy's bruised knuckles. Tam and Andy, as well as Reg, the manager at the Stag, had said Arnott shouted at Andy because Andy had had a row with a punter. "No one pressed charges. Are you talking about the guy Andy hit? What was that all about, anyway?"

Nick relaxed enough to take a sip of his beer. "Everyone was short-fused that night. We were pissed off with Andy for agreeing to the gig, and he was pissed off with us because we were acting like assholes. After the first set, I figured Andy was going to take us outside and tell us off good and proper. But just as we finished playing, this bloke came up and got right in Andy's face. And Andy just went off. I'd never seen him do anything like that."

"Do you know what this guy said?"

"I didn't hear. I heard Andy, though. Everyone did. He was calling the guy a bastard and saying he never wanted to see him again. And then Andy just hauled off and punched him in the nose." Nick shook his head and flexed his own hand, as if contemplating the idiocy of risking such an injury.

"You've no idea who he was?"

"Never seen him before, and I've known Andy since not long after he left school."

Melody took out her phone and showed him the photo of Shaun. "Was it him?"

Nick studied it for a moment, then shook his head. "No. Definitely not."

"Can you tell me what he looked like?"

"About our age. Just ordinary. Thin. A bit scruffy." Nick shrugged. "He had that look. You learn to recognize it if you play in a band long enough. Drugs. Alcohol. Something just a little off." He met Melody's eyes. "I just assumed he was an obnoxious drunk and that between us and him, Andy had had enough. But now, it does seem a bit weird, the way Andy reacted to him. Like it was personal."

"Did you talk to Andy about it, afterwards?"

Nick gave a humorless laugh. "Not bloody likely. Andy wasn't talking to us. Wouldn't even ride back to London in the van. And Tam was doing the whole mother-hen thing over Andy's hand, although I can't say I blame him. I hope he's okay."

"Why don't you try ringing him again now?" Melody suggested carefully. She couldn't repeat anything Andy had told her, and was not even sure she should be playing mediator.

This time Nick smiled more easily. "Nobody wants to be the first to apologize. It's like a bad couple's breakup, you know? One where you know it's coming but it still makes you feel like hell."

"I'm not sure I—"

"The band. It's over, but none of us wants to admit it. In a month or two, we'll be able to go out for a pint and have a laugh about it. But now . . ." He finished his beer and frowned. "You still haven't said exactly what it was you wanted. Although to be fair, I don't suppose I've given you much chance." This time, the glance he gave was assessing, and slightly flirtatious.

Oh, God, she thought. Nick was an attractive guy, but that was a complication she didn't need. Flushing, she said, "It was about the man who shouted at Andy after the row. Did you know him?"

Nick looked blank for a moment. "The white-haired guy? No, I just thought he was some bad-tempered geezer. I really wasn't paying attention, if you want the truth."

"Did you see Andy talk to him either before or after that?"

"No, I didn't notice him before. Then after all the commotion during the break, Tam took Andy outside for a talk. Then we played the second set—a little more professionally, I'm glad to say—and after that, Andy and Tam helped George and me load the van and Tam drove Andy home."

"And the white-haired man—did you see him again that night?"

"I don't think so. I was doing my best to redeem myself, and giving Andy some cover because I could tell his hand was swelling."

"What about the scruffy bloke?"

"No." Nick frowned. "No, I don't think so. But he wasn't exactly the sort you'd notice—although I daresay he had a sore nose," he added, grinning. "Our Andy. Imagine that."

Men, thought Melody. There was nothing that raised them in one another's estimation like the ability to give someone a bloody nose. Then the import of what Nick had said hit her. There'd been no room to slip out of her wool coat, and she was suddenly stifling.

"Look, thanks, Nick," she said, standing. "You've been a big help."

He looked surprised. "I have?"

"Absolutely. But I've got to run. I'll be in touch if I think of anything else."

Nick stood, bumping the table, then had to make a grab for the toppling stack of books. "Maybe next time I can buy you a beer," he called after her as she ducked through the crowd.

Melody pretended not to hear as she slipped out the door. She walked, unmindful of the direction she took, desperate to think.

Andy had told her that the bloke he hit that night was just some drunk punter who'd tried to touch his guitar. If what Nick had said was true, Andy had known him. Andy had lied.

After seeing Andy Monahan in Oxford Street, Gemma spent the remainder of the morning in Brixton, trying to pull the

244 ~ DEBORAH CROMBIE

threads from the two separate investigations into some sort of cohesive whole and having very little success.

She pushed away from her computer and rubbed her tired eyes. They needed to go back to the beginning.

Vincent Arnott had gone to the White Stag on Friday nights on a regular basis, occasionally picking up women whom he'd taken to the Belvedere, and then he'd returned home to care for his ill wife. So what had changed last Friday night?

Caleb Hart had decided to book Andy Monahan's band there, she thought.

Was that a catalyst, or something completely unrelated? Why had Hart said he didn't recognize Arnott when it was very likely that he'd seen him at the pub? Had Hart really left the pub to go to an AA meeting on a Friday night?

It was time she found out, and that meant an official interview with Hart.

She considered asking Maura Bell to question him, but if Hart mentioned that Kincaid had called on him yesterday, she would have to explain that rather unorthodox bit of information gathering to Maura, which she'd prefer not to do. Melody had made things difficult enough without adding anything else into the mix.

So, as Rashid was doing the postmortem on Shaun Francis at the Royal London in Whitechapel, she decided she would stop in at Hart's office herself. She took the tube from Brixton to Liverpool Street station, then walked to the address Kincaid had given her in Hanbury Street by way of Spitalfields Market.

She wondered, as she always did now when she came to the East End, if, when Charlotte was grown, she would remember these streets as home, or if her early years would be swallowed up by the sedate greens and grays of a Notting Hill childhood.

There was certainly no warmth or color in Hanbury Street today. Grim, brown Georgian brick gave way to shoddy postmodern blocks, and the cold, damp wind tugged at her hair and the hem of her coat. Gemma found the entrance to Hart's office and went in.

The reception area was ultrachic, as was the receptionist, who simultaneously managed to look up from her desk and down her perfect nose at Gemma. Gemma felt suddenly disheveled, aware of her hair blown loose from its plait and her wind-chapped cheeks. Kincaid might have warned her, she thought, smoothing a strand of hair and assuming her most brisk manner.

"I'm Detective Inspector James, Met CID," she said, showing her warrant card. "I'd like a word with Mr. Hart."

"He's not here." The girl showed not the least bit of interest, or apology. There was a hint of a dropped *h* in her accent. An authentic East End girl, and all the more trendy for it.

"Do you know when he'll be back?"

"Couldn't say."

"Can you tell me how I can contact him?"

The girl shrugged and handed her a business card from a little silver stand on her desk. "That's his mobile. But he never answers if he doesn't recognize the number, so you'll have to leave a message."

"Great. Thanks." What sort of message did you have to leave to get Caleb Hart to return your call? Gemma wondered. "Maybe you could help," she said to the receptionist with a smile. There was no harm in appealing to the girl's sense of importance. "You're Mr. Hart's personal assistant, right?" She felt sure that *receptionist* would not be well received. "Um—" She let the unspoken query dangle.

"Roxy."

"Roxy. Oh, that suits you." That bit of bubbly enthusiasm earned her a slight relaxing of the girl's facial muscles. "Um, Roxy," she went on brightly, "we're just trying to clear up a few details regarding an incident in Crystal Palace on Friday night. I understand that Mr. Hart booked a band at the pub there.

We were hoping he might have seen something that would help us clarify the time of this, um, incident."

"I heard all about that murder," Roxy said flatly, picking at a manicured fingernail, but Gemma thought she saw a little flare of interest in her eyes. "Caleb said some policewoman came to the studio on Saturday asking about a row the guy had with the guitarist in the band. But Caleb had already left the pub."

"Oh, that's too bad." Gemma did her best to look thoroughly disappointed. "Do you happen to know what time that was?"

"Well, it would have been before ten, because Caleb never misses his Friday night AA meeting at ten. He calls that one *Alcoholic's Prime Time*. Weekends are tough, you know, when you're used to going down to the pub with your mates."

"Yeah, I should think they would be," Gemma agreed. "Did he have far to go?"

"Dulwich. They meet in a community center there. Caleb organized it." There was definite pride in Roxy's voice now. Beneath the girl's brittle exterior lay a kernel of hero worship, thought Gemma. She hoped Caleb Hart deserved it.

"Thanks ever so much for your help, Roxy," she said. "And I'll just give Mr. Hart a ring later on to confirm."

She let herself out, thinking that it was the AA meeting she would be confirming before she got in touch with Hart, and that all roads seemed to lead to Dulwich.

As neither Melody nor Amanda Francis had arrived when Gemma reached the visitors' lounge at the Royal London, she went down to the basement and searched out Rashid in his subterranean den. She always found Rashid's office a wonder—its mass of clutter and graffiti-art-covered walls seemed so at odds with the perfection of his accent—and yet it suited him.

"Gemma!" he said, looking up from a pile of papers.

"Lovely to see you." When he smiled, his teeth were blindingly white against his olive skin. Today he wore a T-shirt which bore the slogan PATHOLOGY: LIVE THE DREAM, and she couldn't help grinning back at him.

"Rashid, you sound as if you've invited me for afternoon tea in the mortuary."

He pointed to a shelf behind his desk. "Kettle. Cups. Why not?"

"No, really." She shook her head. "I don't know what you've had in those. Eye of newt?"

"Gemma, I'm hurt. I put them through the instrument sterilizer every day."

"Now I really will pass." Gemma sat in the gray plastic chair—probably filched from the visitors' lounge—in front of Rashid's desk. "What have you got for us?"

He put his papers, and his teasing, aside. "I've zipped him up already, but do you want to have a look?"

"Not unless it will be useful." Gemma had never succumbed to the fascination of the postmortem.

"Well, he was developing a nice layer of fat round his organs, and some blockage in his arteries. Not good for someone so young. He certainly needed to take up squash and watch his diet, although that's a bit irrelevant now."

"Yes."

"And he was certainly strangled, and with the scarf we found round his neck. But it might not have been necessary, if you look at what I found in the tox results."

"Did he take an overdose of the Valium we found?" asked Gemma.

"Not an overdose, no, although I'd certainly say he was liberal with the prescribed dosage. But it was the combination of things that could very well have killed him without the manual assist. He was loaded with Xanax as well as the Valium, and his blood alcohol was sky high."

"Xanax? But the SOCOs didn't find any in his flat."

"No. Which means either he bought it or took it from someone, or—"

"Could someone have slipped it to him?"

"My thought exactly, unless the guy was a complete idiot who didn't realize you shouldn't mix the two drugs, and especially not with alcohol. My guess would be that it was in the gin and tonics. The bitterness of the tonic would have disguised the taste. And that the gins were doubles. Even if he'd been drinking all day, he'd have metabolized some of the alcohol, so I'd think it was administered over a fairly short time period."

"No wonder he was sick," Gemma said.

"Yes. And that might have been enough to save him, if someone hadn't throttled him."

"Were there any signs that he struggled?"

"No. There was no tissue under his nails, or any bruising to indicate that he tried to fight at the last minute. Although if he was already turned over on his stomach with his hands bound behind him, and his feet bound, there wouldn't have been a whole lot he could do."

"Did he trust whoever tied him up, or would he have been so out of it from the drugs and the alcohol that he didn't know what was happening?"

"Hard to say. He might have been slipping in and out of consciousness."

Gemma tried to visualize the scene. "Could a woman have done this?"

"The strangling, certainly. And the tying up, if he was either willing or too out of it to struggle. My question would be whether a woman could have helped him back from the pub, then got him undressed and onto the bed. He was a fairly big bloke. Fifty-fifty, I'd say."

"Thanks, Rashid. That really narrows things down," said Gemma.

"Glad to be of service," he answered with a grin.

"The barman at the Prince of Wales didn't remember serving Shaun Francis more than one drink. I wonder if any of the other staff will remember someone ordering double G and Ts? We'll have to get someone—" Gemma's phone rang.

It was Melody. "Boss, I'm upstairs, and Amanda Francis is here."

"Hang on a sec." Gemma looked at Rashid. "The sister's here for the ID. Is he ready?"

"I'll have the attendants put him in the viewing room," Rashid answered, already slipping out of the office to take care of it.

"Melody," Gemma said into the phone. "I'll be right up."

Amanda Francis viewed her brother's body in tight-lipped misery. She looked exhausted, her face still puffy and swollen, but her eyes were dry. Gemma suspected she had cried herself out.

After a full minute, she nodded, then reached out as if she might touch his face but pulled her hand back. "I've never seen anyone dead," she said. "My father—not even my mother saw him. They had my uncle make the identification. It's—weird. It's Shaun, but . . . empty. Even the wax figures at Madame Tussauds have more life in them."

"I know," said Gemma, touching her gently on the shoulder. "Are you ready to go upstairs now?" She'd left Melody to organize some tea from the hospital café. When Amanda nodded, Gemma signaled the mortuary attendant that they were finished, then led Amanda from the room.

As they went up in the lift, she asked, "How's your mother doing?"

"The liaison officer you sent has been good with her. He's young and good looking, and she's fawning over him. Disgusting, but at least it's off me. She asks his opinion on the arrangements every five minutes, and his patience is downright saintly."

When they reached the lounge, Melody was waiting with cardboard cups of tea. They found chairs in a quiet corner, and Amanda took her cup. Her hands trembled slightly.

"I've been to your chambers this morning," said Melody. "Everyone is asking after you."

"They've been really kind. They've sent flowers and cards, and Mr. Spencer rang me."

"I can see they think very highly of you," Melody told her. "Will you go back soon?"

Amanda shrugged. "I don't know what's appropriate. And once the liaison officer goes, I don't know how I'll manage my mother. I'll go barking mad if I stay at home with her all day." She went pale at the prospect, looking more distressed than she had at the sight of her brother's body.

"Are you Shaun's executor?" Gemma asked.

"Yes. Thank God he had enough sense not to put that on mother. From what I've seen, his affairs are a mess. Debt, and the flat is mortgaged to the hilt, so the sale of it won't begin to cover what he owed. And this time, there's no life insurance. This"—she looked at Gemma—"what happened to Shaun—it wasn't a convenient . . . accident?"

Like her father's, thought Gemma. "No. We're certain that Shaun was murdered." She caught Melody's quick glance—she hadn't had a chance to tell her Rashid's findings. "Amanda, do you know if Shaun ever used recreational drugs? Nonprescription stuff?"

"He dabbled a bit in his teens, I think, but never very seriously. Why?"

"We have to ask," Gemma said. "And was he in the habit of drinking a lot?"

"That's the lawyer's drug of choice, isn't it?" Amanda had regained a bit of her tartness. "And Shaun liked to drink. But it wasn't in his nature to get really drunk. He liked to be in control of things." She took a sip of her tea and grimaced, then frowned at Gemma. "But if you're sure Shaun was murdered, why are you asking me about drink and drugs? Do you think he was in some sort of trouble? Oh, God, if he was into something illegal and it comes out—"

"We don't know that," soothed Gemma. "We don't know why someone would have killed your brother, so we have to cover every possibility."

Melody leaned forward, cradling her cup in both hands. "Mr. Spencer at your chambers says he doesn't know of any connection Shaun might have had with the other barrister who was killed, Vincent Arnott. Is there any legal matter you might have handled that Mr. Spencer wouldn't have seen?"

"No." Amanda's eyes widened. "This Arnott. You asked me if Shaun knew him. You didn't say he'd been killed. Who was he? What happened?"

"We really can't discuss an ongoing investigation at this time," said Gemma. If it hadn't been for Shaun's death, Amanda would surely have seen the papers. Someone was bound to tell her, however, and it was better that she be prepared. "Mr. Arnott was found in circumstances similar to your brother's. We—"

"You think the same person killed them?" Amanda's voice rose. "Then why aren't you—"

"We don't know that," Gemma broke in. "We're exploring all the possibilities. But in the meantime, I'm sure you don't want the tabloids splashing the details of your brother's death all over the front pages. So, please, Amanda, don't discuss this with anyone. Not even your mother." Especially not your mother, she added to herself. Mrs. Francis would likely be shouting from the rooftops that her son was the victim of a serial killer. A quick change of subject was in order. "Amanda, did Shaun know a man called Caleb Hart?"

"No, not that I'm aware." Amanda was getting the glazed look of someone trying to follow a tennis match. "Who—"

"What about Andy Monahan?" put in Melody, her voice very tight and deliberately neutral.

"No, I don't—" Amanda frowned. "Wait. There was a kid named Andy, I think. One summer in the park. But it was years ago, and I don't think I ever knew his last name." When Gemma and Melody waited, she went on slowly. "He played the guitar. Shaun can't have been more than thirteen or fourteen that summer. I saw them a few times when I went to the park with my own friends, and I asked Shaun who he was. Blond. A pretty boy. I think Shaun was jealous." Her lips twisted. "He thought he was slumming it, my little brother, hanging out with a kid from Crystal Palace. He was a right shit, even then."

"Did they keep in touch?" asked Gemma, watching for Melody's reaction as much as Amanda's.

"No, I don't think so. But there was some kind of trouble that autumn, after term started, at Shaun's school. I'm not even sure the two things were connected, except in my memory. No one told me what it was about—I just remember grown-ups talking in hushed voices, and Dad having meetings with the headmaster."

"The school—where was it?" asked Gemma.

"It's called Norwood College. It's an exclusive boys' prep school. In Dulwich."

CHAPTER EIGHTEEN

Seventy-five years later, the sphinxes and statues adorning the terraces have been transformed from archaeological pastiche to real ruins, but that sense of spectacle is still apparent.

—www.sarahjyoung.com

As soon as Shaun and Joe were inside the flat, Andy knew he'd made a terrible mistake. He felt stifled, as if their physical presence had sucked the air from the space.

And he felt, as he watched them look round the dreary sitting room, ashamed. He did his best to keep things clean and tidy, but the furniture was old and tattered, the walls blotchy and damp stained. He knew from the other boys' clothes and accents that their homes must be very different.

"Nice place you've got here," smirked Shaun, while Joe pulled two large bottles of cheap cider from his paper bag.

Joe unscrewed the cap on one and put the other on the sitting room table. "You'll have to share. We only got two."

"I don't want any," said Andy, wondering how he could get them out again without bodily shoving them, and they were both bigger than he was. "How'd you get that stuff, anyway?"

"*Told you we could get anything we wanted from the shop on the Parade.*" *Shaun was wandering round the sitting room, peering into the kitchen.* "*Where's that electric guitar?*" *he asked.* "*The red one. We've seen you playing it out front.*"

"*Not here. It was . . . borrowed.*" *Thank God he'd left the Strat upstairs in his room, thought Andy. But what if one of them wanted to use the loo? Or Shaun just went upstairs? How would he stop him?* "*Hey, I changed my mind about the cider,*" *he said, desperate for a diversion.*

"*All right, man.*" *Joe handed him the open bottle and he took a swig. It was sweet and made him want to gag.*

"*What do you watch on this thing?*" *Shaun had picked up the remote for the shoddy old television.* "*Blue Peter? Doctor Who? Does it even have color?*"

"*Leave it—*"

But Shaun had already put the remote down and was pulling a packet of cigarettes from the pocket of his jeans. "*I've got something way better than cider.*"

"*You can't smoke in here,*" *protested Andy.*

"*Why ever not? The place reeks of smoke. Your mum will never know.*"

Andy knew Shaun was right, although the first thing he did when his mum had gone to work every day was empty and wash the ashtrays. "*Because I don't like it, that's why.*"

"*You'll like this.*" *From between the packet and its clear wrapper, Shaun pulled a fat joint. Andy hadn't smoked pot but he'd seen kids at his school do it, walking home after class, and he knew what it smelled like.*

"*No. You really can't smoke that in here. My mum would smell it.*"

"*I'll bet she's an old doper, your mum,*" *put in Joe with a snigger.* "*She looks like it.*"

Andy was past responding to insults. He just wanted them out of his house. "*Look, take it in the garden, then. You can smoke anything you want out there.*"

"Okay," said Shaun, his capitulation easier than Andy had expected. "Let's see this garden, then. Give us the grand tour."

Andy let them through the kitchen and down the cracked concrete steps. Light from the kitchen window spilled out onto the barren expanse of seared ground. There was an old push mower in the shed at the bottom of the garden, which Andy had used since he was old enough to manage it, but with the end-of-summer heat there was no grass left to cut. Some broken bricks marked out a little patio area, where he'd placed the plastic stacker chairs his mum had brought home from the pub. And in a corner by the steps, a trowel and the bag of potting soil he'd used to plant Nadine's geraniums.

Shaun lit the joint with a Bic, the sudden flare of light reflected in his flat, dark eyes. The distinctively sweet smoke filled the air as Shaun took a puff and handed the joint to Joe.

The thought of Nadine had made Andy feel reckless again. Why shouldn't he try it, if there was no one to care what he did?

When Joe handed him the joint, he took it and drew the smoke in carefully, not wanting to cough.

"You have to inhale and then hold it, baby boy," said Shaun, watching him.

Andy counted to himself, as if he was holding his breath in the swimming pool. Finally, he released the smoke and let it billow away from him. "Nothing to it. I don't believe there's really anything in this." He took another puff and held it, then another. The boys watched him, grinning. "What?" said Andy. "I don't feel any—" Suddenly, the top of his head went all odd and buzzy, and the world seemed to recede to a distance. He heard Shaun and Joe laughing, but his tongue seemed stuck to the roof of his mouth.

"Some shit, yeah?" said Joe. "This didn't come from the shop on the Parade." He took the joint and drew on it, then held it out to Andy again with a giggle. "Here. Take another hit."

Andy managed to shake his head and back away. "No, man. I feel—I don't want—"

"What's that?" Taking the joint from Joe's fingers, Shaun wandered towards the dilapidated fence that separated Andy's garden from Nadine's. "Someone having a party?"

Andy heard it then, music, coming from next door. They all moved towards the sound, as if drawn by magnets.

"No, it's just my neigh—" Andy stopped, trying to place the song. The slight breeze that had come up with the sunset shifted, bringing the honeyed vocal to them. Sinatra. "Fly Me to the Moon." His dad had had an old Best of Sinatra *album. Buried now, under the rock and pop, but Andy had liked it when he was little. Sometimes his mum had played it when he had trouble sleeping.*

"Some party," said Joe. "Wonder who she's got over for that." There was a familiarity in the way he said "she" that made the hair rise on Andy's neck.

"What do you—"

"Let's see, why don't we?" Shaun had found the loose board in the fence, the one Andy had been meaning to repair. It creaked as Shaun pulled on it and the nails gave way. The board came free, taking the next one with it.

They could see through the gap now. Nadine's flat, unlike Andy and his mum's, was one bedroom rather than two, and all on one level. Both kitchen and bath were on the back of the house, overlooking the garden. The curtains were pulled wide on the kitchen windows, the door to the garden propped open to let in any breath of air.

Nadine stood in the kitchen, illuminated as if she were on a screen, still wearing the poppy-splashed dress. She held a full glass of wine in her hand, and slowly she began to dance, twirling and swaying as Sinatra sang. Her voice, sweet and clear, drifted out to them as she joined in on the chorus.

"Fuck me," said Shaun. "If it isn't our bloody French mis-

tress. I thought she looked familiar." He elbowed Joe in the ribs. "Are my eyes deceiving me, mate?"

"It's her." Joe sounded a little uneasy. "But look, man, we should go. I don't want to get in any tr—"

"French mistress?" Andy hissed. "What the hell are you talking about?"

"She's the upper-form French teacher at our school." Shaun was almost crowing. "She started last term. Mrs. Drake, the merry widow. We haven't had her class yet, but we've heard about her. She's hot, hot, hot—much too hot to be an old bag of a teacher." He stepped through the gap in the fence into Nadine's garden, and they followed as if tethered.

"No, you're lying," said Andy. He felt very strange. The joint had gone out and he smelled burning paper.

"We heard she was giving French lessons to morons over the summer." Shaun put his arm round Andy's shoulders and gave him a squeeze. "What's she been up to with you, eh, Andrew? Tutoring you in the finer French arts?"

"Bugger off." Andy squirmed out of his grasp and shoved at him. "Don't talk about her that way. And shut up. She'll hear you."

"Yeah, lay off, Shaun," said Joe, coming unexpectedly to Andy's defense. "She's nice. She spoke to me once, in the hall."

"Ooh, lucky you." Shaun's voice was suddenly vicious as he turned to Joe. "Fancy the French teacher, do you, Joe?"

The music stopped. They all looked back to the windows, and Andy realized he was holding his breath. Nadine disappeared from view for a moment; then, as she came back into the kitchen, the record began again.

"She likes that old crap, doesn't she?" said Shaun. "I wonder why."

Andy suddenly knew, without being quite sure how. The song reminded her of Marshall, her dead husband. She was dancing for him.

They watched, mesmerized, as she moved from the kitchen into the bathroom, becoming an indistinct silhouette behind the frosted glass of the bathroom window. She bent, and they heard the splash and gurgle in the garden pipe as she turned on the taps in the bath. Then she reappeared in the murky glass, a dark shape, and lifted her arms in a fluid movement.

"She's taken off her dress," breathed Joe.

"Well, go on, then." Shaun took the cider bottle from Joe and gave him a shove. "You want to see bathing beauty? The door's open. Just walk in and have a peek. If she sees you, you can say you were visiting Andy here and you just came in for a glass of water."

"You're crazy." Joe's voice was high. "No way I'm doing that."

"You leave her alone," said Andy, but he had trouble forming the words. His limbs felt heavy, unresponsive.

Shaun turned on him, the glint of malice in his eyes visible even in the dimness. "And you shut up. This is none of your business now." He put his hand on Joe's shoulder and squeezed until Joe grimaced with pain. "I want to see you go in."

"Shaun, please, I don't want to."

Stepping back, Shaun studied him as if he were a specimen on a lab table. "I said, I want to see you go in. If you don't, I'll tell everyone at school what your dad does to you."

"No! You promised." Joe was crying now. "You can't—"

"Leave him the fuck alone," Andy tried to shout, but his words came out in a croak. The effects of the pot seemed to be getting stronger now.

"You going to make me?" With his free hand, Shaun grabbed the front of Andy's T-shirt and swung him hard into the fence. The back of Andy's head hit the boards with a smack and his knees buckled.

He must have blacked out for a moment, because the next

thing he saw was Joe, moving as stiffly as a man going to his execution, walking in Nadine's open door. The music had stopped.

Then there was a scream, and the shattering of glass.

It was dark by the time Melody reached Putney. She pulled up and sat for a moment, watching the green-gold light spilling through the glass panes in Doug's front door. The colors made her think of the way she'd imagined Lothlórien, the enchanted wood in Tolkien's novels. Not that she'd tell Doug that. Not at the moment, anyway.

What *was* she going to say?

She'd talked to Gemma as they'd ridden from Whitechapel back to Brixton on the tube, telling her about her interview with Nick at the Seven Stars. "It wasn't just an omission, what Andy told me about the bloke he hit in the pub," she'd finished miserably. "It was an outright lie. He knew him."

"That doesn't mean it has any connection with these murders," Gemma had said. "We've ruled Andy out, and partly on your own evidence. I've a copy of Rashid's report right here"—she'd tapped her bag—"and he's quite definite about the time of Shaun Francis's death. Not only were you with Andy at the Twelve Bar, there were dozens of other witnesses."

"Yes, but—he's involved in all this somehow, and I—I think I've made a huge fool of myself." She'd shaken her head as Gemma started to speak. "It's not just hurt pride. I'm worried about him. I think something is terribly wrong, and I can't talk to him about it."

"No," Gemma had said firmly. "You can't. You've already gone over the line interviewing Nick. I don't want you speaking to anyone else who has a personal connection with Andy Monahan until we've got this sorted out."

It was a mild enough bollocking, but Melody had known

she'd better pay attention. And that she needed help. Now, taking a deep breath, she got out of the car.

The light from the television flickered through a chink in the sitting room curtains, but when she rang the bell there was no response. After a second ring, she rapped on the glass, then, bending down, she pushed open the letter flap and said into it, "I know you're there, Doug. Answer the damned door."

After a moment, she heard the regular thump of Doug's boot cast striking the floor, and the door swung open.

She looked up at his scowl. "Not only do you sound like Frankenstein's monster, your expression would do him proud. Are you going to let me in?"

"I'm busy."

Melody rolled her eyes. "I can see that. Come on, Doug. Don't pout."

"Me, pout? Whatever gave you that impression? Could it be the fact that I'm laid up here with a broken ankle and you haven't even rung since Sunday?"

"Please. Can I come in? It's freezing out here."

He shuffled back enough to let her in, then led the way to the sitting room, but his scowl was still in place. He'd obviously been settled in the sitting room armchair with his foot propped on the ottoman. The telly was on but muted, and his laptop sat open on the side table.

When Doug had bought the house, the original fireplaces in the sitting and dining rooms had been boarded up. She'd helped him find good-quality gas fires, and similar antique mirrors to hang over both mantels. Tonight the sitting room fire was lit, and the flames sparked off the crystals of the refurbished chandelier she'd helped Doug choose at an auction house in Chelsea.

But spilled paint still stained the carpet. He'd been counting on her, and she was being a bitch. She owed him an apology.

"I am sorry, Doug," she said as he eased back into his chair and lifted his foot to the ottoman. "Really. It was inexcusable, deserting you like that. How are you?"

He sniffed. "The doctors said I did too much the first couple of days. The swelling's up, and I've got to give the ankle a complete rest."

Melody refrained from saying that perhaps he shouldn't have gone chasing round the East End with Duncan. "Do you mind if I sit?"

Grudgingly, Doug nodded towards the sofa.

"Thanks." She sat on its edge, still wearing her coat even though the room was toasty. "I was going to come on Sunday. But I went to do an interview on Sunday evening, and it ended up being . . . late. Then, on Monday morning we found out there'd been a second murder—I'm sure Duncan must have told you—and things just went to hell in a handbasket after that." She swallowed. "The thing is, I screwed up. That interview—I provided the alibi for a person involved in the investigation."

"That guitarist."

"His name is Andy Monahan, as you know perfectly well," she said, exasperation momentarily getting the better of her, "since you went with Duncan to talk to his manager on Monday."

"I was bored." Doug gave her a challenging glare. "And anyway, if you were his alibi for the second murder, and Tam was his alibi for the first, what's the problem?"

Melody rubbed her hands together, a nervous gesture she thought she'd learned to control in boarding school. "I found out that he knew the second victim, Shaun Francis, although he said he hadn't seen him in years. So, that's weird, but maybe just coincidence. Francis lived in Dulwich then, not far from Crystal Palace, where Andy grew up. Andy said he met him in Crystal Palace Park one summer, and Shaun Francis's sister confirmed that. She also said that there was some sort of trouble at Shaun's school that autumn, but she doesn't know that the two things were connected."

"Have you talked to the school?"

"Gemma's made an appointment to see the headmaster in the morning."

"So your guitar bloke—Andy," Doug conceded, "had a connection with Crystal Palace besides the fact that the band was booked to play in the pub there?"

"Yes. But he didn't know Arnott. And we haven't been able to find a direct connection between Arnott and Francis, although there must be one. I don't for one minute believe we've got some deranged killer randomly targeting lawyers."

"Your father would run with that." Doug still couldn't resist the occasional dig about her dad.

"Then we have to hope he doesn't find out. So far we've managed to keep the details of Francis's death from the press, but they're bound to leak at some point."

"Sooner rather than later. Which will mean hell for your team. And you."

Clasping her hands together to keep them still, Melody met Doug's eyes. "It's worse than that. Today I found out Andy lied to me about something. And I had to tell Gemma."

Doug simply waited. Melody thought his interview technique was improving considerably.

"Before Vincent Arnott shouted at Andy in the pub on Friday night, Andy had a row with a punter. Or at least that's what he said—that the guy was drunk and was harassing him about the band's music. He said the guy tried to touch his guitar and he lost his temper and punched him. His hand was bruised—that was one of the reasons he rode home with Tam."

"What do you mean, 'At least that's what he said'?"

"I talked to the band's bass player today. He was standing right behind Andy when it happened. He said that Andy knew the guy, and that whatever they were arguing about, it was definitely personal."

"Okay." Doug shrugged. "So Andy lied to you. What's the big deal? Maybe he was shagging the guy's girlfriend."

That made Melody wonder how much Doug had guessed, or if he was just trying to get a rise out of her. "The big deal is that if he lied about that, he could have lied about anything."

"But you're absolutely sure he couldn't have killed Shaun Francis?"

"Absolutely," she said, hoping he didn't ask her for a minute-by-minute accounting of Andy's alibi. "But— What if Tam lied about Friday night? He has a lot at stake, maybe enough to make him protect Andy . . ." She came to a halt, staring down at her hands.

"What makes you think that? You're making a big jump there, from saying maybe Andy lied to suggesting that Tam lied, too. Duncan trusts Tam. There's something else, isn't there?"

Her mouth felt dry. She wished Doug had offered her a cup of tea. "In the hotel room where Arnott was killed, there was a spot of blood on the sheet that didn't belong to him. And Andy—I didn't think anything of it until today . . . but on Monday, when I went back to talk to Andy about Shaun Francis, I noticed he had a healing cut on his hand . . ."

"Well, if he hit somebody—"

"His other hand."

Doug stared at her. "Did you tell Gemma?"

"No. I just . . . I was . . ." Melody fell silent.

Leaning forward, Doug adjusted his ankle on the ottoman. The firelight flashed off the lenses of his glasses and she couldn't read his expression. When he'd settled himself again, he said, "So. Why are you telling me?"

"Because I want you to help me get to the truth."

"Why should I?"

"Because you're my best friend. And because you are the best person I know at finding things."

"Flattery will get you—"

"Everywhere," she finished for him, and got a reluctant grin. "I can't exactly do footwork."

"You don't need feet." Melody nodded at his computer. "You can log into the case file on HOLMES from here. And—" She frowned, thinking. "What about court records? Could you access Arnott's cases? That seems the most logical place to start."

"You don't want much, do you? And what do I get in return?"

Melody tried to disguise her sigh of relief. "How about beer and pizza, for a start?

Andy pushed himself up and staggered across the garden towards Nadine's door, but the ground seemed to heave beneath him and his feet felt as if they were mired in treacle.

Before he reached the steps, he saw Joe backing out of the kitchen, babbling, "I'm sorry, I'm sorry. I didn't mean to startle you. I was at Andy's next door and he said—he said I could—I didn't know—"

Andy saw Nadine then, behind Joe. She was clutching a pale blue silk dressing gown together at her neck. Her feet were bare, her hair disheveled, and the hem and skirt of the dressing gown were stained with ugly deep red splotches.

"Get out," she said to Joe. There was no slurring to her voice now. "Get out, or I'll call the police."

"I'm sorry," Joe said again, backing down the steps. "I didn't—"

She saw Andy. "You."

He glanced round, not believing that the cold and unfamiliar voice could be directed at him. But Shaun had disappeared through the gap in the fence.

"No, I didn't tell him—"

"You, Andy? You put this—this little creep, up to this?" She was shaking now, her voice rising in rage and shock. Joe stumbled away, and then he, too, had crossed the garden and slipped through the fence.

"How could you? How could you?" Nadine's eyes never left Andy, and when she spoke again, he wished she had kept shouting. "You, Andy. Of all people. I thought you were my friend."

Turning away, she slammed her door, and an instant later the kitchen lights went out.

Andy stood alone in the dark.

CHAPTER NINETEEN

The immensity of the crowd destroyed the possibility of evacuating the area around the tower. Anerley Hill, where the tower was most likely to fall, was one solid, seething mass of people. Mounted and foot police struggled to force the crowd back. Even the fire engines were hemmed in. [. . .]

—www.sarahjyoung.com

Gemma couldn't remember ever feeling so uncomfortable with Melody. They'd taken Gemma's Escort for their appointment with the headmaster of Norwood College in Dulwich, Gemma hoping that the time in the car would give them an opportunity to reconnect after yesterday afternoon's discussion. So far, however, Melody had been uncharacteristically silent.

It had been late the previous evening before Gemma had had a chance to fill Kincaid in on the case developments, including Melody's revelation about her interview with Nick the bassist.

"That's a bugger," Kincaid had said as they finished the last of the washing up in the kitchen. "Tam rang me this morning, after you talked to Andy. Apparently you put the poor bloke in a panic. What did you do, use thumbscrews?"

"Very funny," she'd said. "I thought I was exceedingly gentle."

"Tam said he was even threatening to back out of playing with the girl, Poppy."

"That's odd. He seemed more annoyed than panicked, but the last thing I asked him about was Caleb Hart. Interesting."

"I must say you got on better with Hart's secretary than I did." He'd flicked the tea towel at her.

"It was my overwhelming charm."

"Evidently. She wasn't susceptible to my pretty face."

She'd glanced at him to see if he was really bothered, but he was concentrating on his drying. He'd been in an odd mood all evening, joking and teasing the children more than usual, and she'd had the feeling that he was avoiding her, although she couldn't imagine why. "Tam wanted me to talk to Andy, see if I could find out what's put the wind up him," he went on. "I said I couldn't agree without speaking to you first."

Gemma thought about it before replying. "Well, I obviously am not going to get anything out of him, and I can't let Melody talk to him. Maybe you'll have better luck. Although I still can't see where it will get us. Maybe the punch-up in the pub was a row over a girlfriend—not the sort of thing he'd have wanted to tell Melody if he was trying to impress her."

"Tomorrow, then, I'll see if I can set something up. But I'll need to make arrangements for Charlotte. I'll just give Betty a ring, shall I?"

Gemma had worried over the conversation the rest of the evening, finally deciding not to share Tam's concern over Andy with Melody. She would wait and see what Duncan learned, and in the meantime, she would move Caleb Hart further up her action list.

Now, as they came into Dulwich, she glanced at the car clock. "We've plenty of time before our appointment. I want to make a stop first."

The address of the community center Caleb Hart's assistant had given her was on the eastern side of the suburb, and from the outside, at least, the long, low, sixties-style building was not prepossessing.

"The AA meeting?" asked Melody.

Gemma nodded as she looked for a parking spot. "Damn. Busy place."

"Why don't you circle and I'll go in," Melody suggested.

"Okay. There's a spot where I can pull over on the double yellows if I stay with the car."

As Gemma eased the Escort into a gap not quite big enough for it, Melody hopped out and walked briskly into the building.

Leaving the engine running, Gemma sat rubbing her cold hands and watching as the center's patrons came and went, mostly women wearing exercise gear under their coats. Didn't any of these women work? she wondered, trying to imagine a lifestyle that allowed morning Pilates classes. A few elderly women arrived together, perhaps for bridge or bingo—or power aerobics, for all Gemma knew.

She was glancing at the clock and beginning to worry about their appointment at the school by the time Melody came out.

"Busy indeed," said Melody as she climbed back in the car, bringing with her a blast of frigid air. "Pilates, yoga, meditation. Oh, and a stained-glass-making class. And that's all before the afternoon activities start for older kids."

"And?" Gemma pulled into the flow of traffic, but she'd seen Melody's triumphant grin.

"AA meetings, several times a week, including Friday nights at ten."

"Damn," Gemma muttered. "Hart's story holds up, then."

"Not necessarily. It just so happens that the very helpful activities director attends the group. When I explained that we were verifying Mr. Hart's statement in the course of an investigation, she said that he did arrive at ten on Friday night. But that, unusually for him, he forgot to turn off his phone. He got a call not long after the meeting began, and left hurriedly."

"He didn't say why?"

"No. Just apologized and excused himself. She said it was before half past the hour."

"Ah. So if we know Arnott was alive around eleven, when he checked into the Belvedere, then Hart doesn't have an alibi for the time of Arnott's death." Had Andy Monahan known that Hart had no alibi for Friday night? Gemma wondered. But, as far as they knew, Andy had not even met Hart until Saturday. It seemed that everything they learned complicated things even further.

Their route took them back into West Dulwich, and up the leafy hill between West Norwood Cemetery and Norwood Park. The school itself, so appropriately named, bordered on Norwood Park itself, and was, Gemma realized, just on the edge of Crystal Palace.

This time it was easy to find a parking space in the clearly marked visitors' area. Gemma looked at the complex of warm-colored brick buildings backed by manicured playing fields, and thought what a far cry the place was from the schools she'd gone to growing up in Leyton.

A few boys wearing blazers and carrying satchels scurried between buildings. She could easily imagine Kit in a place like this, with his poise and elegant looks. He had spent the first part of his childhood as the son of Cambridge dons, in an environment where learning and privilege went hand in hand.

But Toby? The thought made her sigh. Her son would racket around like a ball in a pinball machine. And Charlotte? Where did Charlotte fit?

"Boss?" said Melody. They'd reached the doors to the administration building.

"Sorry. Woolgathering. Did you go to a school like this, Melody?"

"Much more posh, I'm afraid. Although on the students' end, that meant turn-of-the-last-century dormitories with mildewed shared baths and a distinct lack of central heating. One pays for the status, not the luxury of the accommodations. I'd take this place in a heartbeat."

"Would you send your own children to boarding school?"

"That's a bit hypothetical at the moment." Melody gave her a quick glance as she held open the door. "But I honestly don't know. Ten years ago I'd have said no way. Now, I'm not so sure. The life does breed a certain self-reliance. And many girls—and boys—do form lifetime bonds. Unfortunately, I wasn't one of them."

"I wonder," said Gemma, "if Shaun Francis was?"

"May I help you?" asked a comfortably motherly woman at the reception desk.

Gemma produced her identification and explained that they had an appointment with the headmaster.

"Oh, yes." The woman smiled, apparently unfazed by a visit from Met CID. "He's with a pupil at the moment, but I'll let him know you're here."

While she spoke quietly into an intercom, Gemma looked round the reception area. The building had obviously undergone some architectural renovation, and glass panels in the ceiling gave the space a light and airy feel.

The door to the headmaster's office opened and a boy about Kit's age came out. He was mixed race and, like the receptionist, gave Gemma and Melody an easy, friendly smile. Considering what Gemma had learned about Shaun Francis, it seemed he would have been the odd one out in this place.

"The headmaster will see you now." The receptionist nodded towards the open door.

"Ooh, called on the carpet," Melody whispered in Gemma's ear, and then they were inside and the man at the desk was rising to greet them.

"I'm Wayne Carstairs." He held out a hand to Gemma. "Inspector James? And—"

"Detective Sergeant Talbot," said Melody as he shook her hand in turn.

Gemma realized she'd been expecting a tweedy-elbowed academic. But Wayne Carstairs, a fair, broad-shouldered man in his late forties or early fifties, looked more like a rugby player than a headmaster, and his accent was closer to her own than it was to Melody's.

He gestured them into chairs, then took his own. "I understand you're here about a former student, Shaun Francis." He tapped a file on his desk. "I've pulled his records for you."

"Thank you for seeing us, Mr. Carstairs," said Gemma. "As I said over the phone, Shaun Francis has died in unexplained circumstances."

"I was sorry to hear that." Carstairs did not sound particularly sorry. "I've seen the papers. I would certainly call murder 'unfortunate.' But I'm not sure how his old school records can help you. It's been more than a decade since he left Norwood."

"Did you know Shaun Francis, Mr. Carstairs?"

"I remember him, yes," Carstairs said, with apparent reluctance.

"Sometimes, when there's no obvious motive in the present, it helps us to look at the victim's history. And his sister mentioned a particular incident, something that happened when Shaun was in perhaps year seven. Do you recall it? It was the beginning of the autumn term, and involved another student here."

"Ah. Well." Carstairs frowned. "You won't find anything in his academic records about that. I wasn't headmaster then, you understand. I was the physics master, and had been here only two years."

"But you do remember the incident," Gemma prompted when he didn't go on.

272 ～ DEBORAH CROMBIE

Carstairs shuffled some papers on his desktop, obviously debating, then said with a slight sigh, "You have to understand that Norwood College was not then what it is now. We were known, not for our academic excellence, but as the school for boys who weren't quite gifted or diligent enough to get into the other college, but whose parents had money and social ambitions."

Gemma assumed he meant Dulwich College, the school's illustrious neighbor. "What you mean is that you got some bad apples, and I'd assume that Shaun Francis was one of them."

"I taught him. And I would say 'bad apple' was a considerable understatement. Shaun Francis was as nasty a piece of work as I've seen in all my years of teaching. No apologies for speaking ill of the dead. But in this case, he wasn't responsible for what happened—at least not directly."

Gemma waited.

"There was another new teacher who had joined the staff the previous term, taking over the upper school French classes for a teacher who had retired suddenly," Carstairs continued after a moment. "Her name was Nadine Drake and she was a young widow." His expression had softened as he said her name.

"A young female teacher in a boys' school?" Melody looked askance.

"Not the best idea," admitted Carstairs. "Nadine Drake was not only young but very attractive. But she had a certain . . . reserve about her. She kept discipline in her classes, and she didn't encourage familiarity with the students. Nor did she make friends with other members of staff, which I think may have been to her detriment in the end." He paused, then went on with a grimace of distaste. "Not long after term started, whispers began going round the school that Mrs. Drake had had . . . inappropriate . . . relations with one of the boys. When the story reached the head, he questioned the boy, who said that over summer hols, Mrs.

Drake had invited him into her home, where she had undressed in front of him and asked him to touch her. This, of course, set him up admirably with the other lads."

"Did you believe it?" asked Gemma.

"Not for a moment. I thought the entire story was preposterous, and that the rumor had been started by Shaun Francis."

"Why would Shaun have done something like that?"

"Because he was the sort of boy who held grudges. I can only assume he'd taken against Mrs. Drake for some reason, and that what happened to his friend was collateral damage."

"What happened to his friend?" repeated Melody, sounding puzzled. "Was he sent down?"

"Oh, no, but it might have gone better for him if he had been. It was Mrs. Drake who paid the price."

After the night in the garden, it took Andy two days to get up the courage to ring Nadine's bell. He'd been too ashamed to face her, and yet he knew he couldn't go on without telling her that he was sorry, that none of what had happened had been his idea, whether she believed him or not.

He rang and rang again. But there was no answer, that day or the next or the next, although her car was parked in front of the flat.

He watched, then, hoping to see her coming or going, and rang her bell at regular intervals, but there was no sound or movement in the flat. She didn't leave or return on her usual schedule—had Shaun and Joe been telling the truth about the French lessons? And did she really teach at their school? Why had she never told him what she did? He didn't know what to think, except that he had lost the only real friend he had ever known.

If she went out at all, it must have been during the times he walked his mum to and from work. His worry for Nadine grew until he felt ill with it, but there was no one he could talk to or ask for help.

Nor did he see Joe or Shaun. They seemed to have disappeared as mysteriously as they had appeared that hot day in the park, and he didn't know their last names or where they lived. What he would have done if he'd found them he didn't know, only that he wanted to hurt them, to somehow make them pay.

But in the end he knew that what had happened had been his fault. Nadine had been unhappy and he'd been too selfish to see it. And instead of helping her, he had betrayed her.

And then the school term began, and with it the weather broke with a vengeance. The rain came down as if it would wash away the sins of the world, but nothing could erase the stain of Andy's guilt.

Nadine's car disappeared. He wondered if she had gone to stay with someone else—perhaps her parents? But he knew only that she'd grown up in Hampstead, and nothing else about her family. He'd never asked.

Then, a few weeks before Christmas, he came home from school to find a to let sign next door. The flat was empty, Nadine was gone, and nothing in his life would ever be the same.

The nursery school interview turned out to be not nearly as intimidating as Kincaid had expected.

MacKenzie had met him and Charlotte, as promised, in front of the white Victorian villa near Pembridge Gardens. The only thing identifying the building as a school was a small brass plaque beside the blue door. When MacKenzie rang the buzzer, they were admitted immediately.

Charlotte, having been told she could visit Oliver's class, went willingly with MacKenzie while Kincaid was ushered into the head's office. "I'm Jane," the woman said, gesturing him to a seat. Middle aged and pleasantly attractive, she wore silver-framed glasses and a long, colorful skirt that looked as if it might have come from one of the stalls in Portobello Road.

He'd expected a long list of questions about Charlotte's background and emotional issues, her level of academic progress, even the state of her toilet training. Instead, Jane scanned a few notes on her desk, then looked up and smiled. "I understand your little girl has had some difficulties. Well, we'll see what we can do for her."

He stared at her for a moment, not certain he'd heard correctly. "You mean— You can take her?"

"It so happens that one of our families is making an unexpected move to New York for business reasons, so there will be an opening in Oliver's class. She could start, um"—she consulted her notes again—"next Monday, I believe, if that would suit you. Although we do provide wraparound care, I'd suggest we begin with mornings only for the first few weeks and see how she does."

Gobsmacked, Kincaid nodded. "Yes. Yes, thanks very much. But what about the—"

"The secretary will give you the admission form and the information on uniforms and fees."

"You don't need to meet Charlotte?"

"I'm sure we'll get well acquainted soon enough, Mr. Kincaid. I like to participate in the children's routine as much as possible. If you think she might need a little help adjusting, you're welcome to sit in with her for a day or two. So I'll expect to see you on Monday as well?"

"Yes, of course. I'm certain I can arrange that." He stood and reached across the desk to pump her hand. "Thanks again," he said with what he felt was great inadequacy.

"Oh, there is one thing, Mr. Kincaid." Jane stopped him as he reached the door, for the first time sounding like his expectation of a headmistress. "Just so there is no misunderstanding. We are not a glamorous school—merely a good one. We don't put children on a waiting list before they are conceived. We don't do celebrity raffles. We don't care if you spent your holiday in Barbados, or if your child's godmother has an Oscar, or what kind of car you drive. In fact, we rather discourage that sort of thing." Her stern expression dissolved into a smile. "Although we do make an exception in MacKenzie's case."

"I'm very relieved to hear both," he'd replied, although he had no idea what she meant about MacKenzie.

He would tell Gemma the good news as soon as she got home, but first he needed to talk to Louise and make certain Charlotte's estate could handle the fees in the interim before the sale of the Fournier Street house was final.

Perhaps, he thought, considering his promise to Tam, he could kill two birds with one stone.

Having made arrangements the previous evening for Charlotte to spend the afternoon with their friend Betty Howard, Kincaid dropped her off and drove to Bethnal Green alone. Louise was resting when he arrived at her flat near Columbia Road, and when she ushered him into the sitting room, he thought she looked a bit better than she had on Saturday.

When he explained about the school, she laughed, and it occurred to him that that was a sound he'd seldom heard from her. "You are one for getting results," she said. "And yes, it should be fine. Actually, I think it's not unreasonable for a fee-paying school, especially in Notting Hill. And if Charlotte can adjust to the wraparound care, that will cost you considerably less than paying a nanny for half days. Although," she added, with a return of her usual acerbity, "it sounds to me as if the place is being elitist by not being elitist."

"How are you feeling?" he asked.

"As well as can be expected. And that, I take it, is a good thing. But I'm pleased for you. It looks as if one of us may be returning to work soon, at least."

She offered coffee but he declined, saying he needed to have a word with Tam, and that he didn't want to tire her. Both true enough, and saved him from confessing that the flat was hothouse temperature and he hadn't the stamina for her coffee.

Next door, he found Michael out with the dogs, and Tam pacing. "He said he'd come, though I had to bloody threaten him. He's always been such a reliable lad, Andy. That's one of the reasons I convinced Caleb to give him a try. And now he's acting like some prima donna. I can't think what's got into him. I havenae told Caleb he's saying he's not sure he wants to record with wee Poppy."

Before Kincaid could reply, there was a light tap on the door. Kincaid opened it to find Andy Monahan, scowling at him. "Tam said you wanted to talk to me."

"If you don't mind," Kincaid said easily. He thought that Andy looked exhausted, the shadows under his eyes dark as bruises. "Do you want to come in?"

Andy threw a glower at Tam. "If it's all the same to you, I'd rather sit outside. Just us."

The day was gray and damp with a chill wind, but Kincaid wasn't inclined to argue. With a quelling shake of his head at Tam, he stepped outside. The chairs were placed on either side of the small balcony, one in front of Tam and Michael's flat and one in front of Louise's. He sensed that arranging them into a conversational grouping would convey an unwanted formality, so he led the way through the gate at the top of the stairs and sat down on the top step.

With obvious reluctance, Andy sat beside him, huddled in the depths of his peacoat. It was Andy, however, who spoke first. "I had no idea Charlotte's mum was a copper. What are the two of you doing, tag-teaming?"

"I'm here strictly because Tam asked me to speak to you. He's worried about you. But you know that if you tell me anything that is relevant to these cases, I'll have to pass it along to Gemma."

"No secrets of the confessional, then?" Andy asked, mocking.

"It looks to me as if you could use some help. I'd guess you haven't slept—or eaten—in a couple of days."

Andy rubbed at the now-fading bruises on the knuckles of his right hand. "Not much of either since Monday. Not since I heard"—he glanced at Kincaid, then looked away—"I guess you know about Melody."

"I know that Melody interviewed you on Sunday night, and that she was with you during the time that someone drugged Shaun Francis at his local pub, took him home, stripped him, tied him up, and strangled him."

"Oh, God." Andy looked as if he might be sick.

"I also know that yesterday Melody spoke to Nick, your bass player, and that she knows you lied to her about the fight in the pub." Kincaid nodded at Andy's knuckles. "Want to start with that?"

Andy gave a choked laugh. "There's no way to start with that." He shoved his hands in the pockets of his coat. For a moment he gazed down into the quiet street and then his shoulders sagged. "I'm tired. I'm tired of keeping secrets. What happened on Friday night was the end, not the beginning. It started on a hot August day when I was thirteen years old."

When Andy had finished his story, Kincaid sat, appalled. He thought of Kit, who had endured much in his young life, but had had someone to turn to, someone to care for him. After a moment, he said quietly, "You never spoke to your mother about any of this?"

Andy shook his head. "She had burdens enough."

"What happened to her?"

"She died when I was sixteen. Her liver gave out, they said, but I always thought she just couldn't find a reason to go on."

"What did you do?"

"The nuns at my school found me a place to stay until I finished my year. I was playing gigs by then. Some of the old-time musicians in Crystal Palace got me jobs, gave me sofas to doss on. Then I met Nick and George in a club, and we put together our band. They both lived at home and their parents let me stay when I needed a place. Then I met Tam and he started getting me enough session work to get by. Eventually I got the flat in Hanway Place." He sighed. "I owe Nick and George. And I owe Tam. I never thought I'd have to choose between the two."

"And the boys, Shaun and Joe? You never saw them again?"

"Not until Friday night. But I didn't lie to Melody. It wasn't Shaun. It was *Joe*. I didn't recognize him at first, when he came up to me in the White Stag. I really thought he was just some drunk punter, until he asked me if I remembered old times. He wanted"—Andy's voice was tight—"he wanted to know why we couldn't be friends."

"So you hit him."

"I lost it. I just lost it. But it didn't make me feel any better." He took his hands from his pockets and rubbed at his knuckles again. "Not worth risking my picking hand. But Shaun, Jesus. I always thought nothing was too bad for him, but— When Melody told me Shaun was dead, like that other guy, I thought I'd gone completely round the bend. I never knew their last names, Shaun or Joe. But I knew it had to be him, and when she showed me the photo, I was certain." Glancing at Kincaid, he added, "You know I don't blame Melody for going to her guv'nor. Your Gemma." He frowned, as if he still hadn't quite managed to get his head round that. "But I can't very well ring her up and say, 'Oh, sorry.'"

"Better if you don't just now," Kincaid agreed. "What about Nadine? You never saw her again, either?"

Andy pulled his coat tighter and shivered. "You'll think I really am bonkers. Not until Friday night, although I swear I looked for her everywhere I went for years. And that night— maybe it was because I'd seen Joe and that brought it all back— but I thought I caught a glimpse of her, in the back of the room at the White Stag. It was during the second set. Then the crowd shifted and she was gone. I thought I'd imagined it . . ."

Kincaid caught the hesitation. "Until—"

"Until Sunday night. When I was with Melody in the Twelve Bar. She looked different, of course, and it was just an instant as she turned back from the stairs. But it was Nadine."

CHAPTER TWENTY

The two high water towers that had been erected were still standing but soon after they were dismantled.

—Betty Carew, www.helium.com

"What happened to Mrs. Drake?" Gemma asked Wayne Carstairs, resisting the urge to fan herself. It was warm in the headmaster's office, and while he wore a long-sleeved navy polo shirt with the school crest embossed on the breast, she and Melody were still in their coats.

"The head dismissed her without references." Carstairs leaned back in his chair and shook his head. "It was cruel. Not only would such an action have kept her from getting a job at another public school, but it would have ruined her prospects at even the lowliest comprehensive."

"You didn't approve?"

"I did not. But Joe Peterson's father, Gary, was on the school's board of governors and he liked to wield his power."

"Joe Peterson? That was the name of the boy involved?"

Carstairs nodded. "A little sycophant, was Joe. Bullied by his father and by Shaun Francis—in fact, I always thought that was what cemented the rather unlikely relationship between the two boys. Joe was already comfortable in the role of toady."

Melody had been following the conversation with a frown. "Did Peterson go to the police?"

"Yes. But after they interviewed the boys and Mrs. Drake, and some of the other members of staff, the police declined to bring charges. I remember the detective was quite sharp, and I doubt he was any more taken in by the story than I was. But Peterson was livid. He hired some City barrister to file a civil suit against the poor woman, claiming she had caused his son 'emotional trauma.' Apparently, there had been some question into the nature of her husband's death, although no charges were brought, and I'm sure Peterson thought he could use that in a civil suit to blacken her character."

"What could he possibly have hoped to gain?" asked Gemma.

"Certainly nothing financially. I don't believe she had two pennies to rub together. But Peterson had money to burn, and like Shaun Francis, he was a man to hold a grudge. I remember seeing him chatting up Mrs. Drake at Games Day, the end of summer term. She looked so cornered that my wife went to her rescue. I always wondered if he had . . . approached her . . . and she had rebuffed him. He certainly didn't do his son any favors by pursuing the matter. Shaun Francis dropped Joe after the whole business, apparently considering him a social liability, and the rest of the school followed suit. Joe Peterson didn't last the rest of the year here. I don't know what happened to him after that."

"And Mrs. Drake?"

Carstairs's lips tightened. "I don't know. She was here teaching one day and gone the next. I—none of the staff—ever had the chance to tell her we were sorry to see her go."

"Did you ever hear the outcome of the civil suit?"

"No. Although I suspect if it had gone to Peterson's advantage he'd have bragged about it at a parents' evening."

A low rumble had begun outside Carstairs's office—the sound of many feet on hard floors and the rising crescendo of children's voices. The classrooms were letting out for lunch.

The headmaster glanced at the clock on his desk. "I'm afraid lunchroom duty calls."

"You've been very generous with your time, Mr. Carstairs," said Gemma with a smile. "One more thing. The barrister Mr. Peterson hired—do you happen to remember his name?"

Standing, Carstairs took a tweedy jacket befitting a more traditional headmaster from a peg behind his desk. "Let's see . . . He was a striking man with prematurely white hair, as I recall. He deposed all the staff, and I'm afraid he found us a bit uncooperative. In fact, the English master composed a rather rude limerick about him that made the rounds of the staff room." Carstairs smiled, murmuring something under his breath that Gemma didn't quite catch, then said, "His name was Arnott, the lawyer. I'll leave the content of that literary masterpiece to your imaginations."

"So there *was* a connection between Shaun Francis and Arnott," said Melody as she and Gemma left the school building and headed for the car. The clouds had come down, obscuring the great Crystal Palace radio transmitters, and a cold drop of moisture touched her cheek like a kiss. "But a bit tenuous, as well as years ago, and we still have no idea what any of that has to do with Andy. Or if it has anything to do with him at all." Glancing at Gemma, she added, "*Someone* needs to speak to him again."

Melody expected to be chastised, but instead, Gemma looked up from reaching in her bag for the car keys, her expression surprisingly sheepish. "Duncan was going to have a word."

"What?"

"Tam rang him last night in a state. He said Andy was threatening to pull out of this big recording deal and wanted Duncan to talk to him."

"So you've put him off-limits to me but agreed that Duncan could question him?" Melody realized how absurd that sounded as soon as the words left her mouth. "No, don't tell me," she said as she slipped into the car beside Gemma. "Duncan didn't sleep with him."

Gemma's lips quirked in a smile. "Well, I hope not. But you're right—I have gone outside channels when I've told you not to do exactly that. But Duncan and Andy seem to have a rapport, and it certainly wasn't there for me. I thought it couldn't hurt for Duncan to give it a try."

"I'm worried about him," admitted Melody. "I know it's stupid and we hardly know each other, not really, but . . ."

"I thought . . ." Gemma hesitated, then went on, "When I talked to him yesterday, I got the impression that the feeling was mutual. And he's— Well, I don't think you're stupid at all."

"Thanks. I feel ever so much better," Melody quipped, but in truth she found that she did. But she was no less worried. "But you haven't heard anything from Dun—" Her phone, silenced for the interview with Mr. Carstairs, vibrated in her pocket.

When she saw it was Doug, she gave Gemma an apologetic shrug and answered.

"I've got something for you," said Doug without preamble. "It's taken me all day, but I've accessed Vincent Arnott's criminal case records, and I came across a familiar name. Ten years ago, Arnott was the prosecutor in a drugs charge against Caleb Hart, your record producer."

"Hart?" repeated Melody. "But he said he didn't know Arnott."

"Well, obviously, he lied. Hart and a young girl singer, his protégé, were found in possession of cocaine and heroin in a drugs bust. Hart had a good lawyer and the bust itself was a bit questionable, so he got off lightly."

"And the girl?"

"A probationary sentence. But I did some research. The case made good fodder for the media—drugs and rock and roll at the very least—and Arnott was apparently vicious as a prosecutor. He smeared the girl's reputation. Apparently she either couldn't handle the drugs or the adverse press. She committed suicide ten months after the trial. Hart then got very publicly sober and has remained so since."

"Bastard," said Melody.

Gemma, watching her intently, mouthed, "What?"

"Did you happen to get a home address?" Melody asked Doug, giving Gemma a slight headshake as she scrabbled in her bag for a pad and pen.

"It's North Dulwich. Crystal Palace, more or less." Doug read it out to her and she wrote it down.

"Thanks. You've been brilliant."

"But," said Doug, who knew her intonations too well.

"You could do something else, if you're not too busy."

"Ha-ha. Very funny. What do you need?"

"Arnott was involved in a civil case about fifteen years ago. The plaintiff was a Gary Peterson, the defendant, Nadine Drake. Can you see what you can dig up on either of them?"

"I live to serve." Doug disconnected.

Melody turned to Gemma. "Not only does Caleb Hart have a lousy alibi for Friday night, it seems he had a very good reason to hate Vincent Arnott."

"I'd like to talk to him without forewarning," said Gemma when Melody had relayed Doug's information. "We're not too far from his home address, although I don't know how likely it is we'd find him there this time of day. But he wasn't in his office when I called in midday yesterday, so I suppose it's possible."

Melody pulled up a map on her phone and examined it. On a hunch, she said, "We're practically a stone's throw from the recording studio. Why don't we try there first? And if he's not there, we could grab some lunch at the White Stag and have another word with Reg, the manager."

"It's worth a try." Gemma started the car and put it into gear, and within a very few minutes they'd reached Westow Street. "Now where?" she asked.

"This little lane." Melody pointed out a turning to the right.

"Bugger," muttered Gemma as they bumped down the incline of narrow, cobbled lane. "I'd hate to try this in icy weather. There's nothing here," she added, peering ahead.

"Take a sharp left at the bottom."

Gemma followed instructions, smiling when she saw the wall murals. She pulled the Escort in behind a new gleaming black Jaguar XF. "Does that look like a record-producer car to you? Maybe we're in luck."

They got out and Melody stood still for a moment, listening. No music drifted down from above. "The recording studio's on the second level, I think, below the rehearsal space." She let Gemma lead the way up the precarious open metal stairs. The memory of Saturday, and her first sight of Andy, was vivid in her mind. Had she been so blinded by instant infatuation that she hadn't done her job? They should have been onto Caleb Hart well before now.

They stopped on the first-floor landing, the wind whipping their hair and their coats. Melody opened the door and the draft almost pushed them into the tiny anteroom.

It was empty. They stood for a moment, catching their breaths. A high-pitched electronic squeal came from behind the closed door of the room beyond. Melody automatically smoothed her hair, then knocked perfunctorily before opening the door.

Caleb Hart sat at a mixing desk, wearing headphones. He looked up, his expression for a moment startled then he gave Melody the bland smile she remembered from Saturday and pulled the headphones off.

"Detective Sergeant Talbot, isn't it? I didn't hear you come in."

Gemma showed him her identification. "I'm Detective Inspector James, Mr. Hart. We'd like to talk to you about Vincent Arnott. I believe you've been less than honest with us."

Hart rolled his chair back from the console and regarded them with what seemed mild interest. "I don't believe I've talked to you about this . . . Arnott."

"You're being disingenuous," said Melody, drawing her eyes from what seemed an overwhelming array of levers and knobs and sparkling lights on the board. "When I spoke to you and Tam and Andy on Saturday, you didn't happen to mention that you knew him."

"You didn't ask me directly, if I recall. You were concerned about an incident in the pub. I wasn't there."

"Stop playing games, Mr. Hart." Gemma's tone made it clear she was losing patience. "We know that you not only knew Vincent Arnott, but that you had very good reason to dislike him, even to hate him. Perhaps even to want him dead."

Hart gazed at them, looking every inch the urbane producer with his neat beard and rimless glasses and his roll-neck sweater.

It was warm in the small room. The only window was interior, overlooking the recording booth. "Now," said Gemma, already beginning to sweat in her coat. "Let us tell you a little story. Melody, I think you have the details?"

Melody made a show of consulting her almost empty notepad. "Ten years ago, there was another promising young singer in your stable. She was arrested, along with you, on a possession of illegal substances charge. You got off quite lightly, and although the young woman received only a probationary sentence, the prosecuting attorney's treatment of her was bru-

288 ~ DEBORAH CROMBIE

tal. The press had a field day, and her reputation was torn to shreds. Later that year, she committed suicide. Was it a drug overdose, Mr. Hart?"

Hart had gone white as paper. His face seemed to float, disembodied, above the dark roll-neck of his sweater. "You don't know anything about it. And her name was Lauren."

"Did you hold Vincent Arnott responsible for what happened to Lauren, Mr. Hart?" asked Gemma.

"No. He was a bastard and he was unnecessarily vicious in his treatment of her. But the only person I held responsible for what happened to Lauren was myself. I got her involved with people who did drugs and alcohol as a matter of course. It's the business. You know what it's like."

"So getting sober was your atonement?" asked Melody.

"There's no way I can ever atone for what happened to Lauren. Getting sober was self-preservation. It was that or die."

Melody wondered if they were finally seeing the real Caleb Hart, or if it was just another layer of self-serving veneer. "And now you have another girl singer, Poppy. Just about Lauren's age, isn't she? Poised on the brink of success. And she's a vicar's daughter, isn't she? Does she know about Lauren? Do her parents? I doubt they'd think you suitable to manage their daughter's career if they did."

Bright spots of color appeared in Hart's cheeks. "Of course they bloody well know. Poppy's father, Tom, was my best friend at university. It was Tom and his family who helped me get sober. I owe them everything, and they know I'll look after Poppy like she was my own daughter.

"That's why I wanted to see Andy Monahan before I put them together. Tam assured me he wasn't into drink and drugs, but I can get a feel for someone when they play. I thought he was all right, and now he seems to be involved in a murder investigation." Hart's laugh was humorless. "I'd dump the whole project if they weren't so bloody good together. You only get one or two chances like this in the music business, if you're very lucky."

"So what you're telling us is that you had a very good reason not to want anything—or anyone—to screw this up," said Gemma. "Did Vincent Arnott threaten you in some way? You can't expect us to believe that, given your history with the man, you frequented the same pub on a regular basis and didn't recognize him."

"Yes, I recognized him," Hart admitted. "But I didn't see why I should get myself involved. I don't think he knew me from Adam, and I certainly never spoke to him."

"You didn't see him on Friday night?"

"I did see him at the pub, yes, but he was drinking alone at the bar. I didn't think it was relevant."

"You don't get to decide what is or isn't relevant when the police are investigating a murder, Mr. Hart," Gemma snapped. "Did you see him after you left the pub?"

"No. I went to my AA meeting. I always go on Friday night. It's a tough time for drinkers."

Gemma merely studied him for a moment, and he shifted uncomfortably. "I spoke to your very helpful personal assistant yesterday," she went on. "Roxy told me about your AA meeting. But we're very thorough, Mr. Hart. We've been to the community center this morning. Apparently, you got a phone call and left during the first half hour of the meeting, which means you could easily have gone back to Crystal Palace and killed Vincent Arnott."

Hart gaped at her. "You're not actually serious? I told you I hadn't spoken to Arnott in years. Why on earth would I have done something like that?"

"I thought you might tell us."

He shook his head. "That's absurd and you know it. You're simply fishing because you don't have anyone else in the frame and you're being pressured to come up with a suspect. I have had some experience with the police, as you've reminded me. I know how these things work."

"Then you won't mind telling us where you went when you left the AA meeting on Friday night."

"I can't. It's—" Hart hesitated. With a manicured fingernail, he pulled at the neck of his sweater as if it felt tight. "Look. If I tell you, you'll have to treat it as confidential. It has nothing to do with your investigation."

"You know I can't promise that. But if that's the truth, I'll do what I can."

Hart nodded. "I suppose that's the best I can hope for. You know that drug and alcohol abuse is rampant in the music business. When I got sober, I had a choice—either get out and give up the only thing I'd ever been any good at, or try to contribute something that would help other people who were struggling with the same demons. For a number of years, I've made myself available to anyone in crisis. That's what the phone call was on Friday night." He named a popular singer who had been much featured in the press, including Melody's father's paper, for her struggles with alcohol addiction. "She needed help. I met her at her flat, made coffee, talked her through the bad patch. I'm sure she'll confirm that if it's necessary, but in telling you I feel I've betrayed her trust. And I certainly don't want it getting out to the media."

It made sense, Melody thought. More sense than the scenario they'd constructed. Why would Hart kill Arnott after ten years, when he would have had easy access to the man on plenty of other occasions? And why kill him in that way, as revenge for a girl who committed suicide? Nor did Hart seem to have any connection with the second murder. "Did you know Shaun Francis, Mr. Hart?" she asked.

He shook his head again. "No. Was he the other lawyer that was killed? Tam told me there'd been another murder."

Apparently Tam had failed to mention Andy's connection with Shaun Francis.

Taking up Melody's lead, Gemma asked, "Where were you on Sunday night, Mr. Hart?"

"I was at home, tweaking the video, then uploading it to the Internet."

The activity would be logged. They could check it if they needed, and he would know that. They could check his story about Friday night as well, but Melody sensed they'd reached a dead end. His involvement seemed even less likely considering that his arrest meant his prints and DNA would be in the system, but there had been no flag on any of the physical evidence from either crime scene.

Apparently coming to the same conclusion, Gemma stood. "Mr. Hart, if we need to talk to you again, I would remind you not to be obstructive. You don't know how much damage you could do by withholding something that you think isn't relevant. You don't have all the pieces."

Gemma had turned to go when he said, frowning, "There was something . . . In the pub on Friday night. It was just before I left, and I'd forgotten. I told you Arnott was drinking at the bar. But there was a woman, alone as well, watching him. At first I thought she might be scoping him out as a prospect for a Friday night hook-up. But her expression . . . It was . . . I don't know. Cold. Made me glad she wasn't looking at me."

"Can you describe her?" Melody asked, feeling a flare of excitement. Could it have been the woman in the CCTV?

"Early to midforties, maybe." Hart shrugged. "It's hard to tell these days. Slender. Very chic. Chin-length dark hair. More striking than pretty, if you know what I mean. But there was . . ." He hesitated, frowning. "This may sound daft. But if you've been in a very dark place, it leaves a mark. You learn to recognize it in other people. And that's what I saw in her face."

CHAPTER TWENTY-ONE

Some of the original remains that can still be seen today are classed as Grade II* listed. They include terraces, sphinxes and the huge bust of Sir Joseph Paxton . . . Other fascinating features include sets of stairs, remains of the aquarium and the base of Isambard Kingdom Brunel's south water tower.

—www.bbc.co.uk

When Melody and Gemma came out of the recording studio, the afternoon had faded to an early twilight. West London, rolling away down the hill below them, was a soft violet beneath the lowering cloud.

A glance at Gemma's face as they got in the car told Melody that her partner felt as dispirited as she did.

"Dead in the water on that one, I think," said Melody.

"For Andy Monahan's sake, I hope so. If Caleb Hart was our murderer, that would be the end of Andy's recording deal. God, I hate winter," Gemma added, glancing up at the sky. "It's not even midafternoon and it's already dark. Not to mention we've missed lunch."

Melody's phone beeped with a text message. She read it, then translated for Gemma. "Doug says he has some new information, and that Duncan is on the way to his house. He wants us to come there, too."

After a moment's thought, Gemma said, "It's that or back to Brixton, and nothing new's come in from the station. I'd just as soon avoid telling the super we've got nowhere. Text Doug back and ask him if he has anything to eat around the place."

Melody did as she was asked. Then, as they traveled north in already heavy afternoon traffic, she tried to curb her impatience. Why had Doug texted rather than ringing her? And why did Duncan want to meet them there? Had he learned something from Andy? Her stomach churned, and she was suddenly glad it was empty.

By the time they reached Putney, the cloud that had hovered over Crystal Palace had descended upon the city, hugging the streets near the river like a great gray beast.

Kincaid's elderly Astra was parked in front of Doug's house, and the little light remaining in the sky was eclipsed by the green-gold beacon of Doug's front door.

By the time Melody and Gemma got out of the car, Kincaid had come out to greet them. He must have been watching for them, thought Melody, and her gut clenched with anxiety. When she reached him, she touched his arm to hold him back for a moment. "Is it Andy?" she said quietly. "Is he all—"

"He's fine." Kincaid gave her a reassuring pat on the shoulder. "Come in and we'll have a powwow."

Inside, Doug was propped in the sitting room armchair like royalty holding an audience, the fire was going, and the coffee table held platters of freshly made sandwiches and fruit.

"The kettle's on," Kincaid said. "I'll just fetch cups."

Melody nodded at the sandwiches. "Your doing?"

"Doug said you needed feeding, so I picked up a few things."

"You're getting to be quite handy to have around," Melody said, still not certain she could do the feast justice.

"Don't encourage him," Gemma put in. "He's already

put my pitiful attempts in the kitchen completely to shame." Picking up a sandwich triangle, she took a nibble and added, "Mmmm, roast beef and horseradish. I could eat the horse."

Doug already had an empty plate beside him and was tapping the arm of his chair impatiently. As Kincaid brought in a tray with mugs and a pot of tea, Doug said, "How did you get on with Caleb Hart?"

"No joy there, I don't think." Gemma's answer was slightly muffled by sandwich. "We found him at the studio in Crystal Palace," she added, swallowing and taking a cup of tea from Kincaid. "Although he admitted to recognizing Arnott in the pub, Poppy and her family know all about his trial and the aftermath. It was Poppy's father who helped him get sober. And we'll check them, of course, but he seems to have reasonable alibis for the times of both deaths."

"I think we'll have to do round-robin," said Kincaid, filling Melody's cup, then topping up Doug's and his own. "Gemma, what about your interview with the head at the boys' college?"

Gemma gave them a rather more concise version of Wayne Carstairs's story, then added, "Which gives us a connection between Vincent Arnott and Shaun Francis, but I still don't see what any of that has to do with Shaun meeting Andy in the park that summer. Are we chasing phantoms, here?"

"No, unfortunately, I don't think you are." Kincaid sat on the edge of the sofa, rotating his cup in his hands. "I spoke to Andy earlier this afternoon, at Tam's. Your Mrs. Drake was Andy Monahan's next-door neighbor.

"Andy was a latchkey kid. Worse than a latchkey kid, because his single mother was an alcoholic and he was her caretaker. He and Mrs. Drake—Nadine—became friends. It seems to have been the first time an adult had ever taken any interest in him or shown any concern for his welfare. And I think, from what Andy told me, that Nadine Drake was just as lonely." He shot a concerned glance at Melody. "It was Nadine who encouraged him to play the guitar, but he said they never talked about personal things. He knew that her husband had died, but he had no idea what she did for a job."

Reaching across him to pour herself more tea, Gemma said, "That seems odd."

"Not really." Kincaid shrugged. "Andy said they talked about books and music and history, the things that interested them both. It's only as adults that we immediately peg people by what they do and who they know. Andy was just thirteen. And as for Nadine Drake, I'd guess it was a way of removing their relationship from reality."

Melody felt cold. "Oh, God, was the story true then? Did she molest the boy from the college? And was Andy—"

"No, no." Kincaid shook his head. "Your headmaster was right. According to Andy, their whole story was a tissue of lies. They didn't just happen to meet Nadine Drake outside school. It was Andy they met in the park, and they attached themselves to him. Bullying him, following him, finding out where he lived. I suppose it might have been envy in a weird sort of way. They had privilege, but he had something they couldn't begin to fathom. An aura of self-sufficiency, maybe.

"Andy said he avoided them as much as possible, but one night he was angry at Nadine because she was drinking and behaving strangely. He let the boys into his house, and from his garden they found a way into hers. It was hot; her doors and windows were open. They could see her, and when she went to have a bath, Shaun Francis dared his friend Joe to go in and surprise her. When he did, she threw the boy out and threatened to call the police. She certainly never touched him. And she never spoke to Andy again."

"But—" Melody tried to fit it all together. "Why did the boys lie about her at the school?"

"I suspect Joe Peterson was humiliated. It might have started as something whispered to another boy to make himself feel better. And then it snowballed."

"Or it might have been Shaun," said Gemma. "Mr. Carstairs

said he was a grudge holder. Maybe he was offended for his friend's sake, or maybe she said something that angered him."

"Could Nadine have thought that Andy countenanced their story?" asked Melody, horrified.

"Possibly," Kincaid answered. "But Andy knew nothing except that she disappeared. He still doesn't."

"Surely the boy's father didn't win the civil suit?"

"It was never resolved," broke in Doug. "Nadine Drake is easy enough to trace before that. Born Nadine Summers, grew up in Hampstead, took a first-class degree in French at Cambridge. Met Marshall Drake, who had a job in advertising. They moved into an upmarket flat in Canary Wharf; then Marshall fell down the stairs in their building and died as the result of a head injury. The neighbors had heard them having a row shortly beforehand. But his blood alcohol was high, and his death was ruled an accident. Apparently, however, he had run up massive debts. Perhaps that was why they were arguing. She lost the Canary Wharf flat, took a job teaching French at Norwood College, and moved into the rented flat in Crystal Palace.

"But that autumn, after she was let go from the college, she simply disappeared. No social security records, no benefits. But speaking of benefits, however, I did track down your Joe Peterson." Doug looked pleased with himself. "He's on the dole and lives in a council flat in Crystal Palace. It's just off Church Road."

"Which is why it makes sense that he was at the White Stag last Friday night," put in Kincaid.

"What?" Melody and Gemma said in unison.

"It was Joe Peterson that Andy punched. He said Joe came up to him and wanted to be mates. He hadn't seen him in fifteen years."

"No wonder he didn't want to talk about it. But why did he tell you?" Melody couldn't help feeling hurt.

"I think he'd carried it for a long time, along with a lor-
ryload of guilt. He thought everything that happened was his
fault. I imagine it would be the last thing he'd want to tell a
woman he fancied." Kincaid flashed Melody a quick smile,
then went on. "But there's more. It seems Nadine Drake may
not have vanished from the face of the earth. Andy thought he
saw Nadine in the pub that night. And again, on Sunday, when
he and Melody were at the Twelve Bar."

Gemma had abandoned her sandwich and was sitting
hunched over her tea mug in concentration. "Caleb Hart said
he saw a woman watching Arnott in the pub on Friday night.
Could it have been . . . good God, she had reason enough to
hate Arnott."

"And Shaun Francis," Kincaid said. "And Peterson, you
would think, more than any of them."

In spite of the fire, Melody's fingers had gone numb. "No,
it's Andy she would have hated the most. But why has she reappeared now, after all these years? And what if—"

A phone rang. Melody recognized it as Gemma's even as
they all automatically checked pockets or bags.

Retrieving her phone, Gemma stood and walked to the hallway door. She turned her back as if the separation helped her
to concentrate. Melody heard her murmur something; then she
came back into the room and picked up a pen and a scrap of
paper from the coffee table.

"Right," Gemma said, writing. "Ta, Mike. I'll let you know
what we find out," she added, and disconnected.

"What is it?" asked Melody, her sense of dread stronger now.

Gemma looked at her, concern in her glance. "I think I can
tell you why Nadine Drake has suddenly reappeared on the
scene. Forensics traced the scarf used to gag Arnott and strangle Shaun Francis. In England, it was sold only in a French
boutique in Covent Garden called Le Perdu. The shop just
opened six months ago, an offshoot of a boutique in Paris

of the same name. The manager of the Paris shop came to London to get this one off the ground. Her name is Nadine Drake."

"Covent Garden?" Kincaid glanced at his watch. "It's only just gone four. We should be able to get there well before closing, even in rush hour."

"We?" said Gemma, raising an eyebrow in an expression that looked remarkably like Kincaid's.

"If there is any possibility that this woman killed two men, you and Melody are not going to interview her on your own." His tone brooked no argument. "You can either have me or uniformed backup. But I promise I'll stay in the background."

For a moment, Melody thought Gemma was going to bridle at having her interview commandeered, but then Gemma nodded. "All right. The more the merrier, I suppose."

As Melody breathed an inner sigh of relief, Doug said, "I take it I'm going to be left behind again."

"I'll have a hard enough time explaining Duncan if things go pear shaped," Gemma told him. "Much less the presence of an officer who's meant to be on medical leave. And you could be most helpful by seeing if you can find a home address for Drake." Turning to Kincaid, she added, "What about Charlotte?"

"I'll just give Betty a ring and see if she can keep her a bit longer."

They were quick, bundling back into coats as Kincaid made his call. Melody spared a moment to look back at Doug, sitting forlornly in his chair, plates and cups and half-eaten sandwiches littered across the room as if the house had suffered a brief invasion by an alien army. "I'll come back," she said. "Help you clear up, and fill you in."

She caught the instant of vulnerability on his face before he gave her a mocking smile. "I won't hold my breath."

"No, really. I promise," she said, and knew she couldn't renege.

Then they were out the door in a flurry of cold air and piling into Duncan's Astra. Melody took the back, next to Charlotte's safety seat, and was glad of the relative seclusion. Thoughts racketed through her mind as they crossed Putney Bridge and entered Chelsea, then drove steadily east along the river through a light mist.

How had this woman found Andy at the White Stag in Crystal Palace? Melody asked herself. Or had Arnott been her target and it was only coincidence that Andy had been there, too? Where was Andy now? Was he safe?

As if reading her mind, Gemma turned from the front seat. "Ring him, why don't you?"

"Right." Melody pulled out her phone and dialed but the call went to voice mail. She didn't leave a message. "No answer," she told Gemma.

"Well, keep trying, then."

The traffic grew heavier and heavier as they neared the city center, until they were crawling and Melody had to fight the urge to get out and walk.

Kincaid glanced at her in the rearview mirror. "It's still early. I should think the shop would stay open until six."

"Maybe we should have called in uniform."

"We're almost there," said Gemma. "And I'd like a chance to talk to her first. Without identification from a witness, we don't have anything concrete. Anyone could have bought that scarf."

Not bloody likely, thought Melody. Then she realized that however damning the evidence seemed against Nadine Drake, there was something that didn't make sense. "Duncan, did Andy say what time he thought he saw Nadine at the Twelve Bar?"

"No. Why?"

"If it really was Nadine Drake, could she have got to Kennington Square in time to pick up Shaun Francis in the Prince of Wales, take him home, and kill him?"

"What time did you and Andy leave the Twelve Bar?"

Melody flushed, realizing that she'd been paying no attention whatsoever to the time that night. "I'm not sure. His was the early set. Maybe somewhere between half past nine and ten."

"It could be done," said Gemma as Kincaid navigated Trafalgar Square. "Northern line from Tottenham Court Road straight to Kennington."

"But from what Rashid said, it sounded like someone had been plying Francis with drugged double gins for a good part of the evening." Melody wondered why she was arguing against Nadine Drake as their murderer. Was it because it terrified her to think that Andy might have been her target that night, and that it was only her presence that had protected him? "And besides," she added, "if Andy thought he recognized her, wouldn't Shaun Francis have recognized her, too?"

"Andy knew her much better," said Kincaid. "He saw her every day for several months. And even if Shaun had recognized her, why would he have been afraid of her? He wouldn't have known anything about Arnott's death, and even if he had, he would have been unlikely to make a connection."

"From Caleb Hart's description, she's very attractive," put in Gemma. "He might have been flattered."

"We don't even know if it was Drake that Caleb Hart saw looking at Arnott," Melody protested.

"It's a logical assumption, if Andy thought he saw her. We have CCTV of Arnott leaving the pub with a woman, and every reason to think that he had a woman with him when he checked into the Belvedere."

Melody sat back, watching the traffic lights change, trying to imagine what could make a woman murder two men so brutally, and trying not to picture Andy the way she'd seen

Vincent Arnott and Shaun Francis. Feeling sick, she punched his number into her phone again, and once more it went to voice mail.

Having inched his way up Charing Cross Road, Kincaid swore as he turned into the one-way system on Longacre. The road was single lane, with widened, pedestrianized pavements on the right and no parking at all. "There's no way I'll be able to leave the car. I'll get as close as I can to the shop and keep you in sight."

But when they reached Le Perdu, the shop was dark and shuttered.

"Bloody hell," said Gemma as Kincaid nosed the car up onto the pavement.

Gemma jumped out with Melody right behind her, and together they banged on the shop door. There was no answer, and no movement within.

The neighboring shops still blazed with light, so at a nod from Gemma, Melody took one side and Gemma the other.

The girl at the sales desk of Melody's boutique looked at her blankly when she asked if she'd seen the woman who managed the shop next door.

"The French shop? Le Perdu?" Melody added.

"Oh. Is that how you say it?" The girl shrugged. "Don't know her. Not very friendly, is she?"

Melody bit back the temptation to say she wouldn't know. "Did you know the shop had closed early?"

"No. Can't leave the shop, can I?"

Melody gave it up and thanked her, hoping Gemma had had better luck, but when she met Gemma outside, Gemma shook her head.

"Call Doug," said Gemma. "See if he's got the home address."

Doug answered on the first ring. "She's closed the shop," Melody told him.

"I was just going to phone you," he said. "She lives right round the corner, a flat in Floral Street." He gave her the address. "Be careful, will you?" he added.

"Somehow I don't think we're going to find her at home."

Kincaid swore when they returned to the car and passed the information along. "Bloody one-way system. I'll have to go round the mulberry bush to get down Floral Street."

"We'll walk and you can meet us there," suggested Gemma.

His lips tightened. "I don't think so. Hop in. I don't think another five minutes are going to matter."

It took longer than five minutes. Melody tried Andy again with no luck. When at last they managed to circle round the right way into Floral Street, they found the address, not far from the back entrance of the Royal Opera House. There was no name beside the bell for the flat number Doug had given them, and when they rang, there was no answer. The windows on the front of the building were dark.

"Try the other bells," suggested Kincaid, who had pulled the car up on the double yellows and got out with them.

No one answered in the other two flats. "Either no one's home from work yet, or these are lease properties that are empty."

Gemma gave the bell one last frustrated push, then turned away. "I'm requesting a warrant to bring Nadine Drake in for questioning. And I want a constable on the shop and on the flat in case she comes back. I wish I had more to give them than Caleb Hart's description." She turned to Melody. "Still no answer from Andy?"

When Melody shook her head, Gemma hesitated, then said, "Maybe he just doesn't want to talk to you. No offense," she added quickly. "But he may feel . . . awkward. Duncan, could you try?"

Melody read out the number to Kincaid, who dialed from his phone. "No joy," he said after listening for a long moment, then clicking off.

Gemma took a breath and straightened her shoulders in the way that meant she'd made a decision. "Could you ring Tam and have him try? In the meantime, I think we should go to Crystal Palace. Maybe Joe Peterson saw something that night. And in any case, he needs to be warned."

Melody had suffered from car sickness as a child. Although Kincaid drove deftly, recrossing the river and winding south and upwards, the patchy fog that curled round the car windows like sinuous ghosts made Melody feel disoriented and queasy.

She thought of a long-ago summer drive with her parents. She had been perhaps nine, and it had been late in the summer hols. They were traveling from the Kensington town house to their country place in Buckinghamshire. The car was too warm, and her father had recently taken up smoking cigars. The smell, combined with the motion, had made her so ill that she'd made her dad stop and let her out so that she could vomit on the verge. He'd never smoked another cigar—at least not in her presence.

She certainly hoped she wasn't going to have to ask the same of Kincaid.

The summer hols . . . something niggled at her. She realized it was the story she'd told Gemma at the beginning of this case, about visiting Crystal Palace Park with her school class. It had been very early in the autumn term, she was certain, because the heat had made it still feel like summer. She and Andy were near the same age—was it possible they had unknowingly passed each other in the park that day?

Romantic rubbish, she chided herself. Yet she found the thought comforting, and she felt a bit better for the rest of the drive.

By the time they neared the summit of Gipsy Hill, they were

driving through dense cloud. Cars loomed at them as they
went round the triangle, yellow lights glaring, and the red and
green traffic lights seemingly winked from out of nowhere.

"Bugger driving in this," Kincaid said. "Are we close?"

Gemma consulted the map and her directions. "There's a
turning to the right just past the White Stag."

The road appeared out of the fog so suddenly that Kincaid
almost missed it. Slowing into the turn, he crept round the corner and down into a loop of road. Blocks of council flats were
barely visible, set in amongst the trees on the steep hillside.

"Not bad for council flats," said Gemma as she looked
round. "Maybe we should try living on benefits."

When Kincaid had found a parking spot and they climbed
from the car, Melody drew her coat collar tight about her
throat. The fog might look soft as cotton wool, but it seared
the lungs and chilled to the bone.

Gemma consulted the building numbers, then pointed. "Up
there. First floor."

They followed her up the slick open staircase with care,
then along a concrete walkway until they reached a battered
door with no name beside the bell. When Gemma pushed it,
there was no sound, so she knocked loudly. They could hear
a television blaring through the thin door. The curtains in the
front window were torn and sagged at the top.

"Not prepossessing, in spite of the view this place must have
in daylight," Kincaid murmured as Gemma knocked again.

The television went quiet and a man's voice said suspiciously, "Who is it?"

"DI James. Metropolitan Police. We'd like a word."

There was no reply. Gemma had lifted her hand to knock
again when the door opened on the chain and a man peered
out at them.

"I want to see some ID," he said.

Obligingly, Gemma held up her warrant card.

The man jerked his head towards Melody and Kincaid.

Melody showed her ID. "DS Talbot."

Kincaid, who stood behind them, merely flashed his and said, "Kincaid," deliberately omitting his rank.

The chain stayed fastened. "What do you want?"

"Can we come in, Mr. Peterson?" asked Gemma. "I'm sure you'd prefer we didn't discuss your business in front of your neighbors."

"Why should it matter with that lot?" he said dismissively, but he flicked the chain off and stepped back to let them in. He didn't deny that he was Joe Peterson.

If he was Andy's age, he'd seen some wear and tear, thought Melody. He was thin, with short brown hair and a scruffy bit of facial hair that couldn't quite be called a beard. He also had a faint, yellowing bruise below his right eye.

The flat looked no better kept, and it smelled of damp and stale smoke. Half-filled boxes lay strewn about the sitting room, empty beer cans littered the tables, and the stained back wall held a Crystal Palace football poster, its top corner curling down like a drooping flag.

"Are you going somewhere, Mr. Peterson?" asked Gemma.

"Nah. Girlfriend's moving out. You know women and their stuff."

Melody pegged his accent as public-school-trying-for-working-class, and it was grating. "Did she give you that, your girlfriend?" asked Melody, touching her own cheekbone.

She saw him hesitate, contemplating a lie, and in that still moment the faint bruising on his nose was visible as well. Then he shrugged. "Nah. I had a bit too much to drink on the weekend. Had a little argy-bargy in the pub."

"That would have been the White Stag, on Church Street?" said Gemma.

Peterson's eyes widened. He hadn't been expecting that. "So happens, yeah. What of it?"

"It was, in fact, your old friend who hit you. Andy Mona-han."

"Yeah. That's right. But I wouldn't exactly call him a friend. I should've pressed charges. Assault, that's what it was."

"You and Andy go way back, as I understand it."

Peterson stepped back, definitely wary now. "I knew him a little when we were kids. Snotty-nosed little bastard, didn't even own a decent pair of shoes, and now he doesn't want to be seen talking to me." Gemma gave a very pointed look round the flat and Peterson flushed. "He had no right to bloody hit me."

"Andy didn't remember you too fondly, either, Joe," put in Melody. "And he doesn't even know what you really did to his neighbor, Mrs. Drake."

His face closed. "I don't know what you're talking about."

"Oh, but I'm sure you do," said Gemma. "You accused her of assault, and your father legally persecuted her. He hired a lawyer named Vincent Arnott to file a civil suit against her when the police refused to charge her. Did you happen to see Mr. Arnott in the White Stag on Friday night?"

"I've no idea what you're talking about," Peterson said again, his accent slipping into public school vowels.

Melody held out her phone, showing him Arnott's photo. "Maybe this will refresh your memory."

He looked, shook his head. "Nah. Don't remember him. That was years ago, anyway."

"And you hadn't seen him in the pub before?"

"Not my regular, the White Stag. Bit too smarmy yuppie. I only went in 'cause I saw Andy's picture on the flyer in the window. Thought it would be a laugh."

Kincaid stepped up behind Gemma, and Melody was glad she wasn't on the receiving end of the look he gave Joe Peterson. "You thought Andy would want to have a laugh over your break-ing into his neighbor's house and scaring her half to death?"

"That's not what happened." Peterson shifted on the balls

of his feet as he glanced at Kincaid, who suddenly seemed to fill the doorway.

"We know what you said happened. Andy says it's not true."

"Little butter-wouldn't-melt Catholic boy? He's the one had been spying on her for months." Peterson glared at them. "What's this all about, anyway? You've no right to harass me like this. I haven't done anything."

"Did you see anyone else you recognized in the pub Friday night?" asked Gemma.

"No. I've told you. Look, I've had enough of—"

"Vincent Arnott—the lawyer your father hired—was in the White Stag on Friday night. We found him dead on Saturday morning." Gemma waited for this to sink in. Peterson shot another glance at Kincaid. The bruise on his cheekbone stood out starkly now.

"So why should I care?" he said finally. His Adam's apple moved as he swallowed.

"Your old mate Shaun Francis was found dead on Monday morning," said Kincaid. "Bit of a coincidence, you see."

"Shaun? Dead?" Peterson licked his lips. "You're having me on, right?"

"No. I'm sorry." Gemma sounded genuinely sympathetic.

"But—I don't understand. I hadn't seen Shaun in years. What has any of this got to do with me?"

"We think there was someone else in the pub that night. Someone who had very good reason to hate Arnott, and your old friend Shaun, and you. Nadine Drake."

Peterson stared at her, then gave a bark of laughter. "Now I know you're having me on. She must be some kind of a hag by now. And besides, I didn't hang around after—" His hand strayed towards his face.

"What did you do?" asked Kincaid.

"Came home. I was bloody pissed off. Had a row with my girlfriend." He gestured at the boxes. "Bitch."

Melody was beginning to think they should leave Joe Peterson to his fate, but Gemma handed him a card. "Mr. Peterson, we should warn you that you could be a target. Please be aware of this if Nadine Drake should approach you. And call the police."

"I think I could handle her." Peterson's expression made Melody wonder just what he had done to his girlfriend when they'd argued on Friday night.

"I wouldn't be too sure," said Gemma, and Melody knew she was seeing Arnott and Francis, naked and strangled. "You might not recognize her, but I'd stay away from strange women in bars. Oh, and we'll need to have a word with your ex-girlfriend. Routine. If you could give us contact information?"

With bad grace, he scribbled a name and a mobile number on a shred of torn-off pizza box. "She's gone to stay with her sister in Streatham. Don't know the address."

"Thank you, Mr. Peterson. You've been most helpful." Gemma gave him her most officious smile, and they left him standing in his sitting room, Gemma's card clutched in his fingers.

"Nasty piece of work," Kincaid said when they reached the car. "I think I can see why Andy punched him."

Gemma glanced back at the flat. "Is he really in danger, do you think? I could have patrol keep an eye on him."

Kincaid frowned as he keyed open the car. "I'd concentrate on Drake. The other two were attacked after they'd been to their locals. And they were fairly high-profile figures, lawyers who could be traced easily enough. How would she find Joe Peterson unless she had access to social security rolls?"

Melody could only think of Andy, whose name and gig dates were on flyers at the 12 Bar, and probably other local clubs as well.

"I think I won't ride back with you," she said, her fingers on the handle of the Astra's back door. Gemma and Kincaid turned to stare at her. "I'll get the train from Gipsy Hill into Victoria. Then it's easy enough to get the tube to Putney. That way, the two of you can go straight home, and I can run Gemma by to pick up her car on the way into the station in the morning."

She didn't want to say that she couldn't bear another hour in the back of the car in evening traffic. Or that she had no intention of going straight to Putney. From Victoria, it was just as easy to get the tube to Tottenham Court Road, and the flat in Hanway Place. She was not going home until she'd made certain Andy was all right.

CHAPTER TWENTY-TWO

In 1963 Regent Sounds Studio was set up at 4 Denmark Street. With the Rolling Stones recording their first album here, the studio took off as the place to be seen to be making music.

—www.covent-garden.co.uk

"Do you think Melody is all right?" Kincaid asked Gemma, taking his eyes from the road to glance at her face.

"I don't know. I can't blame her for being worried. You could ring Tam again when we get home, ask him if Andy was playing anywhere tonight and if he could check on him."

He was crossing the Thames at the Albert Bridge, which would always now make him think of the walk he and Gemma had taken along the Chelsea Embankment after they signed the marriage register in the Chelsea Town Hall.

This seemed as good a time as any, and perhaps the setting would serve as a good omen for what he had to say. "Before we get home, there's something I need to tell you, love."

"What?" Gemma's face was a white blur as she turned towards him. "What's happened? The children—my mum—"

"Oh, no, nothing like that. I didn't mean to frighten you.

It's good news, actually." He reached over and patted her knee through the thick wool of her coat. "But it is about Charlotte. The thing is . . . I didn't want to say anything until I knew for certain. But I think I've found her a place in a good school. It's Miss Jane's. I spoke to the headmistress this morning and she said Charlotte could start half days next week."

"What?" Gemma said again, sounding completely baffled. "But that school is impossible to get in. How could you possibly—"

"A friend got me an introduction."

"A friend?"

"Someone I know from morning coffee at Kitchen and Pantry. MacKenzie Williams. Her son goes there—he's Charlotte's age—and she put in a word for Charlotte."

When Gemma didn't say anything, he glanced at her again. She was gaping at him. Frowning and gaping. "What?" he asked.

"MacKenzie Williams? Do you have any idea who she is?" Her voice rose in a squeak.

He shrugged. "She's nice. And Charlotte likes Oliver. I thought if she was in the same class with someone she felt comfortable with, she might do better."

Out of the corner of his eye, he could see Gemma's hair swing as she shook her head. "Oliver. Just Oliver. Like he was any ordinary little boy."

"Isn't he?"

Gemma pushed at the seat belt strap so that she could turn towards him in her seat. "Don't you ever notice the mail-order catalogs I get? The small, pretty one with the clothes for mothers and children?"

"Um, that's the one you put in the bathroom sometimes, right?"

"How can you not know what that is?" She smacked him on the arm, hard enough to hurt. "OLLIE. It's an incredibly successful mail-order company run by Bill Williams, who just happens to live in Notting Hill. OLLIE is named for his son, Oliver. And his wife, MacKenzie, is the catalog's principal model. Didn't you ever ask her what she did?"

"Um, no." He thought of MacKenzie showing up at his door in her grubby clothes, saying she was on her way to a job. A fashion shoot.

"They are very rich and very famous. Everyone wants to be friends with them. And everyone wants their child to go to the same school as their son."

"Really? Miss Jane said they didn't encourage celebrity parents."

"They have to beat celebrity parents off with a stick." Gemma started to laugh. "It's because you didn't know. You liked MacKenzie Williams for herself. And the headmistress must have known you had no idea who MacKenzie was, or that the school was one of the juiciest plums in Notting Hill."

"I told you MacKenzie was nice." He was a little affronted. "And she goes out of her way to be kind to Charlotte. So, have I made a complete fool of myself?"

"No, love. Or only in the nicest possible way." She patted his arm this time, but when he glanced at her, she was frowning. "But this school has got to be bloody expensive," she said. "It's all very well to get Charlotte in, but how on earth are we going to afford it?"

"Ah, well." Kincaid cleared his throat. "When I saw Louise on Saturday, we had a talk. The Fournier Street house has sold. She told me to look for a better place for Charlotte, and the estate should be able to cover the fees."

"And you didn't tell me this, either?"

"You were on a case, and I didn't want to distract you when I didn't know anything for cer—"

She was shaking her head, and when she spoke there was no mistaking her seriousness. "Don't you keep secrets from me, Duncan. Not for any reason, including for my own good. You don't have the right to decide that. And for all your good intentions, I've missed out on this. Did you not think I would want to see the school and meet with the head? That I would want to worry and anticipate along with you?"

"I'm sorry," he said. "It all happened very quickly."

"Charlotte—" Gemma said after a moment. "Did she—" There was the slightest quaver in her voice. "Did she like the school?"

"She loved it. She visited Oliver's class. And she can't wait to tell you all about it when you get home." He felt on firmer ground now. "If it helps, we're encouraged to go with her to her class the first few days, to help her settle in."

"Oh, God. The bloody case." Gemma rubbed her hands against her cheeks, looking stricken. "I don't know if I'll be able to get away. Although if something doesn't break soon, the super may replace me as SIO."

Kincaid sighed. As much as he hated to add to her worries, he knew there wouldn't be a better time to tell her about Louise. If he kept it from her now it would be unforgivable. "There's something else, love," he said.

Melody heard the music as she came round the corner into Hanway Place. Guitar, coming from Andy's flat. It was loud, even with the windows closed. He was playing an electric, with the amp volume turned up high. The haunting melody teased at the edges of her memory, but she couldn't quite place it.

Her knees felt weak. He was here. He was safe.

The relief that washed through her was followed just as quickly by a flash of anger over the fact that he'd refused to answer her calls. She pressed hard on the flat bell, let up, pressed again. When there was no answering buzz, she took out her phone and typed in a text message: I KNOW YOU'RE THERE. OPEN THE BLOODY DOOR.

After a moment, the music stopped. The downstairs door

buzzer sounded and Melody pushed it open. She climbed the stairs, but when she reached the first floor, Andy wasn't waiting for her in the hallway. The flat door was ajar, however, so, taking a breath, she brushed her knuckles against it in a cursory knock and walked in.

He sat on the folded futon, the Strat on his knees. From the space beside his thigh, Bert, the marmalade cat, glared at her balefully.

"What were you playing?" asked Melody, which was not at all what she'd intended to say. Her anger had evaporated as quickly as it had come. "I liked it."

"Just something I was working on with Poppy."

Searching for someplace to sit, she pulled up a low stool near one of the amps and perched on it. "Why didn't you tell me about Nadine?"

"I couldn't." Andy plucked two strings and the guitar emitted a discordant jangle. "I thought I'd gone mad. Hallucinating."

"Because you'd seen Joe?"

"You've talked to Duncan." It was a statement.

She nodded, waiting.

Slowly, Andy went on. "Because of Joe, and then, on Sunday—I thought it might have been because I was with you."

"Me? Why ever—"

"You'll think it's stupid." Andy glanced up at her, then looked back at the guitar and ran his hand along the neck. "Because I was happy with you, that night," he said so softly that she wasn't quite sure she'd heard him correctly. "And I hadn't felt that way since— Never mind. I told you it was daft."

Melody wrapped her arms round her knees to keep from reaching out to touch him. "I don't think it's daft at all," she said. "What you thought, I mean. But what you saw wasn't crazy, either."

"What are you talking about?"

"Andy, what time was it when you thought you saw Nadine in the Twelve Bar?"

He shrugged. "I don't know. Nine, or half past, maybe. Why?"

Dear God. It *was* possible. Nadine could have left the 12 Bar and gone straight to Kennington, then chatted up Shaun in the Prince of Wales. And taken him home.

But how to tell Andy what they suspected? Melody suddenly wished herself anywhere else, but she knew she had no choice. "We think you really did see Nadine. Tell me what she looked like."

Andy stared at her as if she were the one who was mad. "She looked like Nadine."

"No, I mean—describe her to me."

He gazed into the distance as he thought. "Well, she was older, of course. And thinner, I think. It was just a glimpse, a figure in the back of the room. She—" When he frowned, the outer ends of his eyebrows lifted like wings. "Her hair was cut in a sort of sleek way. It used to be longer"—he touched his collarbone—"and a little wavy. And she looked . . . sophisticated, I suppose. But it was *her* face . . ." He focused on Melody again. "Are you telling me I really saw her?" Hope lit his blue eyes.

"Duncan told us what happened when she lived next door to you, with the boys. But it wasn't your fault that Nadine left." Melody swallowed, wishing he'd offered her tea or even water, anything to wet her dry mouth. "After that . . . incident . . . Joe Peterson started a rumor at her school that she had sexually assaulted him. She—Nadine—lost her job. Then, when the police refused to press charges, Peterson's father filed a civil suit against her for causing emotional damage to his son. The man who berated you in the White Stag on Friday, Vincent Arnott, was the lawyer Peterson hired. And then Shaun Francis—we think it was most likely Shaun who fanned the flames of the rumor, making sure it got to school authorities."

Andy stared at her. "What are you saying?"

"We think that some time after Nadine left Crystal Palace, she went to France. But a few months ago she came back to

London. She manages a designer clothing boutique in Covent Garden. The scarf"—Melody swallowed again—"the scarf that was used to gag Vincent Arnott and strangle Shaun Francis—we've traced it to the shop. Nadine's shop."

"You— You think *Nadine* killed them?"

"Arnott was seen leaving the White Stag with a woman. Caleb Hart saw a woman that night that fits the description you gave me. He said she was watching Arnott. And Shaun, even if he'd recognized her in the Prince of Wales, he might have been flattered. Andy, you need to be careful. We've tried to talk to her but we can't find her."

He stood so quickly that it startled Bert the cat, who disappeared into the workroom with a hiss and a bristle of orange tail. "I don't believe this. I don't believe any of this. Nadine would never hurt anyone." He was holding the Strat by the neck and now he shook it at her. "She gave me this. Did you know that? It was the one thing of her husband's she couldn't bear to part with. She had faith in me. And how did I repay her? I betrayed her. Shaun Francis was a bully and Joe Peterson was a nasty little liar, and I let them—I let them ruin her." He sounded close to tears.

"They used you, those boys. It wasn't your fault."

"That's no excuse. She was my friend. Nadine was— She was the kindest person I've ever known. I let her down. And now you're telling me she killed those bastards and she's going to try to kill me? It's bollocks. Absolute bollocks."

Melody stood, too, frightened by his intensity. "Andy, I know it's hard—"

"You don't know anything." He sat again, as if his knees had refused to hold him up, and held the guitar against his chest like a shield. His face had gone blank. "I need to practice. I've got a session tomorrow with Poppy. I promised Tam I'd do at least one more, and I don't break promises."

"Andy, I—"

He looked at her as if she were a stranger. "Shut the door behind you."

"Andy, I never meant to hurt you."

For a moment, she thought he wouldn't answer; then he said, "We never mean to do a lot of things, but that doesn't undo them."

Midafternoon, she closed and locked the shop, simply because she could no longer bear to speak to anyone, or to summon a smile and a compliment for the customers who came in and ran their hands over the merchandise as if that gave them the satisfaction of temporary ownership.

She'd walked, mindlessly, through Covent Garden and Soho, until she realized that the streetlamps were coming on, and her hair and her coat were beaded with tiny drops of moisture that were soaking through to her scalp and her dress.

The chestnut vendor had set up his brazier outside the Covent Garden arcade. The fire drew her. She stopped and held her hands out towards it to warm them.

Gnarled as an old piece of driftwood, the vendor looked up at her with a toothless grin. "A pound, pretty lady, chestnuts nice and hot," he said, and she thought of men like him in the parks in Paris. She fished in her wallet for a coin and exchanged it for the hot paper bag. When she was out of his sight, she tucked the bag into her coat pocket. She couldn't bear to eat, but the warmth was comforting.

But when she cut through into Floral Street, she saw them outside her flat. She knew what they were, even in plainclothes. There was no mistaking police officers when you'd lived on the streets of Paris. She turned, careful not to hurry, and walked back towards the market. With one hand she turned up her coat collar and tucked her hair into it.

There was no point in checking the shop, not if they'd found the flat. She came out into Garrick Street by St. Paul's, the actors' church, and made her way into Charing Cross Road. Panic rolled over her in waves, making her dizzy and disoriented. A couple in hats and dark coats stood arm in arm, gazing into the window of Patisserie Valerie, and for a moment she thought she was in Paris.

No, no. She shook her head, her heart pounding, and dared to walk faster. Memories clouded her vision as careless passersby jostled her. Then, without being quite sure how she'd got there, she found herself once again in Denmark Street, an oasis of quiet. The guitars gleamed in lamplit windows. She passed the 12 Bar, still shuttered, with her head down. There was no refuge for her there.

Light shone from the church at the street's end. The doors to the nave stood open. It was Wednesday, she realized, clinging to the fragment of rational thought. There must be some sort of evening service. When she reached the great doors, she stopped for a moment, listening, and was reassured by the familiar rise and fall of the liturgy. There were a few people in the pews, she saw, enough so that she could slip into the next but last without being noticed.

She huddled in her coat, struggling to stand when the others did. Memories rose around her, carried by the joined voices, and the past seemed to bleed into the present. She saw Marshall, falling, and clapped a hand to her mouth to keep from crying out. The smell of wine came to her, sour, and on a new rush of dizziness, the sound of her own scream.

Her hands were now so cold that for a moment she thought she was in Paris, that first freezing winter, when she'd learned to find shelter in the empty churches.

Then, as the congregants knelt, she remembered how it was done. She glanced round. There was no one behind her. She bent, as if searching for something, a dropped hymnal or service leaflet, perhaps. As the congregants rose for the final response, she slipped into the cramped space beneath the pew. Curling herself into a fetal ball and pulling her coat round her, she willed herself invisible.

There was a slow shuffle of feet, then the priest's voice, calling a good night to someone. Then, at last, quiet. The doors swung closed with the weight of centuries, and the lights went out.

CHAPTER TWENTY-THREE

It was a strange crowd which came out to see the end of a famous London landmark. There were the connoisseurs forearmed with a knowledge of local topography. There were the sort of young men and women to be seen at almost any free entertainment in the streets. There were vast numbers of cyclists, both men and women. There were youngish men and women with traces of Bloomsbury, Hampstead and Chelsea in their clothes and speech, taking the whole affair very gravely. But among these were to be seen many elderly men and women to whom the destruction of the Palace meant the end of a chapter in their lives.

—www.sarahjyounger.com

Melody hadn't slept well. She'd spent the remainder of last evening at Doug's, using Doug's laptop to read all the court records he'd accessed.

She'd gone home to Notting Hill dispirited, and once in bed, she'd tossed and turned, plagued by fragmented dreams in which something kept eluding her, something she had seen or heard but that slipped away from her like quicksilver whenever she almost grasped it.

When she woke, feeling heavy from lack of sleep and queasy with anxiety, she found she had a text message from Gemma telling her not to bother picking her up, as she was taking the tube to Putney to pick up her car. Melody groaned. She should have been up earlier.

And on top of that, the weather forecast on Radio 2 was dismal—temperatures hovering at freezing with a chance of snow and sleet—so when she'd showered, she pulled on a sweater, jeans, boots, and an old down coat she kept for forays to her parents' country house.

When she reached Brixton, she found Gemma not in the CID room but in her office.

"Bad night?" asked Gemma, glancing up at her.

"That obvious?" Melody rubbed her hands over her face. "God, I must look a fright. Sorry I didn't stop to get coffee, boss. I was late enough as it was."

Gemma gestured to a lidded paper cup on her desk. "I got it for you. You can pop it in the microwave if it's gone cold. Although," she added, casting another glance at Melody, "you look as though you might need to mainline it. Turn up anything new with Doug?"

"No." Melody had rung Gemma on her way to Doug's last night, saying just that she'd spoken to Andy and that he was all right. "I'm a bit worried about Doug's ankle, though. He's keeping off it pretty well but it doesn't seem to be improving much." She frowned, taking in the notes scattered over Gemma's desk. "Any developments here?"

"I've been checking Caleb Hart's alibis." Gemma took a sip of her own coffee, made a face, and put the cup down. "Ugh. Cold. Anyway, I finally managed to talk to the pop singer, although it took speaking to her agent and her agent having her ring me back through the station number, just to ensure I was really the police. But she said yes, she was having a bad night on Friday, and that she did ring Caleb and ask him to come to her flat in Knightsbridge. He arrived there well before eleven and stayed until the early hours of the morning."

"So he's definitely a nonstarter for Friday. And Sunday?"

"I've had forensics pick up his computer to run a check—not that he was happy about that—but I think we'll find he was online when he said he was. The video went up at nine, so I suppose it's possible he uploaded it, then drove to Kennington and somehow drugged and murdered Shaun Francis, but it seems highly unlikely.

"Oh, and I've been on the phone with Poppy's father, Tom, and he confirms what Hart told us. He did help get Hart into rehab, and the whole family has been very supportive of his sobriety. So Hart had nothing to hide."

"And"—Melody found she hated to ask—"Nadine?"

Gemma pushed her chair back and stretched. "You speak a bit of French, don't you? I should have let you take that one. I managed to get the shop owner on the phone at his home, first thing this morning. He's a very excitable Frenchman named Guy, who said—at least I think that's what he said—that we were a bunch of English idiots who couldn't be trusted to find our own arses.

"He found Nadine living on the streets in Paris a year or so after we think she left England. She never talked about what had happened to her, but he saw something in her . . . He said"—Gemma paused, as if trying to remember the conversation word for word—"he said that even in her desperation, she had not lost her kindness. Then he said that if we didn't find her and make certain she was all right, he would personally come to London and twist our heads off. And something in French that I didn't understand but I don't think it was complimentary."

Melody was too busy thinking to smile. "That's what Andy said. That Nadine was kind. The kindest person he'd ever known. Does that sound like a person who would drug and strangle two people for revenge?"

"People change."

"If losing her husband, then being accused of a crime she didn't commit, then losing her job and her home and living rough on the streets in Paris didn't change her, why now? And where the bloody hell is she?"

Gemma's phone rang. "It's Maura," she said as she looked at the ID. "I asked her to track down Joe Peterson's girlfriend."

When she answered, Melody listened to the one-sided conversation and watched Gemma look more and more unhappy. "You're sure?" asked Gemma. She listened for another moment, then added, "Right. Thanks, Maura. We'll get on it."

"What?" said Melody as soon as Gemma had rung off, her stomach lurching.

"Joe Peterson. Maura talked to his girlfriend. Make that ex-girlfriend. She said that Joe's father cut him off completely a few months ago and that Joe had just got worse and worse since then, even on his medication. Temper flare-ups, rows. Apparently they had a bugger of one on Friday and he hit her. She left, told him she was finished, and she hasn't been back since. She's afraid to get her things."

"Friday night?"

"No. That's the thing. Friday afternoon."

Melody and Gemma looked at each other across the desk. "He lied," said Melody. "Andy said he was a liar, even as a kid, and we know he lied about what happened with Nadine Drake. Why did we assume he was telling the truth about Friday night?"

She saw again the flat—the mess, the possessions half thrown in boxes. And then it clicked, the thing that had been nagging at her subconscious. "The poster," she said. "In Joe's flat."

"So?" Gemma looked at her blankly. "What of it?"

"It was the Crystal Palace football team. In their home colors. Navy and maroon. Don't you see? Joe follows Crystal Palace. The scarf."

Gemma's eyes widened in understanding. "The unidenti-fied fibers found at both scenes. Fuzzy navy and maroon. And not only that, but the girlfriend said 'anxiety medication.' Xanax? We wondered where that came from. Bloody hell and damnation."

"And the blood," said Melody. "Oh my God, the blood. On the sheet in the hotel room. Who did we know who bled that night, besides Andy from a cut on his thumb? Joe. Andy punched Joe in the face, hard enough to make his nose bleed. You could still see the bruise on the side of his nose as well as under his eye."

"Christ." Gemma jumped up from her desk and ran for the CID room, Melody right behind her.

"Shara," called Gemma, "get me the CCTV from Friday night. Biggest monitor."

"Right, guv." Changing workstations, Shara typed in the file number, and a moment later they were all looking at the grainy footage.

"I want Arnott leaving the pub."

Shara jumped the film forward, then there he was. The smaller figure beside him was half hidden from the camera by his body, and yet there was something indefinably female about it.

"Nadine," whispered Melody. "It has to be."

Then they saw him, the hooded figure, appearing in the frame as Arnott left it, going in the same direction. No. Fol-lowing.

"That's Joe Peterson," said Gemma with certainty. "Right size, right build, and something about the posture. But what the hell happened in that hotel room? Were Peterson and Drake working together? Her friend in Paris said he found her living on the streets. I suspect that means she knew how to pick men up. And maybe tie them up as well, if that was what they fancied."

"What if . . ." Melody stared at the frozen picture, trying to imagine the scene in the pub. "What if she went to see Andy at the White Stag that night? It wouldn't have been that difficult to learn where the band was playing, even if the gig was scheduled at short notice. And she recognized Arnott. I doubt he'd have realized who she was after fifteen years—she would have just been another case to him, not someone who ruined his life. And he was drunk."

"That makes an argument for her luring him to the hotel and killing him, but it doesn't explain where Peterson comes into it." Gemma turned to Shara. "Can we see the footage from Kennington?"

They all watched carefully, first the film from Kennington Park Road, near the tube station, then the film from Kennington Road, the main thoroughfare on the opposite side of Cleaver Square.

"Look." Shara froze the frame. "There. Coming from the bus stop. It's him." The hooded figure appeared for an instant, in between other pedestrians, then vanished as the footage jumped forwards. But there had been the suggestion of a bulge beneath his jacket that might have been a scarf knotted round his neck. The time stamp showed 7:35.

"He took the bus from Crystal Palace," said Melody. "And he knew exactly where he was going. He must have known where Shaun lived and which pub he frequented. Maybe Arnott was spur of the moment, but Shaun's murder was planned. Why didn't we see him before?"

"Because we weren't looking for him," answered Gemma. She straightened. "If Nadine Drake wasn't involved in killing Arnott, she could be in serious danger. Shara, get uniform to double the watch on her flat and the shop."

"And Andy." Melody's voice caught in her throat. "The headmaster said that after Nadine was fired, Joe Peterson was ostracized at school. Shaun, his only real friend, cut him off.

His marks fell. He had to leave the school, and it sounds like he's been going steadily downhill ever since. Who would he blame?"

"Shaun," said Gemma slowly, thinking it through. "Arnott, possibly as a substitute for his father, who he may not dare to confront even now. And . . ." She looked at Melody, concern in her eyes. "Do you know where Andy is?"

Melody felt as if the air had been sucked from the room. "He said he was recording with Poppy today. I assumed he meant the studio in Crystal Palace."

She woke, so cold and cramped that her limbs were paralyzed. No light yet filtered through the windows of the nave, but her body told her it was near daybreak. Her stomach cramped with emptiness. Carefully, she moved her fingers, then her toes, until she could stretch. Something was digging into her hip, a lump in her coat pocket. She remembered the chestnuts.

When she could lever herself into a sitting position on the pew, she took the package from her pocket and ate the tough, cold, mealy nuts, one at a time, sucking at bits to get enough saliva into her mouth so that she could swallow.

The windows began to appear, faint gray outlines that seemed to shift in shape as she watched.

Nadine felt the city coming to life outside the walls of the church. That, too, was something she had learned in Paris, to catch that hum, the vibration of trains beginning to run and people all around, waking, thinking, moving, talking. Each city had its own particular pulse.

And last night, London had taken her into its arms and given her shelter. With that thought came the realization that her panic had vanished while she slept. Perhaps the city—or this church—had given her more than sanctuary.

As light filled the great windows, her course came to her

with sudden clarity. No more running. No more hiding. She would go to the police and tell them what she had done that night in the Belvedere Hotel.

But first, she had to find Andy.

For the third time, Andy flubbed the intro to the number they were working on and swore.

From the control booth, Caleb said, "Five-minute break, okay? In fact, why don't I go fetch us some sandwiches from the pub while you two compose yourselves?" he added, dripping sarcasm, and Andy suspected he was nipping out to call Tam and ask him what the hell was wrong with his guitarist.

Poppy waited until Caleb disappeared from the booth window, then turned off her mic and reached across to switch Andy's off as well. Wearing a knitted reindeer sweater and an orange Peruvian cap with the earflaps turned up, she looked like an elf that had wandered in from the wrong hemisphere. Fortunately, she'd taken off her bright-pink puffy jacket and draped it over her instrument case.

"What is up with you today, guitar boy?" she asked, with a glance at the now-empty control booth. "You got sausages for fingers?"

Andy flexed his uncooperative hands. "It's the cold, maybe." A lame excuse if he'd ever heard one, and Poppy rolled her eyes.

"Yeah, right. Not cold in here, is it? Buck up, will you?" She took off her cap, leaving her hair standing on end from the static, like Bert the cat when he'd had a fright. "Have you looked at the video today? We've got like a gazillion more views."

He had no doubt she knew exactly how many—she'd been tracking them like a stock analyst. Poppy Jones had brains as well as phenomenal talent, and just now he could see the third ingredient necessary for success, steely determination, glinting in her wide blue eyes. Today he felt far short of the mark.

"Sorry, Poppy. The next take will be better."

This time the look she gave him could have come from someone twice her age. "You all right, Andy? Really?"

"Yeah." He summoned a grin. "Dandy."

"Okay. Just don't blow this. I'll carve up your liver if you do," she added sweetly, going to her jacket and pulling out the water bottle stuffed in a pocket.

"My, you do sound just like a preacher's daughter."

Poppy straightened up, holding a piece of paper crumpled in her hand. "That I may be, but I'm not a very good messenger, apparently. I found this stuck under the door when I got here this morning. I meant to give it to you. It has your name on it."

"What? Let me see." Frowning, he took it from her. It was a piece of cheap notepaper, folded in quarters, with his name printed on one side in black marker. "What the fu—" He caught himself, even though Poppy swore like a trooper. That seemed to be her bit of rebellion, if you didn't count the clothes and the hair. Unfolding the sheet, he peered at the scrawl inside. The paper seemed to have got wet at some point and the marker had run.

"NEED TO TAL—," it said, then something he couldn't make out. Then there was another illegible word, followed by "KNOW WHERE." And then— He tilted the paper one way and then the other, trying to be certain. Was that scrawl running off the bottom of the page an N?

"What is it?" said Poppy. "You look like someone walked over your grave. Let me see."

"No."

"Come on, let me see." She grabbed for the paper, as if he were one of her brothers, playing keep-away.

"No, Poppy, really—"

But she'd snatched at it again and got a glimpse before he yanked it back, half ripping it.

"Ooh, what are you doing? Passing secret messages like the Famous Five or something?"

"No. But *you* probably still read Enid Blyton," he said, trying to make light of it even as he stuffed the torn note into his jeans pocket. "Leave it alone, Poppy."

His heart was pounding in his ears. Was it— Could it be Nadine? But how had she known where to find him? Then he remembered that he'd seen her—or thought he'd seen her—at the White Stag and at the 12 Bar. People knew they were recording—it wasn't impossible someone would have told her he'd be here.

Then he thought of Melody. She'd asked him to promise to be careful. Well, he would be careful. But he didn't for a moment believe those things she'd said, and if the note was from Nadine, there was no way he could refuse.

"Poppy, I have to go out for a bit. Tell Caleb I won't be long."

"But—"

"Please. I'll make it up to you. Tell him it's a family emergency."

Ignoring the disapproval on Poppy's face, he slipped on his jacket and turned towards the door.

Then he stopped. He never left his guitar. Not anywhere. Ever. He put the Strat in its case and slipped the strap over his shoulder.

"You're mad," said Poppy.

"I know." He touched her cheek. "Thanks."

Now there was only one place he could go.

Nadine slipped from the church before full light, hoping that the first person who arrived to prepare for morning service wouldn't be too panicked by the unlocked door. The church, surely, would be safe enough, daybreak on a Thursday morning not being a prime time for vandals.

Head down, she walked into Oxford Street, taking refuge in the McDonald's sandwiched between Tottenham Court Road and Hanway Place. She ordered coffee and a roll, not because she wanted them, but because she knew her body needed fuel if she was to keep going, and because the food and drink provided camouflage. When someone left a newspaper behind, she slid it over to her table and hid behind it, staring unseeing at photos of celebrities she didn't recognize.

When enough time had passed, she left the restaurant and walked back into Charing Cross Road. The air felt dense, and the sky seemed darker than it had at dawn. She went into Foyle's and discreetly freshened up in the ladies' toilet, another skill learned long ago.

Then, when the guitar shops began to open their doors, she wandered back into Denmark Street. She'd perfected the art of aimless browsing as a way to keep warm and kill time, and it served her well. All the salesclerks were men, and after the first—sometimes appreciative—glance they ignored her, as if they knew instantly that she wasn't a serious customer. When they got comfortable with her presence, she asked each, oh so casually, if they happened to know her old friend she'd been meaning to look up since she'd arrived in London.

The luthier in the last shop, a middle-aged man with a ponytail, looked up and smiled. "Andy? Yeah, I hear he's got a good gig going. Some girl singer that's maybe the next big thing. He was in here the other day—had some work done on his Martin. Said he was going to be recording."

"Oh. How smashing for him." Nadine gave him her best smile. "Did he happen to say where?"

"Um, Crystal Palace. That little place tucked away behind Westow Street. Can't remember the name of the lane. You want me to give him a message if he comes in?"

"No, but thanks. I'm sure I'll run into him sooner or later."

She climbed up from Gipsy Hill Railway Station, stopping every few minutes to let the wooziness in her head clear and to ease the pain in her calves. The strange darkness grew. Something icy bit at her cheek and the gray wind funneled down the hill, bringing a swirl of sleety snow with it.

Nadine came to a halt, unable to see above or below as the visibility decreased even further. She felt as though she were suspended in space and in time, a no-man's-land between memory and reality in which she might wander forever.

But she had to finish what she'd begun, had to make things right. Taking a searing breath, she went on. Her feet began to slip as the freezing mixture coated the pavement.

Then, just as she neared the summit, she saw Andy turning into Westow Hill, his guitar case over his shoulder, hurrying.

She followed.

His feet had almost gone out from under him as he clattered out of the studio and started down the metal stairs. "Shit," he muttered, grabbing the rail to steady himself and proceeding the rest of the way down much more carefully. He could see the ice sheen on the steps now, but everything beyond the small parking area below the studio was a gray blur.

A cold drop of moisture touched his cheek, like a tear, then another and another. Freezing rain, turning to snow. For a moment, he was tempted to return the guitar, but he knew he couldn't go back. He hoped he could reach his destination.

Managing to get up the steep lane, he walked as fast as he dared the length of Westow Street, then turned into Westow Hill.

When he reached Woodland Road he stopped, suddenly afraid to go on. Where else could she have meant but the old flats? They had never met in any other place.

And if he was right . . . What would it be like to see her, to talk to her again? Could he face her? But if she needed him, he must go. He'd call Melody when he found out if Nadine was all right.

He half slid down Woodland Road, banging his guitar case more than once. Even returning to Crystal Palace for the gig at the White Stag and the recording sessions, he'd avoided coming this way, and now the sight of the house shocked him.

There was a rubbish skip on the pavement in front, and the windows were partially boarded over. Someone was renovating the place. The thought made him feel violated.

Next door, Nadine's old flat looked freshly painted and well kept. Moving a few steps closer, he saw that the door to his former home stood very slightly ajar. Careful of his footing, he climbed the steps where he had spent so many hours, and stepped inside.

The dimness in the flat was disorienting. Lumber and builder's tools lay everywhere, some on a worktable near the right-hand side of the sitting room. The wall between the kitchen and the sitting room had been pulled down. And there, near the worktable, a flicker of flame. Someone had lit a portable gas heater left behind by the builders.

"Nadine?" he said softly. The room seemed to swallow his words, and the hair on the back of his neck rose.

A figure rose from among the boxes stacked near the heater. "No, sorry, mate. I knew you'd come, but I got a bit cold waiting for you, so I lit us a fire."

"Joe? What the hell are you doing here? Where's Nadine?" Andy set down the Strat, suddenly wanting his hands free.

"Oh, I knew you'd fall for that old trick." Joe giggled. It was the same sound Andy remembered from years ago. He felt sick. "I've no idea where your precious Mrs. Drake is," said Joe. "But I know what she did in that hotel on Friday night, and I know she's going to go down for triple murder."

"You're lying. You always lied. Nadine would never hurt anyone."

Joe unwound the navy and maroon Crystal Palace scarf from round his neck. "Wouldn't she?" he said, running the scarf through his fingers. "You're such an innocent. But it doesn't really matter what you think, does it, Andy lad? As long as the police think she did it."

Andy's shock must have shown on his face because Joe laughed again. "Oh, the police warned you, too, did they? That's hysterical, that's what it is."

"What are you talking about?"

"Because now they're going to think she killed you, too. When they find her—and they will—I don't think things will go well for her. And then that's all of you, finished."

"You're . . ." Andy's tongue felt stuck to the roof of his mouth. "Crazy," he managed to finish.

"Like a fox." Joe cocked his head. "You didn't want to be bothered with me, did you? Did you think I'd forget what you did to me? What you all did to me? No one would talk to me, not even Shaun. I had to leave school the end of that year. They wouldn't stop whispering that 'what happened to poor Mrs. Drake' was my fault. And my father, he—he—" Joe's face twisted in a spasm that might have been grief or pain.

Andy took a step closer. "Look, Joe, whatever you've done, I'm sure there's some way—"

"Whatever I've done? Oh, I've hardly done anything yet. Just wait until they arrest the bitch." Tilting his head again, he seemed to consider Andy. "But I want them to find you first. Maybe I should make an anonymous call. What do you think, Andy?"

Andy tensed, every muscle in his body ready for fight or flight. "I—"

But he'd left it too late.

A piece of lumber seemed to appear in Joe's hands. Before Andy could move, Joe swung it, catching Andy in the forehead.

Andy staggered, stunned, then shook his head and wondered how he'd got on the floor. The room swam. Something wet trickled into his eye as he tried to sit up.

334 ~ DEBORAH CROMBIE

Then Joe was on him, pushing his head back to the bare floorboards with a crack, and something soft and scratchy was pulled and twisted round his neck.

The scarf. Andy scrabbled at it, trying to get his fingers into the space between the fabric and his skin. Joe's weight pinned him, and above him, Joe's face contorted as he grunted with the effort of twisting the scarf.

Spots swam before Andy's eyes. He couldn't let himself black out. Letting go of the scarf, he reached for Joe's shoulders and gave a mighty shove.

Joe fell to one side, rolled, and hit the gas heater.

It tipped and clanged over. Flames sputtered and then began to lick across the floor.

Through a haze of blood, Andy saw his childhood nightmare come to life.

"I can't get the car down the lane." Melody's Clio had slipped and slid going up Gipsy Hill until they'd reached the level surface of the triangle and driven round to Westow Street. The visibility had deteriorated so badly since it had begun to snow that she almost missed the lane altogether. "And there's no bloody place to park here." She felt like screaming with impatience.

"I'll stay with the car." Gemma was already unfastening her seat belt. "You go down and see if Andy's there. Just don't break your neck."

"I'll try not to," Melody answered with as much of a smile as she could muster. Once out of the car, she picked her way carefully down the cobbled lane, thankful she'd worn boots and warm clothes. She'd forgotten a hat. Reaching up, she brushed at the gathering snowflakes in her hair.

As she reached the bottom of the lane, something bright orange bobbed towards her from the direction of the studio.

Squinting through the snow, she recognized Poppy, wearing a ridiculous knitted hat.

"Poppy," she called, a little breathlessly. "Have you seen Andy?"

"He buggered off while Caleb was out getting sandwiches," said Poppy as they met. Poppy, zipped into a puffer jacket that looked suitable for the North Pole, was carrying her bass. "Good thing Caleb decided to call off the session because of the weather, or he'd be royally pissed off with Andy. And I've got to get to the train or I won't get home to Twyford."

"Wait." Melody touched her arm. "Do you know where Andy went?"

"No. He got some cryptic note shoved under the studio door. I managed to read a bit before he took it away from me. Something about a meeting, and then it said"—Poppy drew her eyebrows together—"something like, 'You know where.'" She shrugged. "Whatever that means. But he seemed to know."

"How long ago?"

"Maybe half an hour."

"Right. Thanks."

"Is he all right, do you think?" asked Poppy as they started back up the lane together.

"I'm sure he is," answered Melody, although she wasn't sure at all. "You'd better hurry or you won't be able to get down Gipsy Hill."

Wearing boots that looked as though they were soled with tire tread, Poppy forged ahead. She waved as she reached the top of the hill, then disappeared.

Melody slowed, thinking furiously. What would send Andy tearing out of the studio in the midst of a recording session? And who would leave him a note?

She thought of Nadine, who had seemed to appear and disappear like a ghost all through this case. She still didn't know what part Nadine had played, but if Nadine had wanted to meet Andy, where would she have chosen that he would recognize instantly?

And then she knew. Andy had never told her where he'd lived in Crystal Palace, but she'd seen Nadine's old address in the files she'd looked through at Doug's last night, and she'd looked it up on the map.

Woodland Road.

But if they were right, it wasn't Nadine who was the danger.

Nadine stood at the top of Woodland Road. She thought she'd seen Andy make the turning, but when she'd reached the corner, he'd disappeared. Where could he have gone except the flat?

But why? Surely he didn't still live here, after all these years? She'd never thought to be in this place again, and she'd never imagined the street in weather like this. She'd moved in in the spring and out in the autumn.

Peering through the swirling flakes, she hesitated. She didn't want to go down, didn't want to see the house again. Didn't want to remember.

Lights were coming on, yellow pools shining like floating stepping-stones leading the way. She'd come this far to speak to Andy—she couldn't let herself turn back. Step by step, she started down the hill.

The thin-soled boots she'd put on yesterday for working in the shop were soaked through, and gave her no purchase on the icy pavement.

A last treacherous slip, and then she was opposite the houses, staring at the steps where she and Andy had so often sat in the late-afternoon sun.

But something was wrong. Andy couldn't still live here—his old house was obviously vacant and undergoing renovation. Boards covered the front windows loosely, and she thought the front door stood slightly open.

Had she been mistaken? Had he gone on at the junction? Or farther down the hill?

She stood, shivering, racked with indecision. The minutes seemed to pass as slowly as the chilled blood flowing in her veins.

Then, she saw a flicker of light in the gap between the boards covering the windows. Not yellow. Orange. The light danced, grew brighter.

Galvanized into movement, she slid her way across the street, bumping into the rubbish skip and grabbing on to it for purchase. Panting, she tried to make out the sounds coming from inside the house. Was that voices, or did she hear the crackle of flames?

The steps might have been Everest, but clinging to the side rail, she made it to the top and pushed open the door.

Joe recovered first. He was up and had managed to get between Andy and the door while Andy was still trying to get to his feet, woozy from the blow to the head.

Once upright, Andy stomped at the nearest flames and tried to shout, "We have to get out!" but the words were a croak.

"What? Afraid of a little fire?" Joe was balanced on the balls of his feet, and an extension cord from the builders' debris suddenly appeared, stretched between his hands.

"You're mad," said Andy. "You're absolutely freaking mad." Futilely, he tried swiping at the fire with Joe's scarf, which had fallen to the floor, but the fuzzy threads at the end sizzled and popped when the fire caught them. Andy dropped the scarf, his head swimming from even that effort. "Let me out. This whole place will go."

But when he stepped towards the door, Joe raised the cord. "I don't think so. Or you can try your luck getting past me—"

The door swung open.

She stood, a dark silhouette lit by the white aureole of snow, but now he would have recognized her anywhere.

"Andy? Oh, my God, the fire—Andy, are you all right?"

Nadine started across the room towards him, but Joe, who had been hidden from her by the open door, sprang forwards and looped the power cord over her head, tightening it behind her neck.

She gasped and twisted, but when Joe hissed, "Don't move," she went still.

"Let her go!" Andy glanced at the flames, spreading in little rivulets across a trail of spilled sawdust on the floor. Hadn't he read somewhere that sawdust would ignite? "Do whatever you want with me, but let her go." He was pleading now.

"Oh, I don't think so." Above Nadine's head, Joe smiled. "I wanted her, too—did you think I didn't? But I didn't know where to find her again. And now she's come right to me, thanks to you."

"Joe, please," said Andy, and saw Nadine's eyes go wide in her frightened face. The fire was spreading, popping, and he coughed as the smoke reached his lungs.

"The police will think you killed her. Maybe they'll even think you killed the others. Then you were overcome by the fire before you could get out." Joe gave a vicious yank on the power cord.

Nadine reached for it, trying to pull it away from her throat, but Joe twisted harder. He kept the pressure up until her hands fell away and she slumped against him.

"Bastard!" shouted Andy. The word seemed to echo down the years, entwined with memory and dreams. He'd backed up against the worktable, and now he fumbled behind him, his hand closing on something cold and thin.

A screwdriver blade. He pulled it towards him until his fingers closed tightly over the molded plastic of the handle. Then he launched himself across the room.

Releasing his hold on Nadine, Joe raised his hands to defend himself. His mistake.

Nadine crumpled at his feet. Then Andy was on him. His weight and momentum took them both down, and the blade of the screwdriver found its target.

CHAPTER TWENTY-FOUR

Walking through the ruins gives a taste of what an extraordinary sight the palace must have made. It indicates how powerful the trace of something that has essentially vanished can be. In the case of the Crystal Palace, I think that's because its real power lay not in Joseph Paxton's innovative design for the iron-and-glass structure alone—it was always its appeal to the imagination that mattered most.

—www.sarahjyoung.com

They were halfway along Westow Hill when Melody saw that the traffic ahead had come to a dead standstill. "Pull up on the pavement and put on the flashers," she told Gemma, who had stayed behind the wheel of the Clio. "We'll have to go the rest of the way on foot. And I checked the sat nav. We can't get down Woodland Road in any case—it's one way coming up."

She pulled a Metropolitan Police sign from the glove box and put it against the front windscreen as Gemma nosed the car up onto the curb.

The pavement was less icy as they hurried towards Woodland Road, but when they reached the junction, the north wind hit their faces with a frigid blast.

"Oh, bugger," said Melody, looking down. The road surface was already an inch deep in white powder. They could hear tires spinning as a car halfway up the incline tried to get traction.

"Do you remember the flat number?" asked Gemma.

"I think so. It's not far down."

"Ready?" Gemma gave her a quick look. "Let's go."

They had made it only a few yards when Melody saw it. Smoke, mixed in the dizzying eddies of snow, coming from a house a little lower down on the opposite side of the street. "There," she shouted back to Gemma, pointing. "There's a fire. I think it's the house."

They skidded the rest of the way, regardless of safety, crossing the street when they were opposite the house and could see the smoke pouring from the cracks in the boarded windows.

Melody slipped at the bottom of the steps and pain seared her knee as she went down on the ice-encrusted concrete. Her knee throbbing, she gritted her teeth and pulled herself up by the railing. Behind her, she heard Gemma calling 999 for the fire brigade.

When she heard the high-pitched, keening scream from inside the house, she stopped for an instant, terror gripping her. Andy. Dear God, Andy.

Closer to, Melody could see that the front door stood partially open. She pulled herself up the remaining steps, then stopped before she careened through the door, realizing she was weaponless. Even a standard-issue baton would have given her some defense. Then the scream came again. Feeling Gemma at her shoulder, she pushed open the door and shouted, "Police!"

The smoke blinded her. Blinking, she coughed and ducked lower. The scream came again. Turning towards it, she made out not Andy, but Joe Peterson, curled into a fetal ball on the floor, his hands clutching his stomach.

A hoarse voice said, "Melody." A few feet from Peterson, Andy sat against a wall, his face so covered in blood that he was almost unrecognizable. In his lap he cradled a woman.

A power cord dangled loosely from her neck. Nadine. It must be Nadine.

"He tried to— He tried to strangle her," croaked Andy. "But she's not—"

There was a crack and a burst of flame from the back of the room.

"We've got to get out." Head down, Gemma came to them.

"Are you all right?" Melody asked Andy urgently, frightened by the blood.

"Head cut. Just . . . woozy. Couldn't lift her."

"Right. Come on." She and Gemma eased Nadine from his lap and lifted her up, supporting her under her shoulders. Andy clambered unsteadily to his feet, and the three of them dragged Nadine towards the door. She stirred and began to protest, coughing. "Easy, easy," said Melody. "We've got you. We're almost out."

Joe Peterson's screams had dropped to animal-like cries. "Don't leave me," he moaned. "You can't leave me, you bastards."

"We'll come back. And the fire brigade's on its way," shouted Gemma as they pulled Nadine out the door. They all took gulps of fresh air, then, eyes streaming, Melody gasped, "How the hell are we going to get her down the steps?"

Then figures appeared in the blowing snow, neighbors come to help. There were voices, then helping hands to steady them as Melody, Gemma, and Andy managed to ease Nadine down the steps without any of them falling. Nadine began to cough again.

"Blankets," called Gemma. "Can someone get blankets?"

"Oh, God," whispered Andy. Beneath the blood, his face was ashen. "I thought she was dead."

Melody gave his arm a squeeze. "I think she's okay." She pointed back at the house. "Joe. What happened to him?"

"He was— He was waiting. He jumped me, then tried to strangle me. Then Nadine. I stabbed him." Andy's voice shook. "Screwdriver. I think it was a Phillips."

More smoke rolled out the door. Dread clutched at Melody. "Gemma, come on. We can't wait for the fire brigade or the medics. Andy, you stay with Nadine. We've got to get Joe out or he'll burn."

"Melody, no." Andy grabbed her arm. "You can't go back in. It's not safe!"

"I can't leave him. I'll be all right." She gave him what she hoped was a reassuring smile, then followed Gemma.

Sirens wailed in the distance, but Melody didn't know how long it would take the emergency vehicles to get through the traffic, and even when they did, they wouldn't be able to get down the hill.

"Bloody steps," said Gemma as they reached the bottom. She paused for a moment, then slipped out of her coat and threw it over the first couple of risers. "But I'm not leaving Joe Peterson in that house. If he's murdered two people and almost killed a third or a fourth, I damned well want him to stand trial."

Melody's old down coat covered the rest of the risers. They tamped the fabric down, then climbed the steps and ducked back in the door, locating Joe as much by memory as by sight. The smoke was heavier now, the heat fierce.

"Get one shoulder. I'll get the other. We'll have to drag him," said Gemma through a strangled cough. Melody's eyes were stinging.

Joe was whimpering, but when they got their arms under his shoulders and began to pull him towards the door, he screamed, then started to struggle and swear at them.

"It hurts, it hurts. You bitches! You're killing me." Even

with their arms under his shoulders, he managed to reach for the handle of the screwdriver that they could now see protruding from his gut. A dark, wet patch surrounded it and Melody could smell blood beneath the smoke. "Get it out!" he screamed as Melody yanked his arm back.

"Don't be an idiot. You want to bleed to death? Leave it alone." She and Gemma backed out as fast as they could, and when they were out the door there were again helping hands to transfer him down the steps.

"Careful, careful," Gemma said. "Move him as little as possible."

In the light, Melody could see that Joe's face was contorted with pain, his lips drawn back from his teeth in a feral snarl.

The sirens were close now. When she looked up, she saw blue lights flashing at the top of the street and welcome figures in blazing safety-green jackets moving down the hill.

Her cheeks felt scorched and her knees were threatening to buckle. Leaving others to tend to Joe Peterson, she stepped back, searching for Andy.

Turning, she saw him sitting on the far curb, his face still a smear of blood, a blanket-wrapped Nadine huddled in the curve of his arms. Then their figures were obscured by the whirl of snow and ash.

The first ambulance had taken Joe Peterson, the second, Nadine. Andy, protesting, had also been transported to Casualty at King's College Hospital in a panda car, to have his head wound cleaned and treated.

The fire brigade had managed to run hose down from Westow Hill. They'd kept the fire from spreading to the neighboring houses, but the flat itself was gutted. Gemma hoped the new owners had been well insured.

Having had to abandon Melody's Clio, which was well and

truly stuck on Westow Hill, she and Melody had been given a lift—a very slow lift—to the hospital in one of the area cars. In the hospital toilet, Gemma scrubbed the soot from her face and hands and brushed her hair, but there was no way she was going to disguise the smell of smoke emanating from her clothes. She'd have to explain when she got home, and Duncan was not going to be happy when he learned she'd run—twice—into a burning building. Oh, well.

She came back into the waiting area to find Melody looking pale and exhausted. "Are you all right?" she asked.

"All's well that ends well, isn't it?" Melody tucked a slightly singed bit of hair behind her ear and smiled, but Gemma could see that her heart wasn't in it.

"Andy's going to be all right."

"I know," Melody answered, not meeting her gaze. "Should we see him first?"

"No. I think we should talk to Nadine. There are still some things I don't understand."

Nadine Drake had been treated for heavy bruising on her throat, but the A and E staff had informed Gemma that she was not seriously injured and could be interviewed.

Joe Peterson would not be answering questions any time soon. He was being prepped for surgery to determine the extent of the damage from his abdominal wound.

They found Nadine in a curtained cubicle, sitting, propped up on a gurney. As they entered, an aide was spreading another warmed blanket over her. "She's still a little shocked and cold," the aide told them. "And her throat's very sore, so don't stay long."

It was Gemma's first real look at Nadine. Even with her dark hair still stringy and damp from the snow, and her face pale from shock and streaked with ash, she was lovely. Full lips, a straight nose, high cheekbones—it was the sort of face that aged well. But it was her eyes that held Gemma. Deep and dark, they held intelligence, pain, and, even now, a flash of humor.

Looking up, she gave Gemma and Melody a tentative smile. "I think I have you two to thank," she said, her voice hoarse. "And Andy. Are you sure he's all right?"

"He's fine," Gemma told her. "He's just having the cut on his head seen to. It looks much worse than it is. Now." She pulled up a plastic chair, although Melody remained standing by the curtains. "Nadine—do you mind if I call you Nadine?—I think I understand part of what happened today. Andy got a note purporting to be from you, but it was actually from Joe Peterson, in an attempt to lure him to a place where he could be easily attacked. What I don't know is how you came to be there, too."

"I followed him. Andy, I mean, not Joe. I didn't know about Joe. I still can't quite believe it." Nadine sipped some water from a straw in a plastic cup and cleared her throat. "I asked in Denmark Street this morning until someone told me where Andy was recording. On my way there, I saw him walking along Westow Hill. I wasn't certain he'd gone to the old house, but then I saw the flames . . ."

Pausing, she sipped more water, then shook her head and sank back against the pillow. "Andy could have been killed. We both could have been killed. And none of this would have happened if I hadn't come back to England," she added, her voice catching. "I thought I'd put that part of my life behind me, everything that had happened years ago. But being in London again . . . It began to prey on me. I—" Nadine swallowed and closed her eyes. When she opened them again, Gemma almost looked away from the raw regret in her gaze. "I felt so guilty for abandoning Andy without so much as a good-bye. I knew he was a child at risk, that his mother couldn't care for him, and yet I—I failed him. And myself. That haunted me for years. So when I first saw his name in the window of the club in

Denmark Street, I couldn't believe it. I felt so lost here, and that thread from the past seemed . . ." She sighed. "A sign, I suppose. I convinced myself that was why I'd been brought back to London, to make amends. I started to follow the band's gigs. I just wanted to speak to him once, to say I was sorry and to see if he was all right."

"So it was Andy you went to see at the White Stag on Friday night?" asked Gemma. "Not Vincent Arnott?"

"God, no, not Arnott." Nadine shuddered. "I couldn't believe it when I saw him drinking at the bar. I thought I was delusional. I still wasn't certain it was him until there was some sort of scuffle, then he—Arnott—went over and started shouting at Andy."

She stopped and Gemma waited, not prompting her. The murmurs and clinks of the busy hospital ward flowed around them.

How long had it been, Gemma wondered, since Nadine had talked to anyone about her past—if ever? Guy, her boss in Paris, had seemed unaware of her reasons for leaving England.

"There was a girl," continued Nadine, after some more water. "Maybe in her early twenties. On her own. I watched him start to chat her up and I felt sick. That sanctimonious bastard. And I was angry, so angry that I couldn't think of anything else then, not even Andy. He—Arnott—all those years ago, made me out to be some sort of pervert, a violator of children, when I'd done nothing, nothing but try to be a good teacher. And there he was, trying to seduce a child."

"What did you do?" Gemma asked softly when Nadine fell silent.

"I had to stop him. The girl was laughing, flattered. When she went to the loo, I went after her. I told her I knew him and that I'd just seen his wife come in, looking ready to kill. The girl ran out of the pub after that like a rabbit, and I'm sure Arnott had no idea what had happened to his conquest."

"So you . . . consoled him . . ."

Nadine nodded. "I'd had a bit too much to drink by then. False courage. I only meant to let him make a play, then I was going to laugh at him, humiliate him. But then he . . . he treated me like a common tart. As if I should be grateful for his attention. And he—I could tell he didn't recognize me." She bunched the hospital blankets between her hands. "After everything he'd done to ruin my life, I was nobody. Nobody! That was the worst thing."

"So when he suggested the hotel—"

"I had to see what he meant to do. I wanted to prove that *he* was the one who was the pervert." Nadine leaned forward, still clutching the blankets, her voice rasping with the effort of speaking. "He had me wait at the fire door while he got a room. The place was disgusting, but it was obvious he'd been there often. Once in the room, he undressed and asked me to tie him up. I did what he asked. He was—enjoying it. It was— vile." Her face grew paler and she hesitated before going on. "I played along. I used my scarf to gag him. Then I had him turn over, facing me, and I told him it was part of our little game." Nadine swallowed again, coughed, and took a deep rasping breath. "Then— Then I stood there, looking down at him, and I told him I hoped he'd enjoy explaining himself to the hotel staff in the morning. The expression on his face . . . I felt such triumph. He still had no idea who I was, or what he had done to me, but possibly for the first time in his life, he had no control. And I just—walked out. It seemed like the ultimate revenge." She lifted a shoulder in a gesture that seemed particularly French.

"What happened then?" asked Gemma, leaning forward.

"As soon as I got away from that damned hotel I was already ashamed of myself. Ashamed of what I'd done. Ashamed of how I'd felt doing it. I almost went back, but I couldn't make myself. I didn't know if the band had finished at the White

Stag, but there was no way I could face Andy after that. Not that night. I flagged a taxi on Church Road and went home."

Gemma threw a swift glance at Melody, who still stood by the cubicle curtains, her face unreadable. Then Gemma said quietly to Nadine, "But you still wanted to see Andy, didn't you."

"Not that next day, no. I was so sickened by what had happened. By what I'd done. But I'd seen Andy's name on the schedule for the club in Denmark Street for Sunday night, and by that time I thought—I still thought I owed him some sort of explanation or apology.

"But when I saw him play that night, really play, with his heart in it, I knew he was all right. More than all right." Nadine's expression softened at the memory. "And then"— Pausing, she looked at Melody, studying her as if making an assessment. Then she nodded again, once, and spoke to her directly. "After that first set, when I saw him look at you, I knew he didn't need my interference or my apologies. He'd moved on, and I knew I must, too.

"It was only when I was walking home from the club that I saw on the telly about Arnott. That he was dead. I thought"— Nadine turned a pleading gaze back to Gemma—"I thought I'd killed him. That maybe he'd suffocated from the gag, even though it wasn't tight. I should never have left him like that. It was stupid and childish. But I didn't see how I could explain what I'd done . . . Oh, God." Nadine sagged back against the pillow.

"The police believed you before, when Joe Peterson made those accusations against you," said Gemma.

"Yes, but little good that did me." There was a first hint of bitterness in Nadine's smile. "All week, I'd been frantic with worry, trying to decide what to do. And then yesterday, when I saw the police outside the flat . . . I just . . . panicked. It was only when I'd had time to come to my senses that I knew I had to confess what I'd done. But I also knew I needed one last chance to talk to Andy, after all. I was sure he thought badly enough of me, but I couldn't bear him thinking I'd deliberately harmed someone, even that horrible man."

"And what about Shaun Francis?" asked Gemma.

"Shaun Francis . . ." Nadine frowned. "Oh, he was the other boy, wasn't he? The one who backed up Joe Peterson's story?"

"But you hadn't seen him since?"

"No." Nadine looked confused. "Why would I have—"

"He was killed, too. After Arnott."

Nadine glanced from Gemma to Melody. "But what—I don't understand any of this. Why would someone kill Shaun Francis? And why was Joe waiting for Andy in the house? Why did he attack Andy and me?"

Gemma answered. "Nadine, Vincent Arnott didn't suffocate. He was strangled. Shaun Francis was strangled the same way two nights later, but this time with the scarf you used to gag Arnott."

"What?" Nadine's eyes grew wider. "Dear God. My scarf. So that's why you came to my flat. You thought I killed *both* of them?" She took a moment to think it through, then frowned. "But in the house today, Joe said something about 'the others.' It was Joe who killed them?"

"Peterson was there at the White Stag on Friday night, perhaps for the same reason as you. Maybe he saw Andy's name on the pub flyer and wanted to see what Andy had made of himself. He approached Andy at the break. Andy was furious. He hit him. This was the scuffle that prompted Arnott's outburst."

"Then," Gemma continued slowly, still working things out for herself, "we have to assume Joe recognized you and Arnott. We have CCTV footage of him following the two of you from the pub. I wonder . . ." She paused, visualizing the hotel. "The room at the Belvedere had ground-level windows. Do you remember if the curtains were closed all the way?"

Nadine shook her head. "I—I don't think so. They didn't hang right."

"If Joe followed you to the hotel," Gemma went on, "and saw Arnott let you in the fire door, he could have seen into the room through the cracks in the curtains. And we discovered that the latch on the fire door was broken. So when you left—"

"Oh, God," Nadine whispered. "He just walked in. I gave him the perfect opportunity. If I hadn't—and he took my scarf from Arnott's mouth *after* he was dead?"

"It doesn't matter," Melody said suddenly, sharply, stepping forwards. "It was Andy that Joe was angry with that night. He was always jealous, and Andy publicly made a fool of him. If Joe hadn't followed you, he might have waited for Andy, and who knows what he might have done? He came close enough today. All of this—everything that happened all those years ago, and everything that's happened this last week, these two murders—spiraled out from Joe Peterson's actions. Not yours. Not Andy's.

"Andy never knew, by the way, what the boys had said about you. He didn't know you lost your job or why you left your house. All this time he's thought it was his fault, that you left because you blamed him for what happened."

Nadine's eyes brimmed with tears. "But I never—"

"He wants to see you," said Melody. "He wants to make sure you're all right."

"Oh, no, but I—" Nadine wiped at her tear-streaked cheeks. "How can I face him now, if all this time he's thought that of me?"

"Because he knows the truth. And I think it's far past time the two of you really talked. I'll get him, shall I?"

Slowly, Nadine nodded. But when Melody turned to go, she whispered, "Wait. Will you stay?"

"I'll get Andy," said Gemma, and slipped from the cubicle.

. . .

For a moment, Nadine gazed at Melody, searching her face. Then, her whisper so faint that Melody stepped up to the gurney to hear, she said, "I'll go back to Paris, you know, as soon as I can. I realized, before any of this, that I should never have come back to England. There's no life for me here."

"But Andy—"

"I'll be an old friend." She smiled. "He can write to me, if he wants. I'll follow his career. Maybe someday the two of you can come to Paris."

"But I—but we aren't—"

"I saw you together, at the club in Denmark Street. And today, when you went back into that fire—he wouldn't leave me, but he was terrified for you. I thought—I hoped that you would promise to look after him."

Melody shook her head. "I don't think Andy needs looking after."

"Oh, but that's where you're wrong." Nadine reached out and touched Melody's hand. "We all need looking after. It's the greatest of mistakes to think otherwise. No one knows that better than me."

When Doug Cullen's doorbell rang on Thursday evening, he thought it was about time that Melody had come to tell him in person what had been happening, instead of sending him abbreviated and inscrutable texts.

"I'm coming, I'm coming," he shouted as he hobbled to the door. Maybe he should just have a key made for her, if his damned ankle didn't get better soon.

But when he opened his door, it was not Melody who stood on his slushy step, but Detective Inspector Maura Bell.

In her tan trench coat, she looked just as he remembered, although perhaps a bit more worn. Incongruously, she was holding a bunch of supermarket flowers. As he stared at her, she thrust them out. "I heard you broke your ankle."

"What are you—how did you—"

"Your friend Sergeant Talbot gave me your address. I thought, since you never returned my calls, that maybe with the bum ankle you couldn't avoid me."

"But I— You were the one who—" Doug stopped. The memory of her rejection still made him cringe. He'd thought their relationship was going somewhere until the night he tried to kiss her on the Millennium Bridge.

"You never gave me a chance to explain."

"You didn't have to—"

"Just shut up, will you, Doug?" She gave the exasperated sigh he remembered. "I'd been seeing someone before I went out with you. We'd split up. Before I met you that night, he'd rung, wanting to get back together. I'd thought it might work out, and so I didn't want to— It was complicated."

Doug frowned. "Did it work?" he asked, interested in spite of himself.

"For a week." Maura made a disgusted face. "Lucky it lasted that long. I was an idiot, and all the while I was ringing you and you wouldnae talk to me. Look. I didnae come to grovel. I just thought maybe we could be . . . friends. If you're not going to let me in, at least take your stupid wee flowers. I'm bloody freezing." Maura shivered.

It had started to snow again, great white flakes that drifted gently in the glow from the streetlamp.

Doug pushed his glasses up on his nose. He remembered now, not how hurt he'd been, but how much he had liked this prickly, funny woman, who was never less than honest.

"I seem to be making a habit of acquiring female friends," he said. "I suppose I could do with one more." Opening the door wide, he stepped back. "You didn't by any chance bring anything edible?"

. . .

Melody and Gemma waited at the hospital for Joe Peterson to come out of the operating theater. The afternoon had drawn into night, and when Melody, restless, went to look out the reception area doors, the snow was falling again.

The foyer door opened and Andy came to stand beside her. His hair fell over the square of white gauze on his forehead, making him look quite rakish.

"Is she gone, then?" asked Melody. He'd insisted on staying with Nadine until she was released.

"She wouldn't let me see her back to Covent Garden." He shrugged. "It's very odd. How someone can seem so different and yet the same. She said she'll go back to Paris."

"I know. She told me. There will be some legal things to work out first."

"Will she be all right, do you think?"

"Yes." Melody considered. "I think so." It seemed to her that Nadine Drake had not only survived what life had thrown at her, but that she might at last have found her place in it, and some peace. "What about you?"

He shrugged. "I don't know. I lost the Strat. It was in the flat."

"Oh, Andy." She turned to him. "I'm so sorry." She'd come to realize what the guitar meant to him. It had been his talisman, his connection to the past, his hedge against fate. "They might recover it."

"Time for a new start, maybe," he said, with a shrug. "But Poppy will be livid. She liked the sound." He threw a glance at her. "I was thinking of quitting. The thing with Poppy." Touching a finger to the cold glass, he gazed out at the snow. "I thought that if I let myself care about anything, I would somehow lose it, and I didn't want to take that chance with something I'd wanted so badly. But I think I might have been wrong."

"You can't dream of quitting," said Melody, horrified. "You're brilliant, the two of you. If you don't do this, you'll regret it the rest of your life."

He turned to meet her eyes. "It would mean I'd be touring. There wouldn't be much time for—"

Gemma, coming into the foyer, said, "Oh, there you two are. Peterson's out of surgery, and they think he'll be okay, barring infection. I'm just going to order a guard, although I don't think he's going to be jumping up and running about any time soon, thanks to you, Andy." She sighed, rubbing at a bit of soot left at her hairline. "And his father's shown up, with lawyer, so I'm going to have to deal with them. I'll enjoy telling him that we will be the ones pressing charges, not him. Melody, you might as well leave me to it. I'll see you at the station in the morning." Straightening her shoulders, she headed back for reception.

Melody didn't know what Andy had been going to say, and couldn't bring herself to ask. Instead, she ventured, "I don't suppose there's any chance of me getting my car."

He laughed. "From Crystal Palace, in this weather? Nothing will move in or out of the triangle until it thaws. But we can get the train from Denmark Hill."

"We?" she said, hesitantly.

"Well, as far as you want to go together. I mean—" He colored. "You never told me where you live, you know."

"Notting Hill." Melody thought of going home to the quiet, empty flat. The flat she had never invited anyone to visit, not even Gemma or Doug, because she'd been afraid of their breaching her carefully built barriers.

And what, she thought, had that got her? Nights spent in front of the telly, drinking a few too many glasses of wine and eating ready meals. Suddenly the safety of her solitary existence seemed much less appealing.

She remembered the fantasy she'd had, the evening of the

day she'd met Andy. Standing at the window of her flat, look-ing down into Portobello Road, she'd wondered what it would be like to walk, arm in arm with him, in the cold, brisk air, feeling the warmth of his body through her coat. Now, with a flutter of desire, she imagined much, much more.

She took a breath and said, "We could go to my place, if you like."

CHAPTER TWENTY-FIVE

There have been a number of proposals for the site over the years but all of them have fallen to the way side . . . But Crystal Palace will live on in the minds of those that loved it for a very long time to come.

—Betty Carew, www.helium.com

Kincaid woke early on a dark Monday morning in February, showered, then spent a good deal of time examining the contents of his wardrobe. At last he decided on a suit and tie rather than his usual trousers and sports jacket. He felt he should mark the occasion. It had been so long since he'd dressed for work that he had to brush the dust from the shoulders of his jacket.

"You'll look lovely, whatever you wear," said Gemma, coming out of the bathroom and kissing him on the cheek.

"I don't think 'lovely' is the operative word," he countered, but grinned.

"Wear the blue, then. It brings out the color of your eyes. I can take Char this morning, if you like," she added, continuing the quick, deft plaiting of her hair that always amazed him.

"No, I want to. But thanks."

Gemma had been busy the past few weeks, tying up the details of the Peterson investigation for the Crown prosecutor. Although Joe Peterson and his lawyer were staunchly protesting his innocence, they'd found a fingerprint match in the room in the Belvedere Hotel, and Peterson's blood type and DNA had matched that of the blood spot found on the sheet beneath Vincent Arnott's body.

Kincaid was glad to see Gemma getting the credit she deserved for solving the case—it erased a bit of the guilt he'd felt over what he'd suspected were the real reasons behind her appointment to the South London murder team.

And he'd achieved a major victory—he'd got her to agree to a dinner invitation from MacKenzie Williams for the coming weekend.

Their morning routine went on as usual. The house smelled of bacon and toast. Dishes clattered in the kitchen and the rooms rang with the racket of children and animals, all demanding one thing or another. When it was time, leaving Gemma to see the boys off, he buckled Charlotte into the Astra and drove her the short distance to her school.

He hadn't expected the lump in his throat as he walked her to the door and pushed the buzzer. "Bye, sweetheart." He leaned down to kiss her. "See you tonight." Charlotte had adjusted so well to her new school that she had now begun full days.

"Bye-bye, Papa." She wrapped her small arms round his neck and pressed her face against his, and then she was gone, into the throng of children in their bright blazers.

He'd get used to it, he thought. He would get used to leaving her.

The traffic was light for a Monday, and he arrived at the Yard even earlier than he'd intended. The building seemed unusually quiet as well. There was no one in the corridor when he arrived on his floor, no one to welcome him on his first day back.

For a moment, he considered going up to see his guv'nor, Chief Superintendent Childs, before he went into his office, but he was suddenly and unexpectedly eager for the sight of the small room with its rickety coatrack and carefully organized shelves of books. He'd missed it.

Opening the door, for a moment he thought he'd wandered into the wrong office. He shook his head, baffled. There were his shelves—he'd built them himself when he'd first been promoted to superintendent. But they were empty. Cardboard boxes sat stacked against one wall.

And it *was* his desk, an old oak piece he'd bought at an estate sale to replace the standard police issue when he'd first started at the Yard. But it was bare as well, except for a plain white envelope with his name scrawled across the front.

He felt as if he were sleepwalking. Slowly, he picked up the envelope, lifted the unsealed flap, and eased out the single sheet of paper.

It was a letter of transfer. And his chief superintendent had signed it.